SMALL SCALE REFINING

OF

JEWELERS WASTES

BY

ROLAND LOEWEN

Roland Loewen

FOREWORD

In about 1100 A.D. a monk called Theophilus wrote about various processes and techniques of the time. His philosophy for revealing this information was -

"Wherefore the pious devotion of the faithful should not neglect what the ingenious foresight of their predecessors has transmitted to our present age, and man should embrace with avid eagerness the inheritance that God bestowed on man and should labor to acquire it. Let no one after acquiring it glorify himself in his own heart as though it had been received from himself and not from elsewhere . . . . . . Let him not hide his gifts in the purse of envy nor conceal them in the storeroom of a selfish heart but, thrusting aside all boasting, let him simply and with a cheerful mind dispense to those who seek."

In a similar way it has been said - "We have all warmed ourselves at fires we did not build and drunk from wells we did not dig." This attitude I like and it is a large reason for writing this volume.

Having obtained a degree in Chemical Engineering I worked a dozen years in a chemical plant and then several decades in electric furnace smelters with molten slags and metals. Of many relaxations and hobbies the designing and production of jewelry was the most interesting and resulted in a part time business that lasted many years. With it came some familiarity with silver, gold and platinum and an interest in their metallurgy.

Some 15 or 18 years ago a jeweler in Houston, Texas, a special friend, asked repeatedly how his scrap could be refined to fine gold. I agreed to search the literature, found nothing in the way of direct how-to-do-it material and gradually found enough chemical information to devise a process.

Then came the discovery of a then out-of-print book "Refining Precious Metal Wastes" by C. M. Hoke which told me I was doing things quite correctly and which gave me a very large amount of additional information. I developed a long lasting interest in the techniques of processing precious metals. I became an early member of the International Precious Metals Institute and, as a result of some of my work, an Associate of the Wardens and Commonality of the Mystery of Goldsmiths of the City of London, (Goldsmiths Hall).

Gold refining is very, very old. T. K. Rose refers to Ezekiel (ca 593 B.C.) who described a method for improving the purity of gold. Hoover's translation of "Agricola" p. 465 suggests refining as early as 2500 B.C. In my searches for information useful for the refiner, the latest texts were of little use but older, even antique, books were helpful.

When one remembers that Alchemy, the search for a method of changing base metal(s) to gold was the beginning of the science of Chemistry, this is reasonable. Some one more eloquent than I described Alchemy as "The Daughter of Error and the Mother of Truth." Inorganic materials and precious metals were early studied by the pioneers of the science of chemistry, refining methods gained a new understanding and improvements and new methods were devised.

Today precious metal research continues probably more in the general chemistry than in refining where the major search seems to be for less toxic and less polluting methods.

We are grateful to Art Berg of Houston, Texas for urging us to start refining work, for his patience in our early efforts and for his continuing enthusiasm.

To J.R. (Jimmy) Daniels my partner of many years, my thanks for his patience when I used the shop for experiments and photography.

Our special thanks to Mr. Peter Gainsbury, Dir. Design & Technology, Ret., Worshipful Company of Goldsmiths, London, for urging us to write the original three small books. To the London Assay Office that did numerous assays on experimental lots of silver we give our appreciation.

To Mr. David Schneller of Boulder, Colorado for his ideas, enthusiasm and suggestions on many aspects of precious metals and for his help and encouragement in this project.

To my wife, Lorraine, for her help, suggestions, typing and tolerance.

INTRODUCTION

The work of refining precious metals and precious metal scrap is chemical, electro-chemical and pyrometallurgical in nature. However, a technical eduction in these matters is not required and we will present methods in a non-technical how-to-do-it manner.

It is unlikely that jewelers should set up equipment and do the refining of their own scrap. An understanding of how it is done will, however, give a basis for good business judgment concerning their scrap.

We will describe the methods and the equipment that we use in a small shop we call "ALCHEMY." Our work mostly involves gold with occasional lots of silver and once in a while platinum and palladium. Essentially all of our work is with scrap materials and includes workbench scrap, strip pot sludge and similar high grade wastes. Also low grade materials such as polishing dust (sweeps), shop carpets and flooring, sink trap sludge, jewelry tumbler mud, bombing liquid, scrap watch bands, eye glass frames, watch batteries, etc. are refined.

Some of our equipment is regular chemical ware, some is normally used in kitchens and in other tasks. Being experienced engineers and constructors, we design and build most of our furnaces and other heavier equipment. For those not interested in self-built equipment, commercially available devices are available.

Noble metals are so called because they do not easily go into chemical combination with other elements. Dissolving these resistant materials requires chemicals that can only be described as <u>aggressive</u>. They are corrosive or toxic or both. By-products, both gaseous and liquid, may have similar unpleasant characteristics. The work also involves the melting of metals and other materials and the perils that are a part of such work.

Safety is often considered to be a matter of special clothing, goggles, gloves, guards, protective devices and special procedures. These are necessary, but unless there is an attitude and <u>habit</u> of orderly work, clean work places, neatness and care, such devices are not sufficient. We will make many specific suggestions about safety.

If you have happy-go-lucky housekeeping and work habits and a devil-may-care approach to your work, we suggest that you read this as informative and recreational material, but let others do your refining work.

The by-products of this work tend to be pollutants. The discharge of gaseous and liquid waste (and possibly solids) are subject to legal controls that will vary from place to place, but are often stringent. The control of such by-products is perhaps the most difficult and costly part of the work. We are not able to solve such problems for everyone but we will give suggestions and ideas.

In addition to refining methods, we will present some information on the problems and the methods for sampling jewelers' waste, a difficult thing to do properly.

During the course of years, we have made small tests of other refining methods and have used a few of these on a limited basis. When they did not fit our needs and when our curiosity was satisfied, we put them aside. We will give our experience with them.

Other interesting ideas have come to our attention and because we have no hands-on experience, we consider them to be theoretical, but perhaps of interest to others. We will mention a few.

For those interested in chemistry, we will present chemical formulas as we understand them. We try to give sources of information as specific references. A list of books and publications of possible interest to those wishing to read about precious metal technology will be included.

Our descriptions will be for small scale recovery and refining work and we will try to present the information in a how-to-do-it fashion. However, for those with an interest in chemistry and similar things we will try to give the technical and chemical explanation of what happens in refining work.

Much of this will be in the form of chemical equations which are a shorthand explanation of what occurs during a chemical reaction. These equations make things look quite straight forward and simple. Often this is not so. Although a reaction depicted in an equation probably occurs quite neatly in a laboratory with clean materials and controlled conditions, this may not be so true in an industrial situation. The presence of other materials, differences in temperature, concentration and many other factors can modify the reaction. It may go faster, slower, or not at all.

The reactions we give have been gleaned from tests and references but usually they do not purport to give more than basic facts. Sometimes there may be some question about the exact nature of a reaction then we will give what seems, in our experience, to be reasonable.

In some cases we will write about some rather fundamental aspects of chemistry. This in keeping with our hope that what we have written is uncomplicated and down to earth. To the sophisticated chemist our apologies.

TABLE OF CONTENTS

OUTLINE OF SAFETY AND POLLUTION MATTERS 1

SAMPLING AND ASSAYING 11

REFINING JEWELERS SWEEPS 21

LOW GRADE WASTES 77

GOLD 93

SILVER 133

PLATINUM AND PALLADIUM 157

OTHER REFINING METHODS 169

POLLUTION - AIR AND WATER 193

MINING PRECIOUS METALS 215

REFERENCES AND FURTHER READING 229

INDEX 249

List of Illustrations

Touchstone Kit	Photograph	13
Ingot Drilling Pattern	Drawing	15
Sweeps Burner	Drawing	24
Sweeps Burner	Drawing	25
Sweeps Burner	Drawing	26
Sweeps Burner	Photograph	27
Magnets	Photograph	29
Sample Splitter	Photograph	30
Mixer	Photograph	33
Mixer (Plastic Bowl)	Photograph	34
Magnet and Iron	Photograph	35
Crucible (Exploded)	Photograph	39
Furnace & Dimensions	Drawing	42
Furnace (Small)	Photograph	44
Viscosity Tester	Drawing	49
Viscosity Tester	Photograph	50
Ingot Mold	Drawing	53
Slag and Metal Bar	Photograph	54
Shot Maker	Drawing	55
Shot Maker	Photograph	56
Torch Shotting	Photograph	57
Sweeps Chart	Drawing	58
Phase Diagram	Drawing	66
Phase Diagram	Drawing	68
Jaw Crusher	Photograph	72
Ball Mill	Photograph	73
Screen	Photograph	74
Vacuum Aqua Regia Transfer	Drawing	98
Ultrasonic Equipment	Drawing	101
Buchner Filters	Photograph	103
Vacuum Filtering System	Drawing	105
Aspirator (Eductor) Vacuum Pump	Drawing	106
Water Saving Vacuum System	Photograph	107
Water Saving Vacuum System	Drawing	108
Wash Water System	Drawing	109
Sulfur Dioxide Equipment	Drawing	112
Sulfite Feed Tank	Drawing	113

LIST OF ILLUSTRATIONS
(Continued)

Gold Test Equipment	Photograph	116
Siphon To Decant Barren Solution	Drawing	118
Chart - Gold Pptn.-Dilution Factor	Drawing	128
Wohlwill Gold Cell	Drawing	173
Fizzer Cell	Drawing	174
Cupel Furnace	Drawing	187
Tower Packing	Photograph	195
Muffler	Photograph	197
Scrubber and Hood	Drawing	199
Nitric Acid Recovery	Drawing	202
Aqua Regia Recovery	Drawing	204
Air Lift	Drawing	207

OUTLINE OF SAFETY AND POLLUTION MATTERS

Safety is often considered to be a matter of guards, protection devices and clothing, and formal safety procedures. In fact, a clean and orderly work place, regularly used storage places for supplies and equipment, clear labels on supplies, and careful work habits with care for cleanliness are of major safety importance.

The materials and the equipment required are those used in thousands of laboratories on a daily basis. The caustic and the acids needed are purchased in concentrated form, but are used after dilution. Spills on hands or clothing do little, if any, damage if promptly washed away.

Therefore, the work place should have a source of running water that is readily available. Since eyes are perhaps the most vulnerable, eye protection is the most important. Eye wash to remove splashes should be nearby. Plastic eye wash bottles are available at safety supply shops. Gloves to protect hands from splashes are necessary. A proper fume hood to deal with scrap dissolution and the dilution of strong acids is recommended. Other than this, our usual precaution is to wear clothing suitable for work rather than dress.

Cyanide Wastes

Jewelers often use cyanide chemicals for the work of electroplating, for a jewelry finishing process called "Bombing" or a reverse electrolysis called "Stripping." These cyanidic solutions contain gold in amounts that make recovery worthwhile.

The safety hazards of cyanide are considerable. Avoiding ingestion of cyanide by a faithful habit of no eating, no drinking, no smoking when handling cyanide is required to avoid cyanosis and death. Absorption through the eye is very rapid and the most vulnerable target organ for cyanide penetration. Cyanide can also be absorbed through the skin, immediately through cuts and abrasions. Avoid contact and wash thoroughly if it occurs. Avoid any contact between acid and cyanide because it can produce deadly hydrogen cyanide gas.

The safety precautions for dealing with cyanides, the specific perils of cyanide in its various forms and first aid measures that can be taken are covered in some detail later. See Chapter 4 Low Grade Wastes for specific information before dealing with cyanides.

The destruction of cyanides can be done by several methods. Specific information is given in the section on cyanide in the
chapter about Low Grade Wastes.

Gold Refining

The aqua regia method of refining will occasionally require the use of sulfuric acid. The acids used mostly are nitric and hydrochloric which are mixed to make aqua regia. These strong acids should, at the very least, be handled with rubber gloves and eye protection. A rubber apron and suitable shoes will save clothing for small spatters and droplets are inevitable. Clothing used in this work has a limited life.

Sulfuric acid is not a fuming acid but requires care when diluting with water. Always pour the strong acid INTO water. The heat of dilution is large and can result in dangerous spattering of hot acid if only a small amount of water encounters the acid. Adding acid to water is safe and merely heats the larger mass of water.

Nitric acid is not a strongly fuming acid and it dilutes quietly, if that is necessary. Hydrochloric acid fumes badly. Strong acid should be handled under a fume hood. It also dilutes quietly with water.

Aqua regia, a combination of nitric acid and hydrochloric acid, mixes quietly. Either acid may be poured into the other. It is a very aggressive liquid. As soon as mixed, the aqua regia starts to form and slowly emits chlorine gas for a day or two. Aqua regia containers must NOT be closed. The chlorine pressure in a closed container can produce enough pressure to break the bottle. It should be stored in a suitable fume hood.

The dissolution of metals by aqua regia produces an oxide of nitrogen that is a colorless gas. However, as soon as this oxide of nitrogen reaches air, it combines with oxygen of the air and forms a reddish-brown fume. This is a choking, corrosive and toxic gas.

This work must be done in a fume hood with a good inrush of air and a scrubber to remove acidic fumes. This hood is also suitable for the chlorine emitted from the aqua regia.

The most important safety precaution is the use of eye protection. An eye wash and the trained ability to find it with eyes closed is necessary. Also needed is a safety shower easily found and easily turned on by a pull chain.

The liquids that are a product of aqua regia dissolution contain metals other than gold. When the gold is removed from these solutions, the other metals, notably copper, but also zinc, iron, etc. remain. This very acid solution is an undesirable sewer discard. Treatment to remove metals and modify the acidity is needed.

When precipitating gold from solution that also contains copper (a normal condition), it is possible to add too much of some agents and change the copper from a dichloride to an insoluble monochloride. If this is not removed and is put into the melting furnace, dense white fumes are produced. These are acrid and very, very unpleasant, usually resulting in prompt evacuation of the furnace room.

Breathing such fumes for a while can result in a form of copper poisoning known as false flu. The chills and symptoms are exactly those of influenza but they can pass in a very few hours. There seems to be, in our experience, no lasting ills.

The use of hydroquinone as a reducer does not change the copper and avoids this problem.

Silver Refining

Our small scale refinery method involves the use of nitric acid and produces the same oxides of nitrogen that occur in aqua regia gold refining. Also used in silver work are small amounts of sulfuric acid. Sodium hydroxide is used and this is a base which is a chemical opposite of an acid. Sodium hydroxide (caustic soda or lye) is an aggressive material and perhaps more dangerous to skin and eyes than are acids. Eye protection and rubber gloves are **MANDATORY**. The same eye wash and safety shower mentioned above should be nearby.

The dextrose used in silver refining is a sugar and a food. The addition of caustic soda to a dextrose silver mixture or dextrose to a caustic silver mixture causes a great amount of heat and boiling. Slow and careful addition with at least gloves and eye protection is needed.

During the time of this writing we have tested and adopted a somewhat more simple reduction of silver chloride to silver metal with the use of hydrazine. Hydrazine is a carcinogen and must be handled with care. The precautions are to wear rubber gloves, eye protection and dilute the 30% (as purchased) hydrazine to about 10% and do this in a well ventilated hood.

Hydrazine produces fumes, the stronger the more fumes. The long term effects of these fumes are not good. Details about use, testing and hydrazine destruction are given in the chapter on Silver.

Platinum and Palladium

The recovery of platinum and palladium requires the use of acids, similar to the work with gold and silver. In addition, a fairly ordinary chemical called ammonium chloride is used to precipitate both platinum and palladium. For palladium, a strong oxidizer (one that promotes combustion) called sodium chlorate is used. This should be used in the manner specified and is then no unusual hazard.

The production of platinum and palladium powders from their ammonium compounds requires a heating cycle and a slow increase to red heat. Some smoky clouds of ammonium chloride may appear.

The melting of these powders requires very high temperatures. Oxyacetylene or oxyhydrogen torches are adequate for small amounts. Gas welding goggles are required. An electric induction furnace is preferred and a necessity for large amounts of these high melting point metals.

Safety Data Sheets

It is a legal requirement for chemical suppliers to provide information about the chemicals they sell.

A typical 5-page Material Safety Data Sheet is reproduced on the following pages. This one is for sulfuric acid and was current at the time of this writing. Some such sheets may be revised from time to time if new and pertinent information is developed so this is given as representative only. These are important and can be very helpful in the safe use of these materials.

The following example is included by the courtesy of Van Waters & Rogers.

P1361.1   MATERIAL SAFETY DATA SHEET   PG 1

REVISION OF: 07-21-87

VAN WATERS & ROGERS INC. 1600 NORTON BLDG.   SEATTLE, WA 98104-1564

-------------------------EMERGENCY ASSISTANCE--------------------------

FOR EMERGENCY ASSISTANCE INVOLVING CHEMICALS CALL CHEMTREC
(800) 424-9300.

-------------------FOR PRODUCT AND SALES INFORMATION--------------------

CONTACT YOUR LOCAL VAN WATERS & ROGERS BRANCH OFFICE

-----------------------PRODUCT IDENTIFICATION---------------------------

PRODUCT NAME: SULFURIC ACID   CAS NO.: 7664-93-9
COMMON NAMES/SYNONYMS: SULFURIC ACID;   VW&R CODE: T1362
OIL OF VITRIOL; SULFURIC ACID > 93%; SULFURIC ACID > 66 DEG BE;
SULFURIC ACID > 1.83 SPECIFIC GRAVITY
FORMULA: H2 S O4   DATE ISSUED: 07/87
HAZARD RATING (NFPA 49)   SUPERCEDES: 01/87
    HEALTH: 3   HAZARD RATING SCALE:
    FIRE: 0   0=MINIMAL 3=SERIOUS
    REACTIVITY: 2   1=SLIGHT 4=SEVERE
    SPECIAL: NO WATER 2=MODERATE

-----------------------HAZARDOUS INGREDIENTS---------------------------

EXPOSURE LIMITS, MG/M3

COMPONENT	CAS NO.	OSHA %	ACGIH PEL	OTHER TLV	LIMIT	HAZARD
SULFURIC ACID (DUPONT)	7664-93-9	>93	1	1	1	CORROSIVE
WATER	7732-18-5	BALANCE	NONE	NONE	NONE	NONE

-----------------------PHYSICAL PROPERTIES----------------------------

BOILING POINT, DEG F: A = 529;   VAPOR PRESSURE, MM HG/20 DEG C: A,B =
  B = 590   NIL
FREEZING POINT, DEG F: A = -20;   VAPOR DENSITY (AIR=1): N/A
  B = 30
SPECIFIC GRAVITY (WATER=1): A = 1.835;   WATER SOLUBILITY, %:
  B = 1.84   COMPLETE
APPEARANCE AND ODOR: COLOR-   EVAPORATION RATE (BUTYL ACETATE=1): <1
LESS TO PALE YELLOW, OILY
LIQUID. ODORLESS.

    A = 93% OR 66 DEG BE SULFURIC ACID; B = 99% SULFURIC ACID

-------------------------FIRST AID MEASURES-----------------------------

IF INHALED: REMOVE TO FRESH AIR. GIVE ARTIFICIAL RESPIRATION IF NOT BREATHING. GET IMMEDIATE MEDICAL
ATTENTION.

14:01:24   02 MAR 1988

P1361.1   MATERIAL SAFETY DATA SHEET   PG 2
REVISION OF: 07-21-87

IN CASE OF EYE CONTACT: IMMEDIATELY FLUSH EYES WITH LOTS OF RUNNING WATER FOR 30 MINUTES, LIFTING THE UPPER AND LOWER EYELIDS OCCASIONALLY. GET IMMEDIATE MEDICAL ATTENTION.

IN CASE OF SKIN CONTACT: IMMEDIATELY FLUSH SKIN WITH LOTS OF RUNNING WATER FOR 30 MINUTES. REMOVE CONTAMINATED CLOTHING AND SHOES; WASH BEFORE REUSE. GET IMMEDIATE MEDICAL ATTENTION.

IF SWALLOWED: DO NOT INDUCE VOMITING. IF CONSCIOUS, GIVE LOTS OF WATER OR MILK. GET IMMEDIATE MEDICAL ATTENTION. DO NOT GIVE ANYTHING BY MOUTH TO AN UNCONSCIOUS OR CONVULSING PERSON.

---------------------HEALTH HAZARD INFORMATION-------------------------

PRIMARY ROUTES OF EXPOSURE: SKIN OR EYE CONTACT

SIGNS AND SYMPTOMS OF EXPOSURE
INHALATION: VAPORS AND MISTS ARE EXTREMELY CORROSIVE TO THE NOSE, THROAT, AND MUCOUS MEMBRANES. BRONCHITIS, PULMONARY EDEMA, AND CHEMICAL PNEUMONITIS MAY OCCUR. IRRITATION, COUGHING, CHEST PAIN, AND DIFFICULTY IN BREATHING MAY OCCUR WITH BRIEF EXPOSURE WHILE PROLONGED EXPOSURE MAY RESULT IN MORE SEVERE IRRITATION AND TISSUE DAMAGE. BREATHING HIGH CONCENTRATIONS MAY RESULT IN DEATH.

EYE CONTACT: VAPORS, LIQUID, AND MISTS ARE EXTREMELY CORROSIVE TO THE EYES. BRIEF CONTACT OF THE VAPORS WILL BE SEVERELY IRRITATING. BRIEF CONTACT OF THE LIQUID OR MISTS WILL SEVERELY DAMAGE THE EYES AND PROLONGED CONTACT MAY CAUSE PERMANENT EYE INJURY WHICH MAY BE FOLLOWED BY BLINDNESS.

SKIN CONTACT: VAPORS, MISTS, AND LIQUID ARE EXTREMELY CORROSIVE TO THE SKIN. VAPORS WILL SEVERELY IRRITATE THE SKIN AND LIQUID AND MISTS WILL SEVERELY BURN THE SKIN. PROLONGED LIQUID CONTACT WILL BURN OR DESTROY SURROUNDING TISSUE AND DEATH MAY ACCOMPANY BURNS WHICH EXTEND OVER LARGE POR- TIONS OF THE BODY.

SWALLOWED: VAPORS, MISTS, AND LIQUID ARE EXTREMELY CORROSIVE TO THE MOUTH AND THROAT. SWALLOWING THE LIQUID BURNS THE TISSUES, CAUSES SEVERE ABDOMINAL PAIN, NAUSEA, VOMITING, AND COLLAPSE. SWALLOW- ING LARGE QUANTITIES CAN CAUSE DEATH.

CHRONIC EFFECTS OF EXPOSURE: MAY CAUSE EROSION OF THE TEETH, LESIONS ON THE SKIN, BRONCHIAL IRRITA- TION, COUGHING, AND PNEUMONIA.

MEDICAL CONDITIONS GENERALLY AGGRAVATED BY EXPOSURE: ACUTE AND CHRONIC RESPIRATORY DISEASES.

-----------------------------TOXICITY DATA--------------------------------

ORAL: RAT LD50 = 2,140 MG/KG

P1361.1   MATERIAL SAFETY DATA SHEET   PG 3

REVISION OF: 07-21-87

DERMAL: NO DATA FOUND

INHALATION: GUINEA PIG LC50 = 18 MG/M3

CARCINOGENICITY: THIS MATERIAL IS NOT CONSIDERED TO BE A CARCINOGEN BY THE NATIONAL TOXICOLOGY PROGRAM, THE INTERNATIONAL AGENCY FOR RESEARCH ON CANCER, OR THE OCCUPATIONAL SAFETY AND HEALTH ADMINISTRATION.

OTHER DATA: ALTHOUGH ONE LIMITED STUDY OF REFINERY WORKERS DID SUGGEST A POSSIBLE LINK BETWEEN SULFURIC ACID EXPOSURE AND LARYNGEAL CANCER, THE STUDY WAS LIMITED BECAUSE OF THE SMALL NUMBER OF WORKERS AND THE MIXED EXPOSURES TO SEVERAL OTHER MATERIALS INCLUDING DIETHYL SULFATE, AN IARC AND NTP CARCINOGEN. BASED ON THE OVERALL WEIGHT OF EVIDENCE FROM ALL ANIMAL TOXICITY AND HUMAN EPIDEMIOLOGICAL STUDIES, NO CAUSE-AND-EFFECT RELATIONSHIP BETWEEN CANCER AND SULFURIC ACID EXPOSURE HAS BEEN SHOWN. INDIVIDUALS WITH PREEXISTING DISEASE OF THE LUNGS MAY HAVE INCREASED SUSCEPTIBILITY TO THE TOXICITY OF EXCESSIVE EXPOSURES.

---------------------------PERSONAL PROTECTION---------------------------

VENTILATION: LOCAL MECHANICAL EXHAUST VENTILATION CAPABLE OF MAINTAINING EMISSIONS AT THE POINT OF USE BELOW THE PEL.

RESPIRATORY PROTECTION: WEAR A NIOSH-APPROVED RESPIRATOR APPROPRIATE FOR THE VAPOR OR MIST CONCENTRATION AT THE POINT OF USE. APPROPRIATE RESPIRATORS MAY BE A FULL FACEPIECE AIR-PURIFYING CARTRIDGE RESPIRATOR EQUIPPED FOR ACID GASES/MISTS, A SELF-CONTAINED BREATHING APPARATUS IN THE PRESSURE DEMAND MODE, OR A SUPPLIED-AIR RESPIRATOR.

EYE PROTECTION: CHEMICAL GOGGLES AND FULL FACESHIELD UNLESS A FULL FACEPIECE RESPIRATOR IS ALSO WORN. IT IS GENERALLY RECOGNIZED THAT CONTACT LENSES SHOULD NOT BE WORN WHEN WORKING WITH CHEMICALS BECAUSE CONTACT LENSES MAY CONTRIBUTE TO THE SEVERITY OF AN EYE INJURY.

PROTECTIVE CLOTHING: ACID-RESISTANT SLICKER SUIT WITH RUBBER APRON, RUBBER BOOTS WITH PANTS OUTSIDE, AND RUBBER GLOVES WITH GAUNTLETS.

OTHER PROTECTIVE MEASURES: AN EYEWASH AND SAFETY SHOWER SHOULD BE NEARBY AND READY FOR USE.

----------------------FIRE AND EXPLOSION INFORMATION---------------------

FLASH POINT, DEG F: NONE   FLAMMABLE LIMITS IN AIR, %
METHOD USED: N/A   LOWER: N/A UPPER: N/A
EXTINGUISHING MEDIA: THIS MATERIAL IS NOT COMBUSTIBLE. USE EXTINGUISHING MEDIA APPROPRIATE FOR SURROUNDING FIRE.

SPECIAL FIRE FIGHTING PROCEDURES: FIRE FIGHTERS SHOULD WEAR SELF-CONTAINED BREATHING APPARATUS AND FULL PROTECTIVE CLOTHING. USE WATER SPRAY TO COOL

14:01:24   02 MAR 1988

P1361.1   MATERIAL SAFETY DATA SHEET   PG 4

REVISION OF: 07-21-87

NEARBY CONTAINERS AND STRUCTURES EXPOSED TO FIRE.

UNUSUAL FIRE AND EXPLOSION HAZARDS: EXTINGUISH ALL NEARBY SOURCES OF IGNITION SINCE FLAMMABLE HYDROGEN GAS WILL BE LIBERATED FROM CONTACT WITH SOME METALS. KEEP WATER OUT OF CONTAINERS.

--------------------------HAZARDOUS REACTIVITY--------------------------

STABILITY: STABLE   POLYMERIZATION: WILL NOT OCCUR
CONDITIONS TO AVOID: NONE

MATERIALS TO AVOID: ALKALIS, OXIDIZING OR REDUCING MATERIALS, CYANIDES, SULFIDES, OR COMBUSTIBLE MATERIALS. REACTS WITH MANY METALS. CONCENTRATED ACID REACTS VIOLENTLY WITH WATER.

HAZARDOUS DECOMPOSITION PRODUCTS: MAY LIBERATE CARBON MONOXIDE, CARBON DIOXIDE, AND OXIDES OF SULFUR.

------------------SPILL, LEAK, AND DISPOSAL PROCEDURES------------------

ACTION TO TAKE FOR SPILLS OR LEAKS: WEAR ACID-RESISTANT SLICKER SUIT AND COMPLETE PROTECTIVE EQUIPMENT INCLUDING RUBBER GLOVES, RUBBER BOOTS, AND A SELF-CONTAINED BREATHING APPARATUS IN THE PRESSURE DEMAND MODE OR A SUPPLIED-AIR RESPIRATOR. iF THE SPILL OR LEAK IS SMALL, A FULL FACEPIECE AIR-PURIFYING CARTRIDGE RESPIRATOR EQUIPPED FOR ACID GASES MAY BE SATISFACTORY. IN ANY EVENT, ALWAYS WEAR EYE PROTECTION. REMOVE ALL SOURCES OF IGNITION. FOR SMALL SPILLS OR DRIPS, MOP OR WIPE UP AND DISPOSE OF IN DOT-APPROVED WASTE CONTAINERS. FOR LARGE SPILLS, CONTAIN BY DIKING WITH SOIL OR OTHER NON-COMBUSTIBLE ABSORBENT MATERIALS AND CAREFULLY NEUTRALIZE WITH SODA ASH OR LIME. IF SODA ASH IS USED, PROVIDE ADEQUATE VENTILATION TO DISSIPATE THE CARBON DIOXIDE GAS. KEEP NON-NEUTRALIZED MATERIAL OUT OF SEWERS, STORM DRAINS, SURFACE WATERS, AND SOIL.
COMPLY WITH ALL APPLICABLE GOVERNMENTAL REGULATIONS ON SPILL REPORTING, AND HANDLING AND DISPOSAL OF WASTE.

DISPOSAL METHODS: DISPOSE OF CONTAMINATED PRODUCT AND MATERIALS USED IN CLEANING UP SPILLS OR LEAKS IN A MANNER APPROVED FOR THIS MATERIAL. CONSULT APPROPRIATE FEDERAL, STATE AND LOCAL REGULATORY AGENCIES TO ASCERTAIN PROPER DISPOSAL PROCEDURES.
NOTE: EMPTY CONTAINERS CAN HAVE RESIDUES, GASES AND MISTS AND ARE SUBJECT TO PROPER WASTE DISPOSAL, AS ABOVE.

---------------------------SPECIAL PRECAUTIONS---------------------------

STORAGE AND HANDLING PRECAUTIONS: STORE IN A COOL, DRY, WELL-VENTILATED PLACE AWAY FROM INCOMPATIBLE MATERIALS. VENT CONTAINER CAREFULLY, AS NEEDED, TO RELIEVE PRESSURE. KEEP CONTAINER TIGHTLY CLOSED WHEN NOT IN USE. DO NOT USE PRESSURE TO EMPTY CONTAINER. WASH THOROUGHLY AFTER HANDLING. DO NOT GET IN EYES, ON SKIN, OR ON CLOTHING.

14:01:24   02 MAR 1988

P1361.1   MATERIAL SAFETY DATA SHEET   PG 5

REVISION OF: 07-21-87

REPAIRS AND MAINTENANCE PRECAUTIONS: DO NOT CUT, GRIND, WELD, OR DRILL ON OR NEAR THIS CONTAINER.

OTHER PRECAUTIONS: CONTAINERS, EVEN THOSE THAT HAVE BEEN EMPTIED, WILL RETAIN PRODUCT RESIDUE AND VAPORS. ALWAYS OBEY HAZARD WARNINGS AND HANDLE EMPTY CONTAINERS AS IF THEY WERE FULL.

------------------------FOR ADDITIONAL INFORMATION----------------------

CONTACT DOUGLAS EISNER, TECHNICAL DIRECTOR, VAN WATERS & ROGERS INC.
DURING BUSINESS HOURS, PACIFIC TIME (206) 447-5911

---------------------------------NOTICE---------------------------------

VAN WATERS & ROGERS INC. ("VW&R") EXPRESSLY DISCLAIMS ALL EXPRESS OR IMPLIED WARRANTIES OF MERCHANTABILITY AND FITNESS FOR A PARTICULAR PURPOSE, WITH RESPECT TO THE PRODUCT OR INFORMATION PROVIDED HEREIN.

ALL INFORMATION APPEARING HEREIN IS BASED UPON DATA OBTAINED FROM THE MANUFACTURER AND/OR RECOGNIZED TECHNICAL SOURCES. WHILE THE INFORMATION IS BELIEVED TO BE ACCURATE, VW&R MAKES NO REPRESENTATIONS AS TO ITS ACCURACY OR SUFFICIENCY. CONDITIONS OF USE ARE BEYOND VW&R'S CONTROL AND THEREFORE USERS ARE RESPONSIBLE TO VERIFY THIS DATA UNDER THEIR OWN OPERATING CONDITIONS TO DETERMINE WHETHER THE PRODUCT IS SUITABLE FOR THEIR PARTICULAR PURPOSES AND THEY ASSUME ALL RISKS OF THEIR USE, HANDLING, AND DISPOSAL OF THE PRODUCT, OR FROM THE PUBLICATION OR USE OF, OR RELIANCE UPON, INFORMATION CONTAINED HEREIN. THIS INFORMATION RELATES ONLY TO THE PRODUCT DESIGNATED HEREIN, AND DOES NOT RELATE TO ITS USE IN COMBINATION WITH ANY OTHER MATERIAL OR IN ANY OTHER PROCESS.

---------------------------------REVISION-------------------------------

07/87: REPORTED ADDITIONAL EXPOSURE LIMIT AND OTHER TOXICITY DATA.

**** E N D O F M S D S ****

14:01:24   02 MAR 1988

SAMPLING AND ASSAYING

The most difficult (sometimes impossible) step in the analytical process is accurate sampling. A sample of the unknown material must be obtained and it must be as truly like the original material as possible. This sample should be quite large and it must be reduced to the small size that can be assayed in the laboratory. Somehow this must be done without changing the sample so that it remains a true example of the original scrap. The problems involved in this work are considerable, and this makes sampling the weakest link in the work of analyzing scrap. The portion actually assayed may well be only about one troy ounce and this may be only a very, very tiny portion of the original drum of scrap, or in the case of ore, the mountain from whence it came.

Assaying, the qualitative or quantitative analysis of a substance, especially ore or precious metals, usually brings to mind the ancient and honorable fire assay that today is still the standard for gold commerce. Other assay procedures may involve weights or gravimetric systems or they may involve titrations with liquids or volumetric systems. There are also analytical procedures with instruments; and these would be techniques involving X-ray fluorescence, electron microprobes, emission spectrography and atomic absorption, and perhaps many others. These usually require costly equipment and specialized training. Some are useful mainly to determine very small amounts of values or very small amounts of impurities.

For additional information in this field <u>Beamish and Van Loon</u> gives an excellent review (see references).

TOUCHSTONE

Rapid nondestructive assay of gold artifacts by means of the touchstone is a very old method. It was known as early as 600 B.C.

Those who are expert in this method, who have the experience and proper standards for comparison, are able to determine differences in metal content as small as ten to twenty parts per thousand or the difference between 18 karat and 18.75 karat or 18.51 karat. It is a seemingly simple procedure but is actually quite complex, requiring attention to details and a considerable knowledge of alloys, acids, and several sets of good standards if quantitative accuracy is desired.

The basic principle is quite simple. A dark stone, the touchstone, is rubbed with the unknown to make a sizeable metallic streak on the stone. A standard touch needle of known composition is used to make a similar and nearby streak. The rubbings are treated with a touch acid of the proper composition. The acid dissolves metals, base metals first. A comparison of the colors of the unknown and the known streaks after acid treatment will give a fairly accurate answer of the quality of the unknown material.

Swiss assayers have a reputation for great ability in the use of the touchstone and for being able to determine value or purity quite accurately. For such accuracy, carefully prepared solutions and acids of known strength are required and sets of touch needles of varying fineness and of different colors are required.

Many users of the touchstone rely mainly on a quick look at the speed of complete dissolution of comparative streaks and this may suffice for scrap metal purchases of small individual pieces. But it should be remembered that this only tells how quickly a streak dissolves on the touchstone. It does not tell if the object is gold or silver or other metal.

A preliminary test to find if the article is solid or plated should be done by abrading the article and with magnification, inspect the abrasion to see if there is a substrate or different color. A small drop of nitric acid on the abraded spot that turns green would indicate copper and perhaps brass or bronze. If no color change is noted and a bit of hydrochloric acid or saltwater is added and if it turns white, the presence of silver is indicated. The white color would be insoluble silver chloride.

For a description of the basic process, the simple instructions furnished with test kits available at jeweler's supply shops in the United States are adequate. For a description of the wider and more accurate use of the touchstone, several very complete articles are available. Wälchli & Vuilleumier give a very good account of the touchstone testing methods. Wälchli also wrote about this in the magazine Gold Bulletin. Other articles are "Simple Tests For the Four Precious Metals" presented by the magazine Watchmaker, Jeweler, and Silversmith, an English publication in their September 1955 issue. Also, "Are Acid Tests Reliable" as presented in American Jewelry Manufacturer, November 1981. A book long out of print called Jeweler's Workshop Practices gives directions for this technique starting on page 379.

Hoke has written a second volume on this subject, see references. A photograph of a touchstone kit follows:

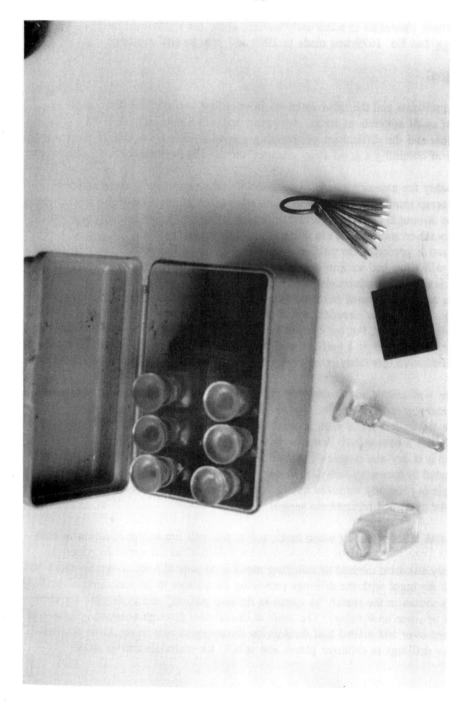

Touchstone Kit

For those interested in some early writing about the touchstone method, a reprint of <u>Badcock</u> 2nd Ed. 1679 was made in 1970 and may be still available.

SAMPLING

The problems and the labor involved in sampling will perhaps discourage most owners of small amounts of scrap. However, without a good sample the assay is meaningless and the difficulties of obtaining a good sample far outweigh the work and problems of obtaining a good assay once the sample has been taken.

Probably the easiest material to sample with some accuracy is metallic scrap. Metallic scrap should, if possible, be sampled as the molten metal. The molten metal should be thoroughly stirred to create uniformity. For silver an iron stirring rod can be used as silver and iron do not alloy to any appreciable extent. The use of a graphite rod is preferred for gold and is a necessity if gold is to be sampled. Gold and iron will alloy and an iron rod in <u>molten</u> gold dissolves to some extent. Graphite rods are available from jewelers' supply shops. Graphite gouging rods in many diameters can be purchased from welding supply shops. These have the disadvantage of having a thin copper covering which can dilute the metal slightly. For scrap this is not usually a problem, but for stirring fine or karat gold, the rods should be cleared of copper. Sandpaper or a half-and-half nitric acid or aqua regia followed by a water wash will remove this fairly readily.

When well stirred and thoroughly mixed, the molten metal can be dip sampled with a small dip ladle of the size that the melt permits. Our preference, however, is to sample the molten metal with a glass tube. A glass tube of 4mm inside diameter is equipped with a rubber bulb that can provide some suction. The glass tube is warmed to be sure it is dry and is quickly dipped into the melt and one half inch or so of molten metal is drawn up into the glass by means of the rubber bulb. The hot glass and sample is promptly removed and is dipped in a small container of water which shatters the glass and releases the sample.

Vacuum tubes that melt when immersed in the melt are commercially available.

A very common method of sampling metal is to pour the metal into an ingot and then drill the ingot with the drillings providing the sample to be analyzed. A drilling pattern is shown in the sketch "A common drilling pattern" and is suitable for most materials of some uniformity. The ingot is drilled half through at several places and then turned over and drilled half through on the opposite side in the same positions. This gives drillings in different places and is o.k. for materials known to be

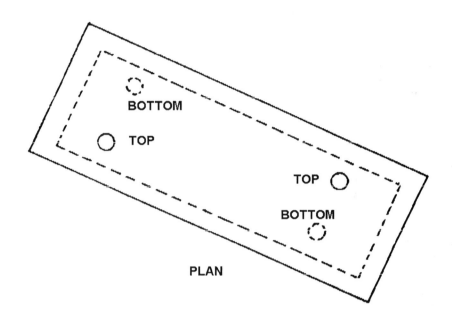

PLAN

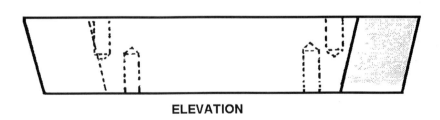

ELEVATION

Ingot Drilling Pattern (Suggested by <u>Rose</u> also <u>Smith</u>)

essentially fine or to have constituents that are not only fully soluble in the molten state but that remain mutually soluble when they solidify. However, some metals when poured into a mold to cool and solidify will have a different composition in the parts that cool first, i.e., the bottom, the edges and the top, than in the center or core, which cools last. Drilling such an ingot will not provide a true sample.

We have seen templates for drilling patterns involving about 20 holes all of them to be completely through the ingot as a means of getting a proper sample. This is a lengthy and laborious task.

Shot made from a well stirred melt may be divided and a portion used for a sample. However, shot made by Torch melting an ingot is not likely to be any better than a drill sample.

One large refiner reported to me that all scrap metal they receive is melted. Even if presented in ingot form, it is remelted and only molten metal is sampled. This appears to have been the result of receiving a large silver ingot containing a small steel crank shaft.

Jewelers Bench Scrap

Most other jeweler's scrap is more difficult to sample than the metallic materials. For instance, the sampling of lemel is complicated because it contains materials other than metal. Sandpaper grit, cigarette ends, bits of paper and similar useless materials must somehow be dealt with. The best way is to first rid this scrap of combustible materials by burning it in a suitable metal pan with some alcohol, or better, with a low volatile petroleum material called charcoal starter fluid. When this has been burned, the iron such as jewelers' saws and similar material are removed with a magnet and then the bulk of the material can be mixed with a flux and melted in a crucible. After a time the metallic portion being heavier settles to the bottom and the useless part has combined with the flux to form a slag. A following section on fluxes and slags will give formulas for a suitable flux to do this work.

All of this material is poured into a mold where the metal goes to the bottom and the lighter slag stays on top. When cool, a tap from a hammer breaks away the slag and the metal can be remelted for sampling.

Jewelers Sweeps

The sampling of sweeps and dust collector material and similar low grade scrap is much more complex. This material must first be burned in a controlled furnace so that it can burn very slowly and not lose valuable, very small particles of gold. The ashes are not accurately assayable unless they are reduced to a homogenous material that makes a valid sample possible.

This requires the removal of scrap that is magnetic and then the grinding of the ashes to pulverize any lumps and to make the entire bulk of material a very small size that can be accurately sampled. The removal of the magnetic material must be done with care because some of the material may well be iron oxide, which is the rouge that often is used for the final polishing of jewelry. This may contain considerable gold and be magnetic so care must be taken to only remove the large particles.

Hammermills and similar dust creating mills are not suitable for grinding these materials because of the losses in the dust. A closed mill, such as a rod mill or a ball mill is used. After reducing these ashes to as fine a powder as possible, some lumps will remain. If these are taken as part of the sample, they will almost certainly destroy the accuracy of the assay. If valueless, they will change the results of the assay to a value lower than correct, and if they contain much gold, they will make the assay too high.

It is a known fact that coarse particles in a material that is to be assayed will always create error, either too high or too low. This is called the nugget effect. The solution is to screen the milled material and remove the oversized particles before the sample is taken. We find that these oversized particles are often quite valuable. However, if a sample must be taken, these coarse particles must be removed.

In our refinery we do not sample sweeps ashes. We just flux, melt, and refine the entire lot as a separate entity with no commingling with other lots.

The techniques of sampling, the equipment involved and the statistical validity are discussed in detail in books about assaying and in books about mining.

For further reading on this subject please see <u>Browning</u>, also <u>Corrigan</u>, also <u>Kudryk</u>, p. 67 and p. 79. <u>Smith</u>, now available as a reprint and most other books on assaying, give information on sampling (see list of references).

The sampling of liquids is generally quite easy. The liquid should be stirred to insure through mixing for uniformity and a sample taken. However, we find that used plating liquids, bombing solutions, and electrostrip solutions often have a considerable amount of solid materials settled out in the bottom which may be of value. In this case, the liquid should be thoroughly stirred and stirred with sufficient vigor that the solids can be sampled with the liquid.

Because jewelers liquid wastes have a likelihood of being cyanide solutions all liquids offered for precious metal recovery must be tested to see if they contain cyanide. Cyanide solutions and cyanide solution samples are then marked and treated with the proper respect and care.

ASSAYING

For the precious metal industry, assaying usually means the ancient and honorable fire assay. This very, very old technique continues to be the standard for gold commerce and is excellent for silver and useful for platinum and palladium. <u>Oddy</u> writes about the assaying of gold by fire as early as 1350 B.C.

Fire assay for low-grade materials, such as sweeps and similar scrap and for ores, consists of essentially two steps. The first step is a gathering or concentrating step in which the precious metals and base metals in the sample are collected by means of lead into a button. In a second step, the precious metal content of this lead button is determined.

Usually the sample is crushed and milled and then carefully divided until a reasonably small amount is obtained for the assay work. The classic sample weight is the assay ton. This is approximately 29 grams and the reason for this amount is that, in the early days, weighing this specific amount avoided pencil and paper arithmetic at the end of the operation. It was merely necessary to weigh the final button which then became a troy-ounce-per-ton result. The ease of using modern calculators makes this procedure unnecessary.

The finely milled and weighed sample is mixed with fluxes and with litharge, which is an oxide of lead. Also, ordinary flour or other carbonaceous material is added and this is a source of carbon that combines with the oxygen of the litharge and changes the litharge into metallic lead. The metallic lead combines with the metals of the sample and removes these metals from the bulk of the material into a heavy metal button that settles out into the bottom of the crucible. When everything is completely melted and quite liquid, the sample is poured into a cone-shaped ingot mold where the metal containing lead button settles to the bottom of the cone and the slag remains at the top. When cool, a simple tap of the hammer breaks away the slag. The lead button is pounded with a hammer so any small adhering pieces of slag are broken away.

In the second step, the lead button is placed in a small shallow porous crucible called a cupel and this is placed in a cupel furnace. The door of the cupel furnace is kept closed until the lead button is completely melted and then is opened slightly to allow air to sweep into the furnace. The lead and the oxygen of the air combine to revert the lead to lead oxide or litharge. While this happens, the base metals such as copper are also oxidized to their respective oxides. These oxides then sink into the porous cupel crucible with the lead oxide and gradually disappear leaving behind the precious metals. At the end of this oxidation step a small sphere or button of precious metals remains and all of the base-metal oxides have disappeared into the pores of the cupel. The cupel is removed, cooled and the precious metal button is weighed and this determines the amount of precious metals present. In order to determine the amount of silver in this button, it is rolled into a thin sheet and then twisted into a spiral which the assayer calls a cornet. This cornet is then placed in chemical glassware and a solution of nitric acid is added, which will dissolve the silver if the silver is there in sufficient quantity. If silver is not there in sufficient quantity, it may be necessary to remelt the button with more silver so that the silver content is in the order of three quarters of the total weight. The nitric acid dissolves the silver leaving the gold behind, often in the same physical shape as the original cornet. This cornet of gold is then washed, dried, and weighed. The proper arithmetic now determines the quantity of silver and gold in the original sample. The presence of other precious metals such as platinum and palladium complicate the procedure but can be handled by a knowledgeable assayer.

In yet another article in Aurum #29, Wälchli presents a description of fire assaying. Some history and a description of this method is given by Deal in the California Mining Journal.

Rose in his 7th edition starting on page 490 describes the assay of ores and bullion and also a few non-cupellation methods. On page 525 he very briefly describes the use of cadmium. A small change in this cadmium method, described to us by a refiner, involves the use of a test tube for melting the cadmium-gold mixture and the use of alcohol over the cadmium with a vacuum on the test tube to avoid the problems of oxidation of cadmium and to avoid the poisonous aspects of cadmium fumes. We have tried this briefly and feel that it is a useful method for some work.

Bugbee is considered by many to be a very practical book on assaying and is still available. Smith covers many metals in his book and this book has been recently reprinted.

Rose, page 531, describes the determination of density of alloys by the method of weighing in water and weighing in air to give an approximation of gold content. Demortier describes the use of X-rays in a Gold Bulletin article.

A nuclear method is described by de Jesus and a review of methods is given by Young. In the books by Young and by Beamish, a larger view is given. Young describes the analysis of about 42 metals including precious metals. Beamish restricts his to a review of methods for the noble metals.

A now very common analytical procedure is atomic absorption spectrography and a somewhat similar plasma arc system. These are especially good for determining very small amounts of materials in a sample. Neutron activation is one of the newer analytical techniques. Emission spectrography is an old and valuable method for some analytical work.

REFINING JEWELERS SWEEPS

The miscellaneous low grade shop wastes such as polishing machine dusts, floor cleanings, sink trap sludge, wiping rags, shop carpets and mats, shop clothing aprons and gloves, vacuum cleaner bags and filters are what we refer to as "sweeps." Mostly these are fluffy, dirty and burnable and look worthless.

Of these materials the polishing machine dust is probably the most consistently valuable.

Gold content of sweeps in our experience varies from about 1/2% to perhaps 5% with most in the 1 1/2% to 2% range.

It is impossible to sample sweeps in the as-collected state.

OUTLINE

The disposition of such sweeps can be done in a number of ways.

1. Sell the sweeps as is.

2. Send the crude sweeps to a reputable refinery for processing and sale or return of the metal contents.

3. Burn the sweeps, grind and screen the ashes, sample and assay and then offer the ashes for sale or melting and refining.

4. Burn the sweeps and melt the ashes. If this is done without mixing different lots, the grinding and screening is not necessary. Melting the ashes separates the valuable metal from useless slag. The crude metal from the melter can be remelted for sampling and toll refining.

5. The crude bar from the melting operation can be refined in-house.

The above sequence is a logical progression of additional work, equipment and complexity. In this section on SWEEPS, we will describe in some detail the methods 1 through 4. The fifth step is essentially the gold refining procedure as described in the later chapter "Gold".

PROCEDURES

1. SELL THE SWEEPS

The very small shop accumulates polishing dust and sweeps very slowly. However, such scrap should be saved because there are those who regularly offer to buy this material. For small lots, this is probably the most reasonable disposition because the jeweler has other more important and worthwhile things to do with his time.

2. HAVE THE SWEEPS REFINED

The crude sweeps can be sent to a refiner. Some refiners accept fairly small lots. It is our feeling that amounts of 20 lbs.(10 kilos) of sweeps and up are best. The time and labor for a small lot of 8 to 20 lbs. (4 to 10 kilos) takes almost as much refinery time and labor as a 60 lb. lot. Our experience is that some shops will send as little as 4 lbs. (2 kilos) of crude sweeps to the refiner and feel that a refining charge of 20-25% is worthwhile.

3. PROCESS AND ASSAY THE SWEEPS

The crude sweeps can be burned and the ashes milled and screened, sampled and assayed so the value is known. The ashes can then be offered for sale or refined based on this known value.

The first step in processing the sweeps is to burn them in a controlled draft burner. This dramatically reduces the volume to perhaps 10% of the original volume and the weight to roughly 60% of the original weight.

Sweeps should be burned slowly so that the very, very small metal particles are not carried out by flames and stack draft. A stove that has few nooks and crannies to hold valuable ashes and is tight so the draft can be controlled to give slow burning is O.K. for this work.

Sweeps usually burn easily and once started, burn rapidly or slowly depending upon the air supplied to the burner. Slow burning as we do it will take about one to two days for 60 to 100 lbs. of sweeps. The burning bed of sweeps requires stirring at least 3 or 4 times for a 60 to 100 lb. lot. Small amounts are stirred perhaps only once.

The burner can be opened and the mass quickly stirred. This always releases a cloud of smelly smoke and there may be a possible loss of some solid particles that could contain gold.

Several small approximately 3/4" diameter holes in the burner will allow the entry of a 1/2" diameter rod so the glowing bed of sweeps can be stirred.

A variety of sweeps burners are used. We have seen arch roofed brick chambers that look like ceramic kilns, smaller units that remind one of old style ovens, larger units where the sweeps are burned in stainless steel pans and others that remind one of trash incinerators. We have seen a very complex and costly rotating burner of Italian origin. We understand that crematory furnaces are used. Most of these have burners and perhaps blowers and some get very hot. It is our strong opinion that a settling chamber so that any dust carryover can be trapped should be a part of such burners. An electro-static precipitator is a very effective but quite costly collector of dust. A sketch of an incinerator type burner follows.

In all cases an after burner is a need because the off-gases smell bad and are smoky.

An incinerator with a settling chamber and after burner is described by <u>Hoel</u> in some detail. Such a burner has the advantage of burning at higher temperature so that very carbonaceous sweeps such as old carpets are thoroughly consumed.

A HOMEMADE BURNER

In our shop we use a homebuilt sweeps burner. This is a piece of 24" diameter by 5 foot long rather heavy gauge pipeline pipe. Wall thickness is about 3/8". The following sketch shows the general outlines and dimensions of this device. The efficiency of the after burner seems to be somewhat dependent on having a good hot ceramic lining that will get hot enough to have a noticeable glow.

The burner itself is not lined and even after some years of use, shows no signs of warping. This is probably a result of the slow burning that does not create high temperatures.

There is no settling chamber and we feel one is not needed if a slow burning rate is maintained. We have taken samples of the very small amounts of material on the walls of the after burner and stack and have found no gold.

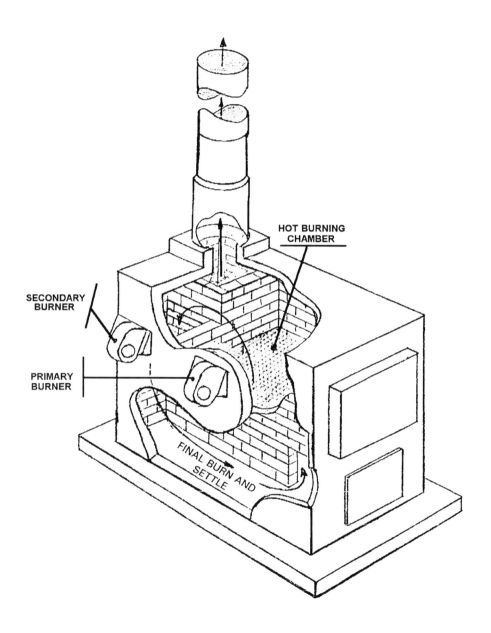

Sweeps Burner (Incinerator Type)

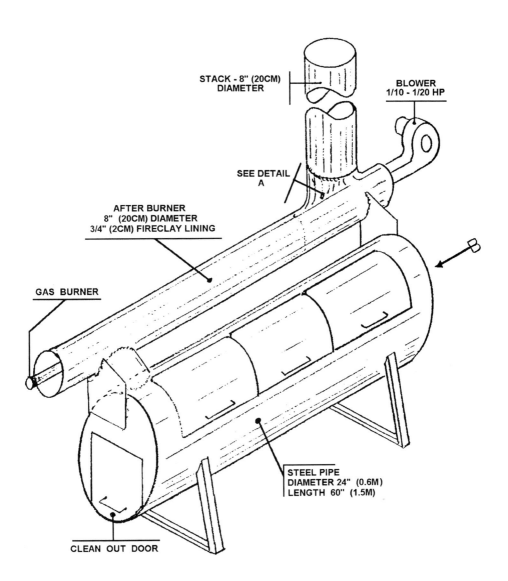

Sweeps Burner

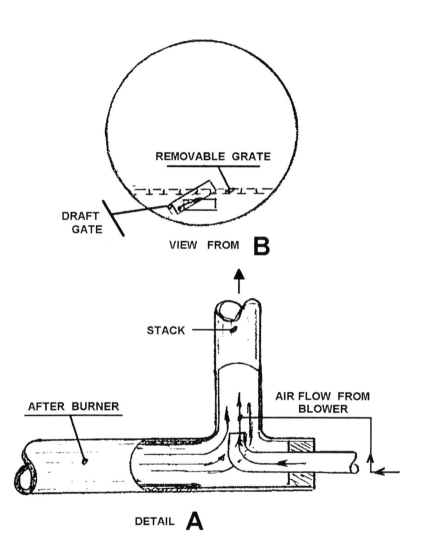

Sweeps Burner (Details)

Sweeps Burner

The grates are made of steel floor mesh as used in some factory cat walks. It is perhaps not necessary to have such grates. However, much of our scrap arrives in plastic garbage bags which we burn as received. This plastic can form a half burned adhering mess on the walls and the grates are helpful in burning the plastic.

Occasionally jewelers send sweeps that also contain wet material such as sink trap sludge or other watery scrap. This burns poorly or not at all. For such once-in-a-while material, we have a small gas jet in our burner. This is near the bottom at the end opposite the clean out door. It is welded to a steel plate and can be moved over a hole in the burner when used or moved away so the plate covers the hole when not used. See "draft gate" in the drawing page 26.

In this case the wet sweeps are piled as close to the gas jet end of the burner as possible so the gas flame dries the lot.

TREATING THE ASHES

When the ashes have cooled, the ashes are carefully raked into a pail through the clean out door. The insides of the burner are scraped with a broad scraper and swept clean with a whisk broom or perhaps a vacuum cleaner. The ashes are dusty and slow care is advised to lose as little dust as possible. See photograph page 27.

The magnetic material is removed with a magnet and screened through a screen with an opening of about 1/4" size. Only the large pieces of iron are discarded. The fine material may be magnetic iron oxide, rouge polishing powder that contains gold. A following photograph shows several of our magnets.

If these ashes are to be sampled for assay and sale or toll refining, they must be milled and screened for sampling.

The grinding and screening is a necessary part of the sampling procedure. A fire assay is the most likely analytical method that will be used. The traditional sample quantity for an assay is the assay ton, 29.16 grams or a little less than a troy ounce.

This is not large and any lumps or large pieces that find their way to this sample will overwhelm the results, too high if valuable or too low if valueless. Therefore the ashes must be milled to pass through a 100 or perhaps 120 or 140 mesh screen.

The grinding is normally done in a rod mill or preferably in a ball mill in order to get a fine enough powder. Hammer mills and other open types are unsuitable

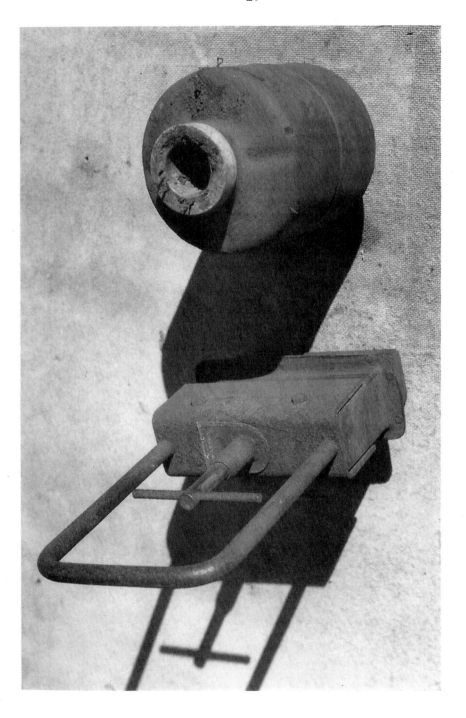

Magnets

Sample Splitter

because fine powders are hard to achieve and dust losses are large. A home made ball mill is shown in a photograph in the section on slags in the latter part of this chapter.

A suitable vibrating shaking or rotating screen for removing oversize is used with careful attention to dust losses. A home made screen is shown in a photograph in the latter part of this chapter.

Some particles cannot be crushed to this fineness and must be removed and do not become part of the sample. These may be lumps of metal which could be gold. We find that these oversize particles may be too valuable to discard.

The milled and screened ashes are now split (repeatedly divided) until a suitable sample portion is obtained. This is divided and half is retained and the other half sent for assaying. See the photograph of a splitter.

An assay is no better than the sample being assayed. Sampling methods, correct splitting methods, sample sizes, etc. are described in detail by texts on assaying. Bugbee and also Smith have entire chapters about sampling in their books on assaying. These are recommended as being presently available as reprints.

When the lot of ashes is offered for sale or refining, the potential buyer or refiner will, of course, resample and re-assay.

4. MELTING THE SWEEPS ASHES

If the ashes are to be melted, the above procedure can be somewhat simplified.

First the grinding and screening need not be done unless various discrete lots are to be mixed together. We burn and melt all lots as separate entities with no comingling.

The ashes are weighed and then put into a small cement mixer. The small mixer available at some hardware stores, Sears Roebuck, etc. is very suitable. See next photograph. We use a mixer with a plastic mixing drum. See photograph. It has an advantage of being easier to clean and does not rust.

We installed a magnet holder in this drum and we also made a tight cover of plywood. This cover is held down with a couple of screen door springs.

With the ashes in the drum, the magnet in place and the lid on, we rotate the drum for half a minute or so. Then wait to let the dust settle, remove the magnet, rake the magnetic material into a pail and repeat. When the magnet finally removes very little iron, we turn our attention to the magnetic particles. One of the following photograph shows a magnet with magnetic particles.

SCREENING THE MAGNETICS

Only the larger pieces of magnetic material should be discarded. By larger pieces we mean nails, bolts, pliers, files, saw blades, etc. The magnetic fines are likely to be rouge polishing powder (magnetic iron oxide). We separate this with a screen with approximately 1/4" to 3/8" openings. A plastic kitchen colander serves well. A dumping type hand magnet for repeatedly lifting and dropping the larger pieces to shake off the fines is useful. A photograph of one type of dumping magnet is shown earlier in this chapter.

The fines are returned to the mixer and the larger pieces rinsed with water. This rinse water is used to later dampen the ash-flux mix for dust control.

SWEEPS QUALITY

The sweeps from jewelers shops often contain a variety of debris. We find nails, bolts, bottles, cans, lunch scraps, files, pliers and once even a 2 x 4 board. The "legitimate" or gold bearing material one can expect is sandpaper, brushes, wiping rags, polishing wheels, rubber wheel debris, old crucibles and melting dishes, stirring rods, polishing dust, etc.

The polishing of jewelry is done with a variety of materials and each shop has its methods and materials. One can expect polishing materials to be a prime contributor of precious metal to the sweeps. <u>Bell</u> states that prepolishing materials are likely to be tripoli (also known as rotten stone, a decomposed sandstone about 75% silica, (SiO_2)), diatomaceous earth sometimes called tripolite, kieselguhr, etc., which are the skeletons of diatoms and may be 81-87% silica, 2-16% alumina (Al_2O_3), with some iron and calcium oxides. Pumice is also used and this is a lava, chemically a complex silicate of aluminum, potassium, and sodium. Corundum or emery is aluminum oxide and when very finely divided can be used for prepolishing. It is also a common material in grinding wheels and sandpaper. Silicon carbide (SiC) may also have a similar application.

Mixer

Mixer (Plastic Bowl)

Magnet and Iron

For fine polishing a variety of materials are available and used. Red rouge (magnetic iron oxide) is usually about 99% iron oxide and is a classic polishing material. White rouge is tin oxide and yellow rouge is cerium oxide, green is chrome oxide, black is lamp black (carbon). There are mixtures of chrome and iron oxides and there may be others.

Casting investment finds its way into some jewelers wastes. Investment in the dry form tends to be 20-25% calcium sulfate ($CaSO_4$), some water of hydration and the rest silica (SiO_2). Such sludge may arrive at the refinery shop soggy but fairly solid and be about 70% dry material and 30% water. Sink trap sludge which may contain investment but also a variety of other trash can be 70% water.

Some large dust collector filter bags come with diatomaceous earth. Diatomaceous earth is reported to be more than 80% silica (SiO_2).

The ash from wood floors and the ash from paper may possibly be similar and be high in potassium (similar to sodium). Lead metal from lead center buffs is a serious contaminant of sweeps ashes. It may also come from soft solder in the scrap although we think this is a very occasional and a very small part of jewelers scrap. If lead is present some manganese dioxide (MnO_2) a high temperature oxidizer should be used in the flux.

Plastic floor tile may contain fibers that act as a reinforcing material. This may be glass strands or in some older tiles asbestos fibers. Carpets made of synthetics are low in ash but burning them is difficult unless it is done in a high temperature burner. Ash from carpets may require additional oxidizer (sodium nitrate) added little by little at the center of the melt during the furnacing operation to remove carbon.

The proper fluxing materials for such a variable mixture is of course largely a matter of guesswork. We like to call it educated witchcraft.

MIXING WITH FLUX

A good flux will react with essentially everything in the ashes and reduce them to a liquid slag thereby releasing the valuable metallic particles.

The only exception to this is the carbonaceous and graphitic melting crucibles and rods that may be a part of the sweeps. These do not melt but the slag coating in them which contains the precious metal does melt and thereby separates them from the valuable metal.

These crucibles should be broken down so that no pockets or cups that could hold metal remain. During the melting work, we stir the hot slag so any crucible chips are actively rolled around.

Flux consists of dry chemicals that will react with the materials in the sweeps at the high temperatures of the furnace. The slag resulting from this reaction should be as thin and watery (low viscosity) as possible. The very small metal pieces need to get together and form drops heavy enough to sink to the bottom of the melting crucible. A thin slag is needed to allow the particles to sink to the bottom.

FLUX RECIPE

A successful flux recipe is as % by weight:

Borax 5 Mol	43	(Pentahydrate)
White Sand	23	
Soda Ash	20	
Sodium Nitrate	10	
Fluorspar	4	

In a later discussion of slags and fluxes we give our quite limited knowledge about fluxes.

The mixture we put into the furnace is half ashes and half flux mixture. A flux mixture can be weighed and mixed and stored in bulk for use as needed. We prefer to mix each lot as needed. We take the weight of the ashes, multiply that by the percentages in the recipe above, weigh those amounts and dump into the mixer on top of the ashes, close the cover and mix.

WATER

This mixture is dusty and unpleasant. Later the flame in the melting furnace tends to blow some of the mixture away. To reduce these problems, we dampen the mixture with water. An easy way to do this is to have a small cup installed in the center of the mixer lid. Water is poured in slowly while the mixing proceeds. The mix need not be soggy or sticky.

THE FURNACE

The ash-flux mixture is melted in a crucible furnace. These are gas fired furnaces with an air blower to provide the volume of flame required to achieve melting temperatures. These are rather commonly available. There is a large list in the large green, many-volume directory of USA manufacturers called "Thomas Register." Our experience is with MacEngelvan. Such factory units are built with safety ignition devices and flame probes to cut the gas if there is no flame. They provide good mixing of fuel and air and are efficient and fast melters.

Commercially available furnaces in the larger sizes are usually the tilting type. The crucible (with a pouring lip) remains in the furnace and the entire furnace and crucible tilts to make the pour. Such large furnaces are not needed for the small scale refining that we do. Our largest furnace will accept a standard #80 crucible. We also have several smaller ones for small lots.

CRUCIBLES

In our experience silicon carbide crucibles are more durable than clay graphite. However in smaller sizes only clay graphite are available.

New crucibles often contain small amounts of moisture and if put into a hot furnace the sudden heat and expansion make some interesting noises and often destroys the crucible. See following photograph.

We always warm a new crucible by placing it near an operating furnace and turning it once in awhile to get all parts quite hot and dry. A new crucible can be started in a cold furnace if the first part of the heating is done with some caution.

"Crucible Charlie Says," tells us that a new clay graphite should be brought up to full temperature rather slowly. Silicon carbide crucibles however (once warm and dry) are best heated very rapidly often in an already hot furnace. This may vary with different manufacturers.

Once heated we find that crucibles do not have to be dried and warmed again if stored in a dry place.

White clay crucibles do not survive very well in a gas fired furnace unless protected by an outer shell of other material. Uneven heating of a gas furnace tends to crack white clay crucibles.

Crucible (Exploded)

MELTING THE ASH-FLUX MIXTURE

The mix is dumped from the mixer into a container (five gallon pails serve well) and into the crucible. The crucible should be filled to about 3 or 4 inches of the top pressed down. An occasional lot will rise in the crucible while starting to melt and a completely full crucible will spill some mix. The crucible is put into the furnace and the furnace started.

As melting proceeds the mixture loses water which escapes as steam. When the furnace is hot enough for the flux and ashes to combine some other gases such as carbon dioxide escape. This usually starts after perhaps 3/4 hour and then more mix can be added. The additional mix that can be added is usually about equal to the original amount put into the crucible.

This can be added with a small hand scoop or the mix can be put into paper bags and the bags added as needed. One must wear heat resistant mittens and suitable heat resistant clothing. Some operators add the mix while the furnace is operating; others let the crucible contents sink fairly low and then momentarily shut off gas and blower to make the addition.

If hand scoop additions are made it is best to swing the lid aside and add carefully to the crucible. If the mix is bagged the bags can possibly be added through the hole in the lid.

Sometimes we make flux additions during a melting run because the slag is not liquid enough. When we have no clue about the nature of the ashes and no reason to add more of a specific material the addition of Borax and/or fluorspar will usually result in improvement. These are both important
liquefiers. Soda ash is often helpful. Some sweeps may be high in silica.

HOME BUILT FURNACES

In our shop we have made our own crucible furnaces in a number of different sizes. The advantage to us has been that we could make them cheaply. They require care in start up and in operation and in some ways are not as convenient. These home built furnaces are all lift-out types. That is, we have to use a crucible tongs to take the hot crucible out of the furnace and pour the melt into molds. This is hot and somewhat hazardous work. Heat resistant garments and sturdy clothing and shoes are needed as well as a tolerance for working within a foot or so of crucibles glowing at 2000-2500°F (1100-1400°C).

To handle the largest of our crucibles (#80) we use a small electric crane and suitable tongs, hooks and pouring handles. A small electric hoist mounted in an overhead rail works well. The smaller crucibles we lift and pour with hand held tongs.

On the following page we give a sketch of some of our home built furnaces. These are welded up from pieces of standard pipe. The linings are 3000°F castable refractory. This is mixed in a cement mixer. A suitable form for the inner wall can be made from heavy paper drums cut and fitted to suit. Pouring this lining is about like pouring concrete. A following photograph shows a small gold melting furnace for the 0 to 3 crucibles.

For any drainage holes and for the air-gas entry hole we insert some foam plastic that has been carved to the correct shape. Refractory mixing instructions should be carefully followed. The setting time and bake out procedures are important and to be done as specified.

One can also make a good lining with plastic fire clay or ramming mix. This is a ready mixed material that can be pounded and rammed into place without forms. The holes can be rammed up around wooden plugs and plugs then pulled out or they can be "sculptured" to shape as the ramming in takes place. Setting up and firing instructions are important and to be followed.

Furnace lids are best made up on some newspapers on the floor. The metal ring of the lid should have some 1/4"-3/8" rods about 2"-4" long welded inside the ring. Space these about 4" to 6" apart. They should project toward the center of the lid. They keep the refractory of the lid from sliding out of the ring.

BLOWERS

A strong force of air mixed with the correct amount of gas is necessary to achieve the temperatures required for this work. Commercial furnaces come with good quality blowers. The homebuilder must provide a high pressure blower.

Small versions of the type used for home heating and air conditioning will not do. The type used in vacuum cleaners are suitable and we use them regularly for the small furnaces. Good quality vacuum cleaner blowers are often available at vacuum cleaner repair shops. Usually inspection or replacement of the brushes will provide a fairly reliable machine. The best quality in our experience is the Kirby.

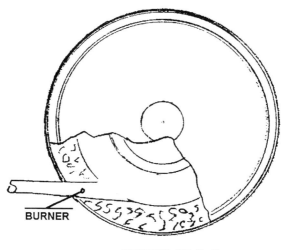

SECTION AT F-F

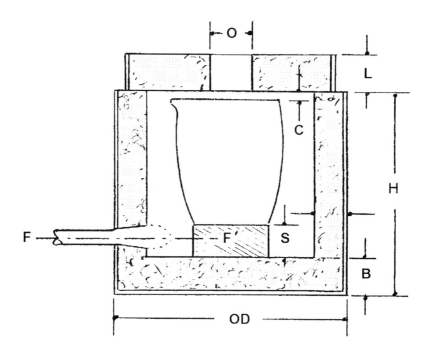

Furnace & Dimensions

Dimensions

Shop Built Crucible Furnaces

Furnace	Crucible No.	OD DIA. OUT.		W WALL THICK		H HGT. LESS LID.		B BOTTOM THICK		L LID THICK		O HOLE DIA	
		IN	(CM)	IN	(CM)	IN	(CM)	IN	(CM)	IN	(CM)	IN	(CM)
Small	0-3	11 1/4	(28.5)	3	(7.6)	11	(28)	4	(10.2)	1 1/2	(3.6)	2 3/4	(7)
Medium	20	18	(45.7)	3	(7.6)	25	(63.5)	6	(15.2)	3 1/2	(8.9)	4 1/2	(11.4)
Large	80	24	(61)	3 1/2	(8.9)	30	(76)	6	(15.2)	5	(12.7)	6	(15.2)

Furnace (Small)

We provide a rather long (say about 12") inlet pipe on the furnace and merely attach the blower with a piece of flexible tube. The long pipe stays fairly cool.

For larger furnaces a larger blower can be purchased. We like the blowers with a set of carbon brushes on the armature for several reasons. They are capable of higher speeds and therefore more pressure and more air than the simpler squirrel cage motors. Also they can be speed controlled with a variable transformer. During the melt cycle when full heat is not needed we reduce the gas and also slow the blower.

A valve in the air line from the blower can also control the air so a speed control blower is not a necessity. Vacuum cleaner blowers usually come with carbon brushes and speed control is easy.

MIXING GAS AND AIR

The fuel gas (natural gas or in our case, propane) must have a specific amount of air to burn. This gas and air must be thoroughly mixed. This is reliably accomplished in commercial furnaces by injecting the fuel in the air stream from the blower to the furnace or in some furnaces into the suction side of the blower.

In home built furnaces some thought should be given to proper mixing if the gas is injected into the air line between the blower and the furnace. We have seen a furnace where the gas and air were both injected right at the furnace wall. All gas-air mixing was done in the furnace. It was hard to start and most of the flame was high in the furnace. It melted slowly, poorly and can best be described as a disaster.

It is our practice to inject the fuel at the inlet of the blower. Blower action and flow through the pipe to the blower results in good mixing and a good hot flame.

STARTING THE FURNACE

Commercial furnaces will have starting equipment and starting instructions. They will also have flame monitoring devices and automatic fuel shut-off in case of a flame-out. This is a real safety advantage of the commercial unit. Such devices can be purchased for home built furnaces.

Home built furnaces have been our choice for strictly monetary reasons and we have used scrap pipe and iron and have done our own welding. The care needed to safely start and operate a home built is somewhat greater. We start our furnaces, both large and small, with a special starting pipe. A flexible hose is attached to a separate gas valve some 5 or 6 feet (2 meters) or more away from the furnace. A 1/8" (approx. 3mm) pipe about 5' (1 1/2 meters) long is clamped to the other end of this hose.

The gas valve is opened a little and the gas coming out of the 1/8" pipe is lighted. The valve is adjusted so the flame is stable and perhaps 12" (30cm) long. The pipe is inserted into the top of the furnace between the crucible and the wall of the furnace and allowed to burn in that position. We then start the blower at about 20-25% capacity by adjusting the blower speed or restricting the air flow valve. The 1/8" pipe starter flame must continue to burn. If it goes out, start over with more flame or less blower air.

The main furnace gas valve is opened slowly. At the proper air-gas ratio a somewhat noisy flame starts burning in the furnace. The 1/8" starting pipe is removed and turned off. We run the furnace at this low speed and low flame for 5 or 10 minutes to help warm the refractory lining somewhat slowly. Then the gas and blower are both increased together to keep a mixture that will continue to burn. Having some of the furnace lining red hot helps keep the flame going even if the air-gas ratio is not the best.

Please note that too little blower air will cause problems. There must be enough air velocity so that when the furnace gas is turned on the flame will burn in the furnace and not burn back into the pipe or in the blower.

If this occurs, shut off the gas, <u>increase blower air</u> and go through the starting procedure again.

CAUTION

<u>DO NOT</u> try to start these furnaces with matches, paper torches or any procedure that gets you close to the furnace. The theoretical flame temperatures for these gases is in excess of 3700°F (2500°C) and actual temperatures can approach this. An accumulation of a combustible mixture can start as a small explosion that turns face and hands into a <u>medical case</u> in a fraction of a second.

MELTING THE MIX

Running the furnace with the best air-gas ratio is a matter of experience and observation. Natural gas and butane do not burn quite the same but their flammability limits in air are in the 3% to 10-14% range. Within this range there is a best ratio.

We judge this by the length of the flame coming through the hole in the lid and by observation of the crucible and interior of the furnace. A flame 8" to 12" (20-30cm) out of the top of our large furnace (#80 crucible) and 4" or 5" (10-13cm) out of the top of the small bullion melter seems best.

With a little experience the flame can be quite accurately adjusted for the best temperature remembering that white heats are hotter than red heats. We suggest that dark glasses be worn and always the same pair so that differences in dark glasses do not impair your judgment of the flame.

The flame temperature is a matter of the right air-gas ratio not how much air and how much gas is used. However, during start up of a cold furnace and during melting of a cold charge more heat is needed to get things hot and molten. Heat and temperature are not the same although a high temperature forces heat into cold objects faster.

The first part of each melt cycle is run at a rather high flame. Once the ash-flux lot is all in the crucible, the mix can be stirred with an iron rod. Do this with good heat protection and heat resistant mittens (not leather). Stir slowly and with caution and care. If some of the mix is still raw and cold, it can start to react very, very actively and boil over. Careful stirring does, however, speed up the melting procedure.

Once the material is all melted the air and gas can be reduced. Everything in the furnace is now hot and we only need to maintain the temperature. Our usual procedure is to keep it in this molten condition for about one hour. This depends somewhat on the liquidity of the melt. A thick slag that does not improve with additions of selected flux materials (See section on fluxes and slags) is kept longer. Very small lots that are good and liquid may be poured in 45 or 50 minutes.

SLAG LIQUIDITY

Slag liquidity is important and good judgment about this is soon learned. How fast the slag runs off the stirring rod and how a layer clings to the rod are good visual clues.

A fairly good measurement can be made using a simple measuring device. Our device for comparing slag liquidity is based on a description of a simple measuring device, page 779 <u>Fine and Gaskel</u>. The viscosities that are so measured are not scientific in that they cannot be translated to a standard scale. However, if done in the same way each time, they give a quick and easy comparison with slags that have been found to be O.K.

The sketch following shows the slag viscosity trough that we made up from materials on hand. A steel angle was welded up with a stiffening web at the bottom. Without this web the heat of the slag makes the trough bend into a sagging curve. This varies from test to test and thus the effective slope of the trough varies unless a web is welded in to keep it straight. Splash guards and a generous end plate avoid losses at the upper end when the sample is poured.

In actual use the upper end is set onto a wooden block to give a total rise of 4."

A thick cast iron dipper stays so cold that a heavy solidified layer of slag limits the size of the sample and distorts results. An ordinary steel food can does not melt but it becomes hot almost immediately. Almost all of the slag it carries pours easily into the trough. After several uses or when it gets distorted we discard the can. We use a crucible tongs to hold the can.

To make a test we open the furnace and quickly dip out a canful of slag. Care is used not to include any floating pieces of graphite crucibles that may be on top of the melt. The hot slag is promptly poured into the trough. Each test should be poured into the same spot in the trough and we manage this by pouring the slag against the end plate each time. See photograph, that follows.

The slag then runs down the slope of the trough until it solidifies. The thinner the slag the farther it runs. When cool we measure this distance and tip out the slag which we weigh. The distance divided by the weight is the result we look at. This is inches of run per pound of slag (or centimeters per kilo.) It is not possible to dip and pour the exact same amount each time so this ratio makes a correction for a varying amount of slag dipped and poured.

A food can 3" (about 7 1/2cm) diameter and 4 1/2" (about 11cm) high will get a sample that weighs about 2 lbs. or about 1 kilo. In our particular device with the wall thickness of our trough and a slope of 4" (10cm) in 84" (200cm) a value of about 2 feet per 1 pound (or 130cm per kilo) of slag is a quite satisfactory liquidity. This will not compare to a trough made in a different way.

We do not make this test on a routine basis. We use it when it seems that a slag is different.

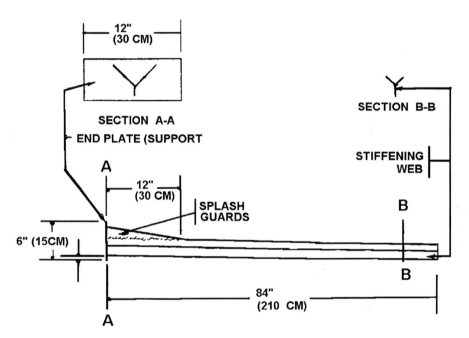

Viscosity Tester

50

Viscosity Tester

If a slag is too thick we try to thin out and liquefy it by making additions of some of the flux chemicals. The sweeps ashes may be quite different from lot to lot because different shops use different polishing materials, also the other debris may be quite different.

A classic old polishing material is red rouge (iron oxide). Too much soda ash will reduce this to iron metal (very undesirable). Should the ashes have a large amount of tripoli which is very high in silica (this is chemically the same as sand), there will be an insufficiency of soda ash to make a thin glass. Instead a thick glass is formed. The cautious addition of soda ash often dramatically thins out such slag.

A green polish, that we understand is a chrome compound, is occasionally found. The addition of more sand seems to be the answer for thinning such slags. There may be a certain amount of aluminum oxide, a grinding material. This is very difficult to thin.

Borax has a thinning effect on almost all slags as does fluorspar (calcium fluoride, CAF_2), the classic and almost universal liquefier of almost all slag.

POURING THE SLAG

When the mix has been molten for an hour or more the crucible can be poured. If the furnace is a tilter the molds that receive the melt are arranged so the slag will go directly from the crucible lip into the mold(s).

If the crucible must be lifted out, the tongs, pouring rings and molds are arranged in safe and convenient spots for the work. Protective clothing, gloves, eye protection, etc. are put on. At the very least the clothing should be fire retardant treated. Ordinary clothing can burn rapidly and severe burns are the usual result. Radiant heat is the most uncomfortable part of pouring lift out crucibles and heat protective clothing, rather than merely flame resistant, should be used.

The molten slag-metal in the crucible is best poured in such a way that the metal forms a rather thin bar. This is to be remelted and this shape is convenient for melting in a smaller furnace or for melting into shot with a welding torch.

THE SLAG METAL MOLDS

A Vee-shaped mold welded up from a piece of steel angle and a few pieces of steel plate has served our needs for many years. The sketch following gives dimensions for a fairly large Vee mold. This will hold only part of a full #80 crucible. A larger one can be made to hold the entire contents but such a mold is very heavy.

An old water heater split lengthwise with a cutting torch is used for slag. We first pour about 3/4 of the crucible carefully into this slag "mold" and then empty the crucible into the Vee mold. The metal sinks to the bottom of the Vee and slag stays above it.

No preparation is needed for the slag trough other than to support it on a small brick at each end and to place 2 bricks at the sides as chocks to prevent it from tipping. The Vee mold is painted with a commercial mold wash that can be obtained from foundry supply shops or it can be coated with carbon with a smoky acetylene torch flame.

The Vee mold must be dry. To be sure we always stand the mold on end against the side of the furnace for about half an hour to warm and dry it. If water mixed mold washes are used this drying procedure <u>must be done with attention and care</u> and drying must be complete.

About an hour after the pour the mold can be tipped and the slag and metal dumped on the floor. A few taps of a hammer separate the slag and metal although small amounts of slag sometimes adhere to the metal. The following photograph shows slag and metal from the Vee mold.

REMELTING THE METAL

If the metal is to be sold as a bar it is remelted in a smaller furnace. Any slag is skimmed. Some white sand can sometimes be added to make a thick, pasty slag that can be picked up with a rod. The melt is thoroughly stirred and the molten metal sampled with a small dipper or a glass tube. It is then poured into a standard brick shaped ingot mold.

If it is to be refined it is poured into a "shot pail." For this we pour the metal slowly into a cross flow water stream near the top of a 10-gallon aluminum pot. A sketch following shows this arrangement. The photograph shows metal being poured.

Sometimes (especially with small bars) we just melt the bar with a #8 welding torch. We let the drippings of metal fall into the same 10 gallon pail of water. Torch melting is shown in another following photograph.

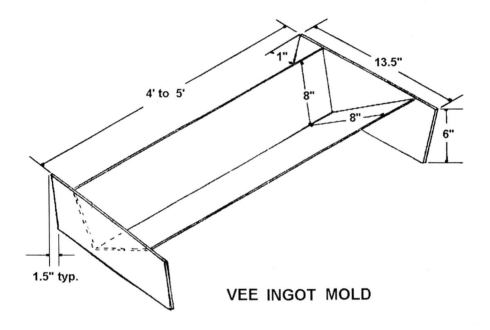

VEE INGOT MOLD

Ingot Mold

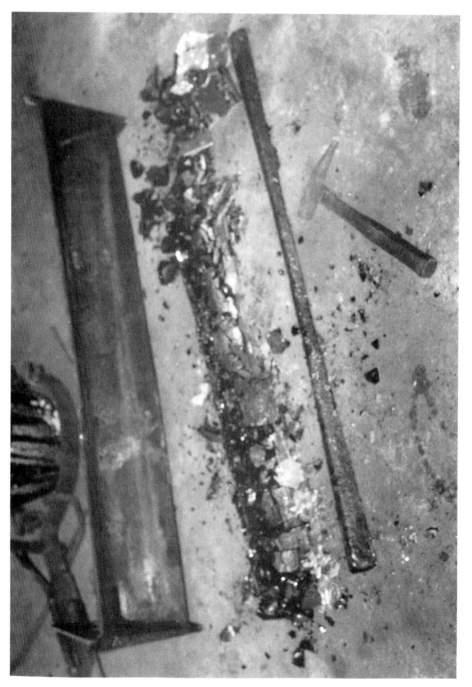

Slag and Metal Bar

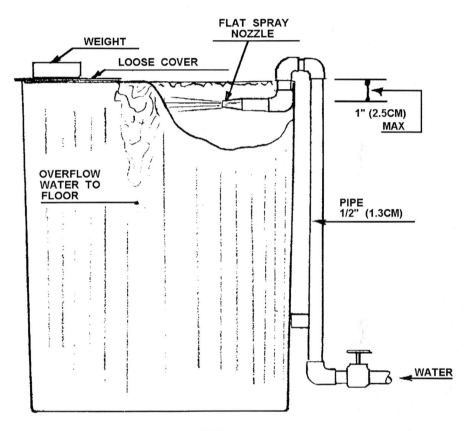

Shot Maker

Shot Maker

Torch Shotting

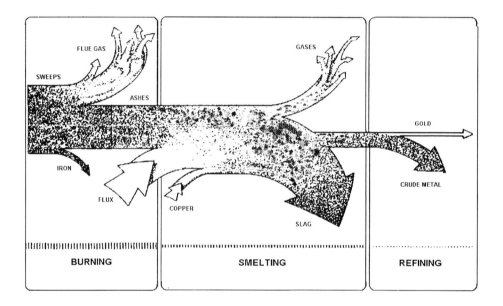

Sweeps Chart

Large bars of metal dissolve so slowly in aqua regia that this shot making procedure is necessary.

We find that the metal shot is usually so hot even at the bottom of 10 gallons of water that it burns through plastic and often sticks to iron pails. It does not stick to aluminum and we use a heavy restaurant type cooking pot.

The next procedure is to refine the crude metal shot to recover the contained precious metals. This process is described in the chapter on Gold.

SWEEPS PROCESSING CHART

On the preceeding page is a flow chart of a typical lot of sweeps. The width of the paths in this chart are in scale as determined by weighing the materials in and the materials out of this particular melting job. Gases out are by difference. The parts shown as contributed to melting gases by the flux chemicals and by the ash are based on chemical reactions assumed to occur in the heating and activity for flux chemicals and may be only approximately correct.

This technique is a method of setting up conditions so that a gravity separation of the heavy metallics from lighter unwanted materials occurs. The metals start as metals (not as compounds as in ores) and coalesce as metals. The unwanted portions of the scrap react with the added fluxes to form silicates, borates, oxides and combinations that are liquid at furnace temperatures. It is basically a melting rather than a smelting process.

TECHNICAL ASPECTS OF SWEEPS, SLAGS AND FLUXES

The burning of sweeps and the fluxing and melting of their ashes is chemistry at elevated temperatures. The materials involved are numerous. Reactions that may be simple in an uncomplicated situation may become obscure in the variety and complexity of slag formation. We present what we have learned and what we think we know.

SWEEPS ASHES - GOLD SEPARATIONS

Recovery of gold from sweeps ashes has been a matter of self education. Our first attempts were to get the gold from the ashes with aqua regia. It was our hope to avoid operating furnaces. Recovery was poor. With the idea that sweeps burning was creating a coating over the gold particles and that this might be high in silica we tried a pretreatment with hydrofluoric acid, an active dissolver of glass and quartz.

Recovery was improved but still unacceptable. Hydrofluoric acid is a terrible material and we abandoned that idea with relief.

At an elevated temperature certain chemicals will react with sweeps ashes to form a liquid (a slag). Such chemicals are called fluxes, a word that comes from Latin meaning "a flowing".

Several characteristics are required of such flux materials. Since the ash itself will not melt at temperatures attainable in a crucible furnace the flux must react with the ash and form a melt (slag). The flux chemicals must not reduce base metal compounds to metals. For example too much soda ash and/or too little silica can result in reducing iron oxide (red rouge) to iron metal. On the other hand it may be desirable to oxidize a base metal to a compound that will enter and depart with the slag. The use of manganese oxide to oxidize lead is an example.

Slags are chemical compounds, usually metal oxides or other metallic chemical combinations. Metals and slags do not dissolve into one another but remain physically separate. Slags are usually light and many metals especially precious metals much heavier.

A fundamental requirement of fluxes is to form a liquid slag that will permit the very small precious metal particles to find each other, combine into drops and globules that will sink to the bottom of the crucible. It is a gravity separation technique.

FLUXES

Much flux and slag information is available for iron and similar low cost metals. The gold refiner finds some of these materials useful but he can also afford to use more costly chemicals than can the iron and steel processor.

In our searches for flux and slag information we have never found a formula specifically set up for jewelers sweeps. However the flux chemicals used for assay work, Zadra cell product, and other precious metal work are also successful in the fluxing of jewelers sweeps ashes.

Following are some commonly used fluxes for this work:

Silica (SiO_2) (Sand). This alone is not a suitable flux because of a very high melting point (1700°C) (3000°F) and high viscosity. Reaction with soda lowers both melting temperature and viscosity.

Soda ash (Na_2CO_3) is a convenient source of Soda (Na_2O) to react with silica. These are the two major raw materials that react to make ordinary glass. A by product is carbon dioxide gas (CO_2).

Silica is acidic and soda basic and their reaction at an elevated temperature can be thought of as a reaction between an acid and a base in aqueous chemistry. It is desirable for other base metal oxides to react with the flux but the silica soda combination reduces this capacity.

Bugbee p 6 says sodium carbonate (Na_2CO_3) melts at 852°C (1565°F) and is a very fluid material. At about 950°C (1740°F) it loses a small amount of CO_2.

Another aspect of soda ash (sodium carbonate) is that it will react with some metal compounds to release the metal. Silver chloride and soda ash to produce silver metal is a classic process. Soda ash with iron oxide (red rouge for example) will result in a gassy reaction and metallic iron. See Scott p 212 and Gee p 375. A sufficiency of silica avoids this.

Boron oxide (B_2O_3) is almost as acidic as silica. Its lower melting point (450°C) (840°F) is more favorable for this work. The exact nature of its action in a flux mixture is uncertain but its use is favorable and effective.

Anhydrous Borax ($Na_2B_4O_7$) also called borax glass can be used. The formula can be written $Na_2O \cdot 2B_2O_3$ showing it a source of boron oxide and soda. Actually anhydrous borax is very hard to find so we use the hydrated form and depend upon the furnace to evaporate the water.

Borax 5 ($Na_2B_4O_7 \cdot 5H_2O$) is available and specified in our recipes. The amounts are larger than anhydrous recipes to account for the water.

Borax 10 ($Na_2B_4O_7 \cdot 10H_2O$) is the common form and may be used if Borax 5 is not available. Use 30 % more borax 10 than borax 5.

Boric acid (H_3BO_3) well known to jewelers may be useful. This decomposes to form water and B_2O_3. According to Lange this occurs at 185°C (365°F). We find it useful in a final gold melting flux. We have not found it in other flux recipes.

Fluorspar (Ca_2F) is a very aggressive liquefier. It is almost universally used for this purpose and recipes often specify 4 to 8% fluorspar.

Sodium nitrate ($NaNO_3$) (and the more costly potassium salt) is a useful oxidizer of some metals so they will enter the slag. When sweeps are not completely burned a scum of carbonaceous material floats on the melt. We specify a small amount of sodium nitrate in our recipe for this reason. If such a scum persists it can be burned away with sodium nitrate. It should be added in small amounts in the center of the crucible. It is not kind to crucibles and large amounts smoke badly.

Manganese dioxide (MnO_2) is also an oxidizer but works at a higher temperature. It is often used to oxidize iron. Lead which may be present in sweeps ashes oxidizes only at a high temperature and manganese dioxide is therefore helpful with lead removal. The reaction of manganese dioxide with lead metal is:

$$MnO_2 + Pb = MnO + PbO$$

Lime (CaO) may be useful in small amounts. Smith says that lime reacts with silica to make a better melting material. Fusibility of lime plus silica is aided by the presence of another base. Levin Fig. 485 indicates an eutectic (lowest melting point) at about 870°C (1600°F) when CaO is about 4 % in the system $Na_2O \cdot CaO \cdot SiO_2$. In our experience too much lime can be harmful.

Iron oxides (FeO, Fe_2O_3, Fe_3O_4) may in some cases help liquidity. These are not flux additives but are often a part of sweeps ashes. These are basic materials.

Alumina (Al_2O_3) acts as a base if the slag is acidic and as an acid if the slag is basic. It increases viscosity and melt temperature and is always a nuisance. It is not a flux additive but may be a part of sweeps, crucibles or refractories.

We have no words of wisdom about flux materials to help liquify alumina. Sometimes cautious additions of soda ash help. When in doubt more borax and fluorspar may help. Higher temperatures improve liquidity. Another refiner reports that a glassy slag is essential. When a crystalline slag shows up they remelt with additional materials to make a glassy slag and gold recovery improves.

We found slag information in the Encyclopedia Britannica 11th ed 1910 p 583-584, Bray p 31-38, Liddell p 697-711, Hoke p 219 and Smith p 113-135. Levin is of course full of phase diagrams that may give useful clues.

Adamson pp 344-346 and Stanley pp 897-899 give an interesting and lucid explanation of some of the reactions that occur in slag formation. Both books give essentially the same information. In the following paragraphs we outline some of their information.

Silica (SiO_2) consists of SiO_4 units where each silicon atom is surrounded by 4 oxygen atoms and each oxygen bonded to two silicon atoms. The addition of a metal oxide to the molten silica results in the metal oxide entering the network, breaking the bridge and creating some disorder. If we designate MO as a general term for metal oxide an equation can be:

$$\text{-Si-O-Si-} + MO = \text{-Si-O-}M^{2+}\text{-O-Si-}$$

Borax also reacts with metal oxides in a similar manner. A flux of equal weight proportions of silica and borax (sodium tetraborate) is considered to be a good starting point for flux. This is essentially the ratio in the flux suggested in "Sweeps" when the Borax 5 is corrected for water content.

Fluorspar (calcium fluoride) is a strong network breaker. The fluorine (F) enters the matrix:

$$\text{-Si-O-Si-} + 2F = 2(\text{-Si-F}) + O_2$$

The oxygen increases the oxide activity of the slag.

Manganese dioxide reacts with metals (M):

$$MnO_2 + M = MO + MnO$$

Sodium nitrate with metals react as follows:

$$2NaNO_3 + 3M = Na_2O + 2NO + 3MO$$

Adamson p 344 gives Table 7 that lists free energies of reaction for some metal oxides. Stanley p 897 gives similar data as a chart. These indicate that with strong oxidants silver can form oxides and enter the slag. We find this interesting because it explains that traces of gold and silver found in slag from sweeps processing are no longer present in the ratios expected in karat gold. Instead the silver is relatively high being equal to or often higher than the traces of gold. We imagine that the gold is there as tiny particles of metal while much of the silver is there as silver oxide.

Other reactions that may occur in slag formation are:

Soda ash plus silica (sand).

$Na_2CO_3 + SiO_2 = Na_2SiO_3 + CO_2$. In actuality the neat compound shown may be a rarity. Others are possible and the reaction of soda ash and silica is glass forming and the characteristics of the glass varies depending on the ratio of soda ash to silica. High soda ash favors liquidity.

Sodium nitrate with carbon:

$$2NaNO_3 + 4C = Na_2O + N_2 + CO$$

and in the air the carbon monoxide CO goes

$$2\,CO + O_2 = 2CO_2$$

An undesirable reaction where there is an excess of sodium carbonate and when red rouge is present is perhaps as follows:

$$2Na_2CO_3 + 2Fe_2O_3 = 2Na_2O + 4Fe + 2\,CO_2 + 3O_2$$

It is a very gassy reaction and the crucible is likely to boil over. The iron that results complicates the refining work.

A similar reaction occurs when silver chloride (AgCl) is melted with soda ash. See the following section about silver reactions.

At one time we used a rather strange self devised flux using Barium salts. When barium sulfate was used a matte (a sulfide) was very frequently formed.

We felt that perhaps sulfates were not stable at high temperatures. However it may be more likely that there are high temperature reactions. A study of high temperature reactions between calcium sulfate (gypsum) and carbon and also silica was made by Hoffman and Mostowitsch in 1909 and in 1911.

One reaction of possible interest is where calcium sulfate from casting investment and carbon from incompletely burned sweeps are present. It is:

$$CaSO_4 + 2C = CaS + 2CO_2 \text{ at } 700°C\;(1292°F)$$

then $\quad\quad\quad 3CASO_4 + CaS = 4CaO + 4SO_2$ at 800°C (1472°F)

if SiO_2 is present

$3CaO + 2SiO_2 = CaSi_2O_7$ at 850°C (1562°F)

there are other reactions. They may be of interest when there is casting investment in the jewelers debris.

PHASE DIAGRAMS

Phase diagrams give information about the composition and melting temperatures of many materials. They have been useful to us and therefore we give a short discussion about their use.

A limitation is that a diagram is presented on a flat piece of paper and can present only 3 or 4 variables (one of which is temperature). Useful flux recipes usually have many more ingredients. Our sweeps flux has 5 and more are added by the sweeps ashes. A phase diagram can therefore give only a little information about what happens in our sweeps melting work. In spite of this these diagrams have helped a little in understanding some of the witchcraft of flux work.

The first of the following diagrams is the system $SiO_2 - 2Na_2O \cdot SiO_2$. This is glass and is part of the material in sweeps slag.

The numbers at the left side are temperatures in °C. The numbers along the bottom are amounts of Na_2O and SiO_2 in percent. SiO_2 is 100% at the right end and 30% near the left end, while Na_2O is 70% near the left and is zero at the right end.

We are interested in the proportions of SiO_2 and Na_2O that have the lowest melting temperature. By operating the furnace well above this lowest melting point we expect to materially increase liquidity. Although this superheat is helpful it is not the only factor in viscosity because the characteristics of the material themselves strongly affect liquidity.

This chart shows a lowest temperature (a eutectic) between areas 8 and 9 with a melting point of about 800°C (1470°F). We believe the furnace can go to 2000 - 2500°F (1100°C - 1350°C) and therefore give such a melt considerable super heat.

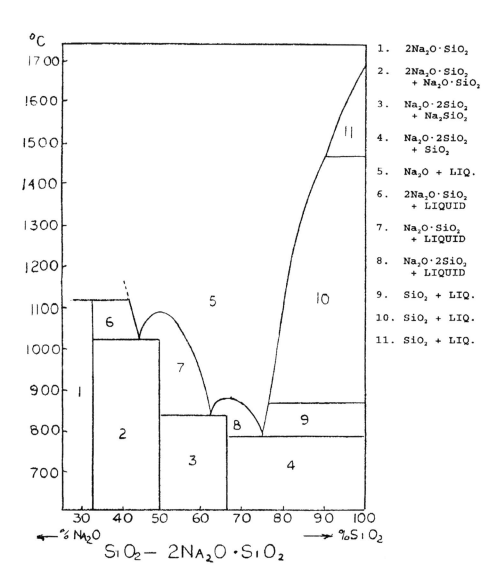

Phase Diagram

The second diagram is a much simplified triangle for a system of Al_2O_3, SiO_2, Na_2O and temperature. Temperatures here are given as curved lines in the body of the drawing.

The method of presentation is that SiO_2 is zero at the bottom left going up to 100% at the top. Al_2O_3 is zero at the top and progresses to 100% at the bottom right. Then Na_2O is zero at bottom right and increases to 100% at the bottom left. Melting temperatures of the pure materials are given. Na_2O sublimes and does not melt.

Assume that we are interested in the amounts of Al_2O_3 that are tolerable in a melt. Al_2O_3 is a known problem. We look for the lowest melting temperature and find one at about 760°C which we show as a small circle.

We can find the composition of the material at this spot by drawing 3 lines through the circle that are parallel to the 3 sides of the triangle (see 3 dotted lines on the chart).

The dotted line parallel to the side that faces the Al_2O_3 apex gives % Al_2O_3. See where it intersects the Al_2O_3 line at top right, about 10%. The horizontal line parallel to the bottom is opposite the SiO_2 apex (top) and intersects the bottom at 34% Na_2O. The total of the 3 ingredients is 100%.

This diagram also shows that if we reduce the amount of Al_2O_3 the temperatures will still be low but an increase rather quickly gives high melting points.

As a practical matter in setting up raw materials for such melts Na_2O is not really available as such. One would use soda ash (Na_2CO_3) and this would react with silica and lose CO_2 to form Na_2O.

There are other diagrams for other materials such as B_2O_3 (Borax system); iron oxides, calcium oxides and many others. When these various systems are mixed in a slag system they affect each other to some extent but drastic changes do not seem to happen. We have found them useful in telling us the general part of the woods we are in and helpful in making additions when thick slags show up.

FLUX RECIPES

When we wish to try a new flux recipe or when we are faced with a really unknown situation of considerable size we make a small scale test. For such a test we use a small crucible (often a small "gold melting" size) in our smallest furnace.

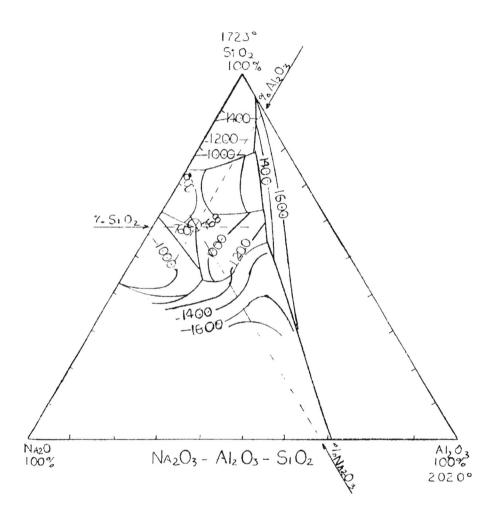

Phase Diagram

A standard known recipe is made up and a mixture of the test recipe of a similar size is made up. Both are melted at the same temperature for the same time and characteristics observed as carefully as we know how. This homely and simple experiment has been helpful in devising better melts.

Jewelers sink trap sludge is a variable material. Usually it goes into the furnace as part of the ashes. In one case we were able to test a lot separately and it was 70 % moisture. A flux recipe consisting of 32% soda ash, 8% fluorspar and 60% Borax 5 used as an equal part of the 30% dry portion of the sludge gave good results.

Jewelers investment is reported to be 25-30% calcium sulfate and the rest quartz and crystobalite (silicas). A small test that gave good liquidity was:

Investment	100 parts by weight
Soda Ash (Na_2CO_3)	78 parts by weight
Borax 5	40 parts by weight

A large captive refinery reported that when Torit dust collectors began to contain diatomaceous earth gold recovery at the smelter was poor. A suggestion to raise the soda ash (to react and make a lower melting glass with the silica in the diatomaceous material) was followed. They increased the soda ash from 8 to 11 parts per 100 and reported satisfactory results.

Soda ash additions have been helpful in melting ashes from plastic floor tile which may contain fibers of glass or even asbestos.

Broken glass is sometimes useful and we have occasionally used it to advantage. It was originally made by melting white sand with soda ash.

Gold and silver are now often recovered electrolytically from cyanide leaching solutions in what is known as Zadra cells or cells similar to those designed by Zadra some years ago. In these cells the precious metal is electrolytically deposited on steel wool cathodes. When loaded the cathodes are melted with a flux that oxidizes the iron and produces a reasonably iron free bullion.

These fluxes contain considerable nitrate to oxidize the iron. A recipe that has come to my attention is:

Borax glass	42%
Sodium nitrate	32%
Sand	26%

The Homestake Mine in Lead, South Dakota treats these cathodes with 10 % sulfuric acid for 24 hours to remove as much iron as possible and then melts with a flux containing the above three ingredients. The amounts are determined experimentally in one ounce crucibles. They state it should be acidic and usually shiny. We believe glassy, shining slag is desirable or even necessary for good metal recovery.

The fluxes used in assay work usually involve the materials previously mentioned plus litharge and a carbonaceous material such as flour. These latter two have no place in melting sweeps ashes.

Anyone interested in these should consult <u>Smith</u> or <u>Bugbee</u> or <u>Shepard</u> or <u>Dietrich</u>.

Metal melting fluxes for melting pure materials may be useful. Pure gold should usually not require fluxing. However some flux recipes for this work have been given and we give one for gold.

Borax 5	4 vols.
Soda Ash	1 vol.
MnO_2	1 vol.
SiO_2	1 vol.

Verbal communication by <u>Lashley</u> says this was once used by the U.S. Mint to remove traces of silver as silver silicate. Reportedly once published in an Encyclopedia Britannica of the early 1930's.

The Bureau of Mines has used a flux of 38% potassium nitrate, 36% borax glass and 27% silica to materially increase gold fineness in a laboratory experiment. The equivalent in more readily obtainable materials is:

Sodium Nitrate	29 %
Borax 5	47 %
Sand	24 %

Our best experience for gold melting is with a simple boric acid - borax flux. This forms a slag that is quite easy to remove. If all does not break away a dilute sulfuric acid usually takes the last traces rather quickly.

The recipe is equal parts by weight of Boric acid and Borax 10. If borax 5 is used the ratio of 1 Boric acid to 0.6 Borax 5 is okay.

SLAG REPROCESSING

A small amount of metal remains in the slag and we felt that with a simple process recovery and a fairly large accumulation of slag that reprocessing would be worthwhile.

We found that sampling and fire assay gave such variable results that we refused to depend on them. Refurnacing the slag followed by further recovery by another method in another refinery gave interesting results.

Based on information from <u>Roberts</u> we made some experiments and set up a small homemade recovery system.

1. A small 4" X 6" (10 X 15cm) 1 HP jaw crusher. Which, at closest setting, will crush to about 1/4" (0.65cm) by down.
2. A ball mill made from a small Essick cement mixer. This particular machine was selected because it has high quality replaceable drive gears. Also the pinion gear drive shaft sleeve bearing is easily replaced by pillow block ball bearings. The bowl will wear out after a few months but is easily replaced by a heavier straight sided bowl. The grinding balls are 1" (2.54cm) steel.
3. A small 1 1/2 X 3 foot (45 X 90cm) homemade screen. Vibration is by a motor driven shaft and eccentric weights.

The following three photos show this equipment.

The operating schedule is to crush the lumpy slag in the jaw crusher. The crushed slag goes into the "ball mill" in 60 or 70 lb. (27-32 kilo) batches. The load in the ball mill is about 3 parts balls and 1 part slag by weight (this is less than 1 to 1 on a volume basis). The grinding is very dusty and a plastic cover held in place over the mouth of the bowl with a rubber band

Jaw Crusher

Ball Mill

Screen

keeps the dust in the mill.

The ball mill is run until the next day, (20 to 22 hours) and then dumped. A 3/8" (approximately 1 cm) screen over the mouth of the bowl lets the milled slag out and keeps the balls in the bowl.

Our screening has been done in a 30 mesh screen and original samples indicated this was a reasonable split with little value in the -30 mesh material. Later work shows that there is considerable metal (gold) in the -30 plus 200 mesh size.

A recovery of values from this fine material has not been devised at this time. Several methods are being tested.

The use of a 200 mesh (or perhaps a 150 mesh) screen instead of 30 mesh may give acceptable gold recovery. Screening will be slower and more difficult.

PROBABLE FUTURE METHOD

Until we make several dozen runs on any new method we keep running into surprises. This has been true with our work with slag as described above. Original assays of the -30 mesh slag indicated a very low value in this material.

However careful samples of more -30 mesh material showed interesting amounts of both gold and silver did go into this fine material. We then did some test work to learn more about this slag and the values it contains.

As a result of this work we have reason to believe that:

1. Milling and screening through a 30 mesh screen results in a recovery of over half the gold content of the slag.

2. Screening to 140 or 150 mesh could possibly improve recovery to 70-75%. This would require more ball milling time.

3. A concentrating table (as used in the mining industry) was tried. About one half of the values in the -30 mesh was concentrated in about 5% of the fine slag. This was also the coarsest part of the -30 mesh slag.

4. A pressure cyanide extraction test run by the Bureau of Mines in the Reno laboratory achieved almost 90% recovery.

5. We believe much of the metal in the fine slag is not free separate pellets. Microscope examination did not reveal small pellets.

Operating estimates were made for milling and screening costs, for additional work to make -150 mesh material, for furnace costs to recover metal from concentrate, pressure cyanidation cost and possible rates of recovery for these several methods.

Recovery, even using the concentrating table for final treatment, was only about 50 to 70%. In our quest for further information we were advised to consider a plant in Sparks, NV called G-D Resources. They use a litharge - lead cupellation process and have the extensive processing and lead pollution control equipment needed.

Although costly to ship and process we find that the recovery is good and the economics of this method worthwhile.

We understand that copper refineries can recover precious metals from such slags and that some gold refiners have arrangements to send their slags to these copper plants.

LOW GRADE WASTES

The most prevalent low grade jewelers scrap is sweeps and a method of dealing with that has been described.

Over the years we have been offered other low value debris. We list this below:

1. Gold filled or rolled gold scrap
2. Watch bands
3. Eyeglass frames
4. Electrostrip solutions and solids (sometimes called electropolish) - <u>contains cyanide</u>.
5. Plating solutions - <u>cyanide</u>
6. Bombing solutions - <u>cyanide</u>
7. Miscellaneous shop and laboratory solutions - can sometimes contain <u>cyanide</u>
8. Sink trap sludges
9. Tumbling mud and liquids from rotary and vibratory machines
10. Used casting investment
11. Used rhodium plating solutions
12. Electronic scrap, telephone scrap, gold plated scrap.
13. Automobile muffler scrap
14. Ore-gold, silver, etc.
15. Watch batteries

We will comment on these and will give our methods for those that we occasionally process. These methods are essentially all self devised. We have little knowledge of how others handle such scrap.

<u>Gold Filled, Watch Bands and Glasses Frames</u>

The first three items in our list are all processed in the same way. In fact they often come to us as a mixture. Gold filled is often more valuable than watch bands or frames. Only one or two lots of gold filled come to mind and contained in the order of 5% gold. Watch bands are variable the older the more gold they contain. We remember a lot of very old watch bands that yielded about 0.56% gold. White gold watch bands may well be stainless steel and unless this scrap is sorted by a knowledgeable person gold recovery will be low. Eye glass frames sometimes come carefully selected and sometimes full of lenses, plastic frames, etc. Our experiences is that gold content is from less than 1/2% to about 2%.

Although we have tried the furnacing method (see later comments) our system is to dissolve the entire lot in acid. We have experimented with dissolution of as much as possible in sulfuric acid rather than aqua regia. Our present regular technique is to just dissolve the entire lot in aqua regia.

The batches of scrap are usually quite large. Considerable surface area is presented and acid reaction is vigorous. The aqua regia must be added with care in frequent small amounts. When the reaction vessel is quite full we let the liquid cool and stand, usually overnight.

Most of this spent acid is then carefully removed. We use a small siphon and leave a heel of liquid in the bottom. The reason for this is that the gold in this kind of scrap is usually a surface layer. The acid attacks the base metal first and gold remains in the bottom sludge. It should not be poured out or siphoned away with the top liquid which is usually of no value.

Aqua regia is again added with care and the cycle repeated. This may go on for a number of days. When dissolution is perhaps half done there is a tendency for the partly dissolved scrap to cement itself together. Acid action is then very slow unless the scrap is actively stirred. We use a stout plastic rod to break up the lumps.

The amount of aqua regia required may vary but a typical batch used 33 gallons (125 liters) for a 50 lb (23 kilo) lot of watch bands. If samples of the liquid are spot tested with stannous chloride one will find that it will test "no gold" until about 90% of the metal has been dissolved.

The reason for this is that the base metals are chemically much more reactive than gold and are preferentially dissolved until the gold is more concentrated and becomes a considerable portion of the undissolved mass.

Often if a spot test is made during dissolution the test will be positive but later when the reaction has ceased and the solution is quiet and cooler a second test will be negative. The reason for this is that any gold dissolved during the heat and turmoil of acid action will be displaced (cemented out) by base metals when things quiet down.

There is however another angle to this cementation reaction that can lead to gold loss if liquids testing no-gold are summarily discarded. The gold precipitated by

The dissolution of all base metals by acids other than aqua regia to leave the gold has been suggested. Our tests told us that this was incomplete and quite slow. For a time we did this to remove the acid soluble part of the scrap. We no longer do this in favor of the speed of aqua regia.

We have speculated that a melt with lead could perhaps dissolve the gold and that this could be recovered by a small version of the Parkes process (see Mining chapter).

Gaskell p. 231, describes a mechanical device for concentrating valuable material from non-precious metal containing particles. Although this was devised for ore it may possibly be of use if the scrap were broken up in say a hammer mill.

Cyanide Containing Solutions - Cyanide Information

Items 4, 5, 6, and possibly 7 in the previous list contain cyanide. The hazards of dealing with cyanidic materials are large. **THE SMALL REFINER SHOULD NOT REFINE THESE WASTES**. Special knowledge, care & skills, special work areas, equipment and supplies are needed, Residues after gold is removed must be treated and tested for legal disposal.

"Cyanide" in general terms may refer to a solid, a salt, sodium or potassium cyanide or it may be a metal cyanide complex. It may be the solid material or a water solution of these materials. Electrostrip and bombing solutions contain cyanides and may be quite strong. Some laboratory solutions may be cyanidic. **WE KNOW OF NO FORM OF "CYANIDE" THAT IS NOT POISONOUS.**

Ballantyne and Marrs, Chapter One, gives a lengthy list of materials with potential for cyanide exposure and properties and chemical reactions including information about electroplating, p. 11.

Cyanide can kill by absorption through the skin and is especially rapid if the skin is abraded, scratched, or cut. Cyanide enters the body very quickly through mucous membranes (the mouth for example), very rapidly from contact with the eye (see Ballantyne and Marrs pp 61-2 and 64).

Swallowing results in rapid poisoning and entering through a cut is almost instantaneous. Inhalations can cause death very quickly especially the hydrogen cyanide gas that can form when acid makes contact with cyanide materials. Hydrogen cyanide gas can be absorbed through the skin quite rapidly (about 3 minutes). A neutral or acidic material penetrates the skin about 30 times faster than a strongly alkaline material, Ballantyne and Marrs p. 132, 133, 139. This means the time lag from contact to toxic reaction through healthy skin can be 3 minutes instead of say 90.

If only a small portion of healthy skin is contacted by basic cyanide the body may metabolize, i.e. destroy and eliminate, cyanide fast enough to avoid any toxic symptoms. There are differences from person to person but it is thought that a healthy 154 lb. individual will metabolize cyanide at the rate of about 30 mg. per hour. It is important to know that an American postage stamp weighs about 57 mg. This amount is a lethal dose which is considered to be about 50-100 mg. Obviously even very small amounts of cyanide can cause death.

There is a general belief that cyanide smells like bitter almonds. This may be true for some people but many report an entirely different odor. About 40% do not smell cyanide at all. (Ballantyne & Marrs pp. 17, 41, 184, 209, 210, 213, 214, 222-3, 242, 316.)

A strong dose of hydrogen cyanide gas can smell acrid, corrosive, rough but not acidic. One breath of this is enough to result in very definite poisoning symptoms within about one minute. An acquaintance went through similar symptoms but states that he smelled nothing unusual. Only 3000 parts per million can cause collapse in as little as 15 to 30 seconds.

This author was severely poisoned when he took a second sniff to try to identify an unexpected and nasty odor from a solution he thought was completely destroyed. The fact that he had cyanide first aid training and a cyanide first aid kit and oxygen in the shop surely saved his life.

THE REFINER SHOULD NOT TRY TO PROCESS CYANIDE WASTES.

There are some compelling reasons for avoiding these wastes. In the first place the methods for processing cyanide wastes are very different from the methods used in the regular refinery.

These cyanide wastes must be processed in a separate facility. For both safety and legal reasons the acids and acidic conditions of the refinery must be separate from any cyanide. This can be costly.

The special first aid equipment and training for cyanide work is different from that in the refinery.

Our refinery has over the years been offered the occasional cyanidic scrap. From time to time we have tried different gold recovery and cyanide destruction methods. The area that we once devoted to this occasional work is now used for other things. our advice is **DO NOT DO CYANIDE WORK**.

Safety Considerations

The refinery may receive materials that are not marked, incorrectly worded or otherwise be mysterious. These can be solids or solutions. They could be dangerously toxic.

Solutions identified as plating, bombing, electrostrip or otherwise cyanidic are of course dangerous and must be so handled. Cyanide solutions are often quite basic, but some solutions are somewhat acidic (perhaps pH 4-4.5). A test for acidity does not tell whether a solution does or does not contain cyanide.

These are test kits available for determining the presence of cyanide. One is:

> EM Quant By EM Science, Box 70,
> Democrat Road, Gibbstown, NJ 08027

This will give some indication of the amount of cyanide present.
Another kit is a test paper by Cyantismo, (Machery-Nagel of Germany). The USA distributor is Gallard-Schlesinger Industries, Inc., Carle Place, NY.

This is essentially a yes or no test for the presence of cyanide and quite quick and easy to use. Instructions are given with each kit. These instructions do not mention that there are interfering elements. If these are present in the cyanide solutions, cyanide is not detected even if it is there.

We understand that when chlorine or hypochlorite, etc. are used to destroy cyanide the residual chlorine will interfere with cyanide tests.

Metals such as silver, iron, copper, zinc, etc. form stable complexes that resist destruction and remain in solution. For instance gold forms $NaAu(CN)_2$ which is very stable. We know of no easy way to break down this complex. It resists mineral acids and is apparently one of the most stable cyanide complexes.

The simple tests for cyanide do not detect the presence of these metal cyanide complexes.

Rose p. 306-312 gives some cyanide chemistry including some information about metal complexes.

Tests for so called total cyanide are given in <u>Smith</u> p. 461, in <u>Lenahan and Murray—Smith</u> Chapter XIX and in <u>Rose</u> p. 325.

Very recently a method using picric acid has come to our attention. This method was devised by INCO.

Unknown solid wastes can probably best be tested by dissolving a little of the unknown material in water that <u>has been made basic</u> with a little caustic soda (sodium hydroxide), (Never use acid) and then testing this solution for cyanide.

If it becomes necessary to accept store and test cyanidic materials this must be done in a special room and in the proper way.

1. A special room must be used and this must be away from acids so that acids and acid spills cannot reach cyanides. Also cyanide spills cannot reach acid areas. This means that spilled liquids <u>must not flow under room partitions</u> into another room. Storage of acids and cyanides must be separate.

   Drains from the cyanide area must not flow to refinery drains, sinks, or floor traps or visa versa. There is a very real danger of making poisonous hydrogen cyanide gas if acids and cyanides mingle and react in sewers and drains. This may be a legal requirement.

2. Be sure to identify and clearly mark the material.

3. Do not work alone.

4. Ventilation must be brisk and active. An air flow rate of 100 feet per minute into a hood is considered a reasonable minimum.

   In our experience an air flow rate that is much higher than this may sometimes not be sufficient. This can happen when a person is working with a fume producing material in front of him and the air flow coming from his back. In this situation a persons body will create eddy currents that can carry fumes to the face. Air flow to the side or to the front is often better.

5. Be sure to have an oxygen resuscitator for forced breathing and also have a cyanide poisoning first aid kit. Lilly M76 cyanide antidote kit. A prescription is required for both of these.

6. Be sure you and several others know how to use the first aid equipment.

First Aid

Watch for symptoms in yourself and others. These symptoms may or may not always be present. Red eyes seem to be the most common symptom. The following list of symptoms may be of help in detecting cyanide poisoning.

- Reddened Eyes
- Irritated Throat
- Palpitations
- Difficult Breathing
- Numbness
- Nausea
- Headache
- Weakness in Arms or Legs
- Giddiness
- Salivation
- Loss of Coordination
- Rapid Breathing

Further progression will likely cause loss of mental and physical capabilities, convulsions, unconsciousness, breathing stopped, heart stoppage and death. This is down hill progression caused by oxygen deprivation.

Speedy Treatment is Essential

1. Call for nearby help.

2. Move victim to fresh air.

3. Quickly determine the victim's condition.

4. Give first aid immediately.

5. Send for trained medical help (to administer sodium nitrate and sodium thiosulfate, if necessary).

In our training we were told that because poisoning is so quick an ambulance call or a run to a hospital is probably too slow. Even if a very rapid run to an emergency room is accomplished, cyanide usage is unusual and emergency rooms rarely have the knowledge or equipment to deal with cyanide poisoning as quickly as needed. Severe oxygen deprivation can cause brain damage in as little as six minutes. Death follows shortly thereafter. Our personal experiences with cyanide poisoning indicates that this is true.

We urge any user of cyanide to obtain from the DuPont Co., Chemicals and Pigments, Wilmington, Delaware 19898, the bulletins, "Sodium Cyanide, Properties Uses, Storage and Handling," also Plating Product Bulletin #42 and also their Material Data Safety Sheet. First aid information is given. The previously mentioned Lilly M76 antidote kit gives some instructions.

Ballantyne and Marrs, Chapter 16, "The Choice of Cyanide Antidotes," gives much information p. 391 has a paragraph about amyl nitrite the material in the Lilly M76 kit.

We understand that other areas, Great Britain for instance, suggest trained medical intervention rather than first aid as used in the USA. The thinking is that many useful cyanide antidotes have other effects and could need medical monitoring. Amyl nitrite is reported to do little harm (Ballantyne and Marrs p. 391.)

Gold Recovery Comments

The recovery of gold from cyanide solutions has been done for quite a long time. Several methods have been developed. We will mention them briefly.

The use of zinc for, "cementation displacement" of gold has been used since cyanide was first used by gold mines early in this century. This is usually known as the Merrill-Crowe Process. Rose p. 375-388 gives information. Many books about cyanidation have been written and these usually give information about zinc as used for gold recovery. The cyanide solutions used by gold mills is quite dilute but zinc will probably be effective in strong solutions. We are not entirely sure.

Aluminum as a precipitant was suggested by Rose p. 318, 319, 388. The use of aluminum to precipitate gold from plating solutions was studied in detail by GAL-OR and Calmanovici. This method is quite straight forward and may be of interest. In our shop we have in the past used both zinc and aluminum. We have also used copper, however, since copper leaves another metal cyanide complex in solution this is no longer done and copper should not be used. Destruction and disposal is probably very difficult. Our experience is not such that we feel able to give reliable data on recovery efficiency, etc. The use of activated carbon to extract gold from cyanide solutions was investigated by the US Bureau of Mines shortly after World War II. This has been developed into a useful and now much used process. The original surplus gas mask activated carbon is long gone but gold recovery activated carbon is now produced in large amounts.

It is possible that stirring activated carbon particles (usually about the size of rice grains) into gold cyanide will take up the gold in the carbon. Separating the carbon from the solution can be done by simple straining through a suitable screen instead of a filter. The solution needs to be tested to be sure that metal recovery is complete.

The carbon granules can be water washed and then burned. We have used a shallow pan with a 3 or 4 inch layer of carbon in a jewelers burnout oven at red heat with ventilation. The residual ashes are mostly gold.

Although we have done this it was done with a fairly strong cyanide solution. The mining mill solutions are much more dilute and we have no data on the efficiency of recovery from stronger solutions.

Destruction of Cyanide

No matter how the gold is removed from the cyanide solution the remaining barren solution and its disposition has a strong requirement of responsibility both ecological and legal.

In our case as a small refiner with very occasional need to dispose of cyanide wastes our very best solution was to employ a professional shop that had the knowledge, equipment and legal authority to accept and destroy these solutions. We believe that this way it the best for any refiner dealing with cyanides.

The so called "destruction" of cyanide by strong acids has been suggested. <u>This is very, very dangerous</u>! There is a large evolution of gaseous and toxic hydrogen cyanide. Even if the process is apparently complete hydrogen cyanide can still be dissolved in the acidic solution and later agitation result in an unexpected evolution of poisonous gas.

The acid will probably not destroy all of the metal cyanide complexes resulting in poor recovery and a residual cyanide content. <u>DO NOT USE THIS TECHNIQUE</u>.

Probably the most often mentioned destruction method (for smaller amounts of cyanide) is alkaline chlorination. Details of this can be gotten from the DuPont Corporation, Chemicals and Pigments Department, Wilmington, Del. 19898. DuPont also has a hydrogen peroxide method. We understand that the hydrogen peroxide method does not destroy all metal cyanide complexes leaving a residual poisonous metal cyanide in solution. This may also be true of chlorination.

A chlorination destruct only goes to completion if all metals are removed from solution first. If they are not removed completely before chlorination, the destruction is very incomplete and the residual material is very difficult to treat.

We understand that household bleach (sodium hypochlorite) can be used as the source of chlorine for this chlorination. This method does require attention to a number of details. Fairly low (below 1%) cyanide concentration and a specific pH range is required to avoid making an intermediate toxic material called cyanogen chloride. The toxicity of cyanogen chloride is equal to or exceeds that of hydrogen cyanide. It is a strong tear gas. We understand first aid is the same as for hydrogen cyanide. Acid is used to make pH adjustments. Unless this is done with dilute acids and active stirring in a very actively ventilated place it is possible to make localized surges of HCN gas - very dangerous. The idea is simple, the procedures fairly complex.

The presence of chlorine interferes with cyanide testing so the point of completion is difficult to determine. In our opinion metal complexes are probably not destroyed but remain in their toxic form.

A recently devised cyanide destruction method uses air, sulfur dioxide and a small amount of copper as a catalyst. This is patented and subject to license by INCO. An article in the Journal of Metals, by <u>Devuyst, Conrad, Verqunst and Tandi</u>, describes the method. (See pages 44 and 45 of the December 1989 issue. More information is available from INCO see <u>Devuyst</u> in the references section.) Our question about its ability to destroy metal complexes resulted in conflicting answers.

According to Compressed Air Magazine (a technical publication of Ingersoll Rand Company), December 1994, p. 11 the US Bureau of Mines has isolated bacteria that decomposes cyanide to non-toxic materials.

<u>Others Methods of Cyanide Destruction</u>

We have heard of some 9 or 10 other methods of cyanide destruction. See articles by <u>Groshart</u> and by <u>Morris</u> for information and comments.

Cyanide Destruction Chemistry

The very dangerous and undesirable reaction of cyanide with an acid (any acid) is:

$$NaCN + HCl = NACl + HCN \text{ (a poisonous gas)}$$

In this example we use hydrochloric acid (HCl). Other acids work in a similar way.

As mentioned earlier metal complexes of cyanide resist destruction. An example of a complex with gold is :

$$NaAu(CN)_2$$

The displacement of gold by zinc (cementation) is:

$$2\ NaAu(CN)_2 + Zn = Na_2Zn(CN)_4 + 2\ Au$$

Other reactions can occur.

It is reported that aluminum does not complex but that its use requires additional caustic soda. See <u>Rose</u> p. 388.

Activated carbon removes gold and silver from cyanide solutions. We understand this is physical not a truly chemical exchange.

The reactions that occur in the chlorination of cyanide are several. First is the hydrolyses of the bleach (NaClO):

$$NaClO + H_2O = HClO + NaOH$$

The hydrolyzed bleach then reacts with the cyanide.

$$NaCN + HClO = ClCN + NaOH$$

The ClCN is cyanogen chloride, as poisonous as cyanide and a strong lachrymator (tear gas). If the pH is high enough and solutions are dilute (all under 1%) and well stirred a second reaction proceeds rapidly and the cyanogen chloride is safely destroyed.

$$ClCN + 2NaOH = NaCNO + NaCl + H_2O$$

The cyanate (NaCNO) can be destroyed at a lower pH with additional chlorate.

$$2NaCNO + HOCl + H_2O + O_2 = 2\,NaOH + HCl + 2CO_2 + N_2$$

The exact step-by-step chemistry of the INCO sulfur dioxide treatment is not given. That paper discusses several aspects of this chemistry. They do give the following equation as the ideal overall stoichiometry of the method:

$$CN^- + SO_2 + O_2 + H_2O = CNO + H_2SO_4$$

Their paper, (Devuyst), says that the metals and precious metals present are recovered as hydroxides by adjusting the pH to about 9-10. Our present information about this is confusing.

This could make it possible to simultaneously destroy cyanide and recover precious metals. Further investigation and chemical tests are needed to see if this could be worthwhile.

RECOVERY FROM OTHER LOWGRADE SCRAP

Sink Trap Sludge, Tumbling Liquids and Mud, Used Casting Investment

Sink trap sludges are often received with or as a part of jewelers sweeps. They are watery or semi solid. We dewater the sloppiest portion by filtration. We do not dry these sludges but put them into the crucible furnace with sweeps ashes and sweeps flux.

We generally assume them to be 30 to 40% dry solids and add flux on this assumption. Some adjustment by extra additions of mixed flux, borax or fluorspar is once in awhile needed.

Tumbling mud is a term we use for the solids that come from vibratory or rotary polishing machines. It sometimes comes to us as a quite dry solid, sometimes as a wet sludge but more often as a soapy liquid. If this liquid is clear we decant using a siphon and deal only with the bottom layer of liquid and the solids.

A small amount of acid very effectively acidifies this solution and promotes settling and filtering. The solids are added to sweeps ashes and furnaced.

Casting investment is rarely offered for refining although there may be some in sink trap sludges. Casting investment must be concentrated so that the bulk of the investment has been discarded and a small portion containing the valuable metals retained or the processing cost exceeds the value of the recovery.

Schneller p. 283, Jewelry Mfg. Technology 1987, describes some rather extensive tests on value and recovery from used investment. A recommendation for a rather simple concentration and recovery system is given. In outline it is that the caster provide a 35 mesh screen in the quench tank and that the caster quench his flasks so that the investment mostly goes through the 35 mesh screen and that the plus 35 mesh coarse fraction be saved for gold recovery. This should be done at quench time not later. Used investment will form lumps (of no value) and a screening operation later is laborious and costly. Wet ball milling for a short time followed by rescreening will eliminate most of the investment.

Investment (dry basis) is about 60-70% silica and 30-40% calcium sulfate. If melted separately the use of soda ash and some regular sweeps flux works quite well. We rather prefer to run it as part of a sweeps ashes melt.

Rhodium Plating Solutions

Rhodium plating solutions are often used for a hard, good color plate on white gold. In our many years of work we have never been offered any of this as scrap. The concentrations of rhodium in the solutions is quite low and the extraction and refining work complex. Such scrap should go to a platinum metal refiner. Refining charges will be substantial.

Electronic Scrap, Gold Plated Material and Telephone Scrap

Electronic scrap and most gold plated material is bright, shiny and delights the eye. It looks very valuable but the gold content is usually very, very small. The gold is a microscopically thin electroplated surface layer. Recovery work needs to be on a very large scale to be fiscally worth while. The methods we use are not the ones that work well on such scrap. A large refiner said that such scrap would have 2 to 10 T/oz gold, 40 to 100 T/oz silver and 0 to 1 T/oz platinum group metals per ton.

We understand that much of this work is done by cyanide dissolution of the gold after the scrap has been suitably broken up so that all gold surfaces are available to the cyanide solution.

There is a tendency for base metals to predissolve and interfere with the solution of the gold. Several gold recovery enterprises offer additions that help prevent this interference. Patent No. 4,483,739, November 1984, covers the use of mercaptobenzothiazole as an additive for this use. We have been verbally informed that 3 nitrobenzene sulfonic acid-sodium salt is useful.

Older telephone scrap contains considerable palladium and we have recovered such palladium by traditional methods - see chapter on Platinum and Palladium. We doubt that there is much of this scrap around. Unless a very laborious concentration by hand clipping contact points is done, it is probably not a worthwhile refining job.

Automobile Mufflers

Catalytic automobile mufflers contain small amounts of platinum group metals. Generally these are platinum and palladium and perhaps traces of rhodium. Research in this field is continuous and the metals, the amounts and the base on which these are deposited for use in the mufflers will change.

This scrap is of no interest to the small refiner. The values in the muffler material are small and a successful recovery plant will have to be large to process the material in large amounts to be financially successful.

There are numerous articles concerning the various possible methods of recovery. Some information is in publications of The Metallurgical Society and also in various volumes published by the International Precious Metals Institute. We will not attempt to make specific references to the many articles available.

The problem of accumulating a steady flow of auto catalyst to keep a necessarily large plant is considerable. Unless such a steady flow of raw material can be maintained the large plant is in trouble.

One method of recovery of values from auto catalyst is processing the catalyst in a copper smelter. A Belgian copper smelter does this as a regular part of their operation. The platinum, palladium, etc. proceeds through the plant and finally reports to the tank house sludge in the electrolytic refining of copper together with the precious metals naturally present in the copper. Some adjustment of fluxes to make proper slags may be needed to compensate for changes in the feed to the smelter but a steady supply of catalyst is not a necessity.

Ore-Gold, Silver, etc.

On rare occasions precious metal ores appear at the small refinery. There is no useful service that can be done to recover gold or silver from ore. The refiner deals with the purification of impure bullion (metal). Recovery from ore is a separate problem. (See chapter about Mining that outlines such work).

Watch Batteries

Small batteries come from watches, cameras, hearing aids, etc. These are usually silver oxide batteries in a stainless steel case. Silver recovery is not greatly worth while considering the price of silver. However, for special customers who send worth while amounts we do recover this silver.

Our system is to dissolve the lot in aqua regia which destroys the cases and releases the silver probably as silver chloride. The silver chloride is treated as described in the chapter, Silver.

The silver is not of great purity and is normally sold on the basis of weight and assay.

GOLD

Gold can be refined (purified) in a number of ways. There are special reasons for the use of these different methods. Some processes are very, very old; a few were devised in the late 1800's. Some methods are fairly new but these tend to be applied to specialized needs.

This section will be devoted to one venerable refining technique, the aqua regia process. It has the advantages of being able to refine discrete lots with no co-mingling from batch to batch, it requires a minimum of furnace melting of metals, it is useful for very small amounts of, say, a few ounces as well as large amounts and it is quite efficient (good recovery).

The disadvantages of the aqua regia method is that it requires strong acids, produces rather vile fumes and the leftover barren solution is a pollution problem.

OUTLINE

The aqua regia process is basically uncomplicated. Although straightforward and simple, a number of details require specific attention. We will try to include such matters in the details of the description.

The scrap gold is dissolved in an acid mixture known as aqua regia, the Royal Water of the ancients. It is easily made by mixing nitric with hydrochloric acid. It is one of the rather limited number of things that will dissolve gold. It does this quite rapidly.

Scrap gold will usually contain a number of other metals such as copper, silver, nickel and zinc. There may be some iron in the scrap, perhaps tin and lead, possibly platinum and palladium, aluminum, etc. Aqua regia dissolves these metals as well as the gold. The silver in jewelry gold is attacked but the silver chloride formed is quite insoluble and remains as a precipitate.

SAFETY

The materials involved in these processes are not what those experienced in chemical and metallurgical work would consider especially dangerous. They are, however, strong acids and produce acrid fumes and solutions that can badly burn and stain the skin. These deserve respect. Very valuable materials are also involved and it makes sense to have the equipment and procedures set up to avoid loss.

The acids used, nitric and hydrochloric, are both somewhat volatile and emit fumes and should be well stoppered to keep fumes out of the work areas. The acids (especially hydrochloric) emit some fumes when poured for measuring and mixing. These corrode equipment and make breathing difficult, and this work should be done in a chemical hood or in clear open spaces.

The acids, if spilled on the clothes, will eat holes and produce stains but not instantly. Acid on bare skin will soon sting and burn, but also not instantly, and spills should be promptly washed away with water. Reasonable precautions are to wear rubber gloves, an apron or work clothes and shoes, and always to wear glasses or goggles, as a splash in the eye can be serious. Contact lenses tend to concentrate foreign liquids or fumes that contact the eye. Use goggles or regular glasses. Emergency showers and eye washes are necessary in areas where this type of work is carried out. Such equipment may be an official requirement in many places.

A box or two of ordinary baking soda (sodium bicarbonate) should be kept at hand because it effectively neutralizes acid that spills on to floors and clothing. It is in itself harmless. Baking soda is, however, too strong for and NOT to be used in the eyes.

The hydrochloric and nitric acids mix quietly without spatter no matter which acid is poured into which.

The aqua regia container must be glass or plastic. Plastic has the great advantage of being less breakable. No metal will hold aqua regia except very costly tantalum. The container must be open or vented to allow the escape of the chlorine.

Although aqua regia does not rapidly attack plastics, Teflon is the only plastic truly resistant to the oxidizing attack of hot aqua regia. Polypropylene is quite resistant and ordinary plastic pails and similar ware last for quite a long time. We use them and after awhile throw them away.

The brown fumes generated during aqua regia digestion are toxic but are so acrid that their presence is soon detected. A good fume hood with a moving current of air to a stack or washer is required for this operation. Essentially all the fumes produced in the process are heavier than air but will be swept out by a properly designed hood.

While it is not a matter of personal safety the matter of gold solution spills can be so costly that it is worthy of serious thought. The containers for this are normally glass and the time will come when they break.

The floor of the fume hood should be acid resistant and sloped to a trap or a plastic catchment so any valuable gold solution spilled is not lost permanently. Using a glass vessel inside a larger plastic pan is a good way to retrieve the occasional boil over or spill.

Hard sinks, tables or floors where glassware is handled are best lined and covered with pads, liners or permanent covers of rubber or soft plastic.

Inspect the glassware regularly for cracks. Tapping the vessel lightly when it is being washed often reveals cracks by the changed sound of a bad container.

Gold chloride is formed when aqua regia digests gold scrap. Gold chloride has photochemical properties similar to the properties of the silver salts used in photography. Very minute amounts of this solution will stain the skin. Any work with this gold solution will almost surely result in the hands being stained a dark purple. The stain only appears hours after contact. It is not dangerous, just very visible. It is prevented by consistently wearing rubber gloves.

Gold stains on the skin can be removed by washing with household bleach, but the long-term effects of repeated contact with this chemical are not known. Our regular use of full strength bleach (Clorox) a 5.25% sodium hypochlorite solution for many years has caused us no problems.

The refined gold must be melted and care with heat and fire is essential. The melting crucibles must be thoroughly dry before they are heated in the melting furnace. If not properly dried out, the crucible often disintegrates explosively in the furnace. Because this happens in the furnace, it is rarely dangerous but it is noisy and costly.

All stirring rods and tongs should be thoroughly warmed before putting them into the crucible. A cold tool in hot metal sometimes results in strong ejection of metal.

Pour molten metal only into thoroughly dry and very warm molds. Small amounts of moisture create steam instantly and explosively throw out molten metal with dynamic force.

A pair of dark glasses will very much help observe the progress of the melt and also protect the eyes. The strength used by operators of industrial furnaces or gas torch welders are satisfactory.

Eye protection is very necessary. Accidents in this melting work are rare, but hot metal in the eyes can cause severe and permanent damage.

A pair of heat resisting gloves or mittens are really needed for comfort. There is enough radiant heat to curl leather gloves. Long sleeves and decent shoes are reasonable precautions for spills of hot metal. A welders type apron protects the body and clothing.

Although there is a chance of explosions if molten metals are poured onto damp surfaces, this is not a danger when pouring small amounts of molten metal into large volumes of water to make shot. Under these conditions the metal cannot trap steam under it so therefore it does not erupt. The metal must however, be poured <u>slowly</u> in a small stream about the size of a pencil or smaller. An active jet of water helps to break up the molten stream and makes this even safer. Slag, however, <u>sometimes</u> splatters when it touches water.

Be sure to use only good crucibles. Examine them before use. A broken crucible or anything that causes a large amount of molten metal to drop into the water can trap water and cause a steam explosion.

Be sure to wear eye protection for this work.

REFINING PROCEDURE

If the scrap contains combustible material, it is probably best to burn it before any further work is done. This can be done in a shallow pan (a frying pan is suitable for small batches). Usually a very coarse sieve with about a 10mm (3/8 inch) opening is used to separate the fine scrap and only the coarse portion is burnt. The burning is then much more efficient.

A traditional fuel is alcohol, but the author prefers a petroleum fuel of a non-explosive nature and has found the type known as "Charcoal Lighting Fluid" is good.

After burning it is well to remove all iron (saw blades, etc.) with a magnet. Iron in large quantities can be a problem and large magnetic pieces should be removed. These problems will be taken up as the process is described.

Massive pieces of metal take a very long time to digest in aqua regia. Any such large pieces should be made into shot as described later. Strip pot sludge should be well washed with water to remove cyanide residues before acid is added to it. A thorough wash with bleach to destroy any residual cyanide in strip pot sludge is strongly advised. Some metal cyanides (eg silver) can remain after a water wash. Soak the strip sludge in a bath of bleach over night. Do this at a pH of 10 to 11 under a well ventilated hood. See cyanide information in chapter Low Grade Scrap.

"Green gold" has a high silver content and resists dissolution because of the formation of silver chloride that covers the surface. Such gold should be melted with copper to allow the aqua regia to work.

MIXING AQUA REGIA

This and many of the operations described here should be carried out under an efficient fume extraction hood.

Aqua regia is a combination of nitric acid and hydrochloric acid (sometimes called muriatic acid). It is made by mixing 1 volume of concentrated nitric acid with 4½ volumes of concentrated hydrochloric acid. This mixture is quite stable and in our experience will last for many months. If aqua regia is to be used in a rather short time, a week or two, a mixture ratio of 1 nitric to 3 hydrochloric acid by volume reduces some of the work and expense of effluent water treatment later. It is reported that a 1 to 3 volume mixture is self destructive over a period of time. See Chemistry Section.

The precautions for mixing the acids are simple. Avoid splashes, protect eyes and work in the open or under a fume hood. These acids mix quietly.

Both acids and especially hydrochloric emit acrid fumes. No heat is evolved when mixing, but the aqua regia at once starts to emit chlorine gas, which evolves slowly for several days. DO NOT STOPPER aqua regia bottles. A closed aqua regia vessel can develop enough chlorine pressure to burst. Store in the open or in a fume hood.

The aqua regia can be mixed by just measuring and pouring the acids together. Vacuum can be used to transfer the aqua regia to small bottles for use. See page 100.

The aqua regia can be used immediately or in days or weeks and possibly months after preparation, especially if mixed in a 4½ to 1 ratio.

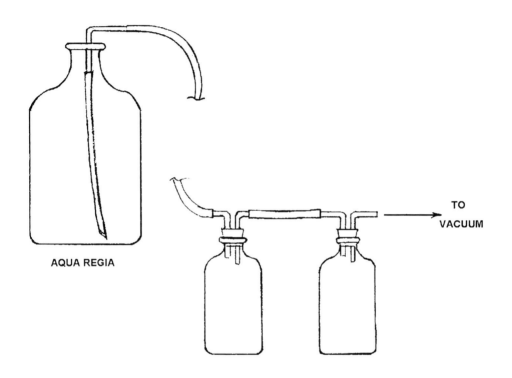

VACUUM TRANSFER TO AQUA
REGIA USAGE BOTTLES

Vacuum Aqua Regia Transfer

DIGESTING THE SCRAP

The scrap gold is placed in the digesting vessel. Glass may be used for small batches. Teflon plastic is also suitable for the strong oxidizing conditions of the aqua regia and Teflon will tolerate gentle heating if done with care. Ordinary plastic containers last for many runs and are less costly. We use them for a while and then discard. They cannot be externally heated.

The amount of aqua regia required for a given batch varies and depends on the proportion that is acid soluble and the quality of the metal present. It has been found that from 3.5 to 5 liters of aqua regia are required per kilo of scrap. (Approximately 1/2 gallon per pound.)

If the scrap is the usual filings and dust from jewelers' benches, the aqua regia will react very rapidly and may boil over, so the acid must be added slowly and with care.

If the scrap is in the form of old jewelry or metal shot or other large pieces, the reaction will be slower and a considerable amount of aqua regia can just be poured on to the scrap. Care is advised as the reaction is often quite slow to start and then after some minutes becomes very, very active. The container may get quite hot which increases the reaction speed. Generally, cold aqua regia works slowly but at about 140°F. (60°C.) it is very active.

When there is jewelry with diamonds, rubies, sapphires and similar acid-resistant gems these can be left in place and recovered from the filter.

The reaction of the aqua regia with the metals in the scrap produces nitrogen oxides. These are colorless but take up oxygen as soon as they reach air and then turn red-brown. These fumes are acrid, choking and toxic; they dissolve quite easily in water and in caustic solutions; they are heavier than air and the aqua regia digestion should be done under a GOOD FUME HOOD. See sketch and description in the chapter "Pollution".

The preferred practice is to add the aqua regia to the batch in two or three separate additions. About three-quarters of the expected amount of aqua regia is added and the mixture is allowed to stand for some time. Occasional agitation is good, especially with finely divided material. When brown fumes are no longer evolved and the bubbling of the solution is quiet, the solution is carefully siphoned or poured into a filter. More aqua regia is then added as before and the cycle repeated until the addition of fresh aqua regia produces no reaction, i.e., no more brown fumes and bubbling.

Enough aqua regia must be added to dissolve all of the gold. However the excess aqua regia that is required to accomplish this will later have to be removed so large excesses should be avoided.

The reaction also slows down near the end because of the amount of fine sludge present which tends to restrict the contact between aqua regia and undissolved gold, so frequent agitation is helpful.

When pieces of jewelry or larger pieces of metal are being dissolved, it often seems that the jewelry is not being attacked because it is still there in its original shape; however, such pieces often crumble if crushed with a stirring rod. Most jewelry alloys contain silver and the aqua regia dissolves the gold and other alloying metals leaving insoluble silver chloride as a residue in the original size and form. It is good to break these as there may be a yet undissolved core that will dissolve more quickly if exposed. Sometimes bending or cutting large pieces reveals a core that then dissolves. In extreme cases, insoluble lumps must be remelted with scrap copper. We use a melting dish and a welder's torch for small amounts and a small crucible in a small furnace for larger amounts. The remelted material usually emits clouds of smoke. This can be alleviated by adding some soda ash (sodium carbonate) while melting the copper and scrap. Stir thoroughly with a graphite rod and pour slowly into water to make shot.

When the gold alloy contains about 8 or 10% silver an adherent layer of silver chloride forms and "protects" the metal from dissolution. Green gold is much higher in silver content and is essentially aqua regia insoluble. Melting and dilution with copper is the only reasonable way of dissolving high silver material.

When the gold content of the scrap is below 30% any silver and copper present can be dissolved with nitric acid. See Parting in the chapter Other Refining Methods.

We have made preliminary tests with ultrasonic vibration and find that it effectively creates aqua regia dissolution of marginal material. We do not know the effective limits.

The following sketch shows the ultrasonic equipment we have set up. Our first test unit was in our opinion quite well sealed but rapidly failed in the NO_x fumes of aqua regia dissolution of the scrap. This somewhat complex nest of beaker, tank seals

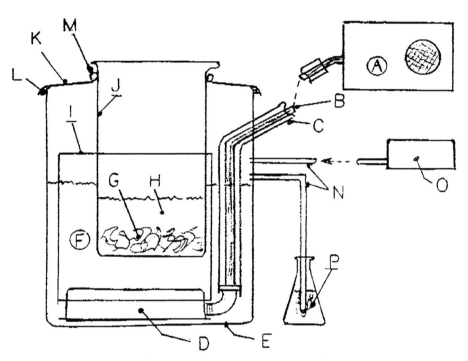

A - ULTRA SONIC POWER UNIT
B - COAXIAL POWER CABLE
C - FLEX TUBE CABLE COVER
D - SUBMERSIBLE TRANSDUCER
E - PLASTIC TANK APPX. 5 GAL (29L)
F - WATER - BASIC pH
G - SCRAP GOLD
H - AQUA REGIA
I - SHEET METAL CYLINDER
J - GLASS BEAKER
K - PLASTIC COVER
L - SEAL
M - O RING SEAL
N - PLASTIC TUBE
O - SMALL AIR COMPRESSOR
P - BUBBLER

Ultrasonic Equipment

and air purge seems to survive.

Sometimes the last few particles in a refining batch are relatively large lumps and the self heating characteristics of larger amounts no longer works. Dissolution continues but is very slow. Ultrasonic vibration is quite effective on such small amounts.

Suslick gives an interesting general description of ultrasonic work.

FILTERING

The aqua regia now contains various metal chlorides in solution and insoluble silver chloride as well as a lot of unwanted material in the sludge, and this mixture must be cooled and filtered. The reason for cooling is that silver chloride, though quite insoluble in water, is slightly soluble in strong acids and this solubility is lower in cold acids.

It may be helpful although not essential to dilute the solution at this time. Silver chloride is somewhat soluble in strong acids but less so in diluted solutions. Some solutions filter very slowly so that the increased volume of diluted solution may seriously extend filtering time.

It is good practice to add a little sulfuric acid to the dissolution vessel before filtering. When there is lead in the scrap (as occasionally happens) it forms a very hard to filter gelatinous material. (This is also true of tin).

Lead sulfate is somewhat easier to filter so the addition of sulfuric acid can help filtering.

Sulfuric acid should be diluted with about 4 parts of water (acid into the water). About a cupful of this is put into the pregnant liquid with care a little while before filtering.

The aqua regia solutions are filtered with a Buchner filtering funnel and a 4 liter vacuum filtering flask. Two sizes of funnel are used, a small one about 125mm diameter, and a larger one about 250mm diameter. Buchner Funnels are shown in the following photo. Buchner Funnels are vacuum filtering devices that help increase filtering speed.

Buchner Filters

Experience has shown that the paper discs usually used in these filters by chemists tend to float away when the filter is filled with liquid, but coffee urn filters obtainable from hotel and restaurant supply shops have proved very satisfactory. These should be large enough to line the bottom and sides of the filter funnel, inserted dry, wetted thoroughly with water and firmly seated and pressed into the corners to avoid wrinkles and vacuum leaks. Two plys of filter paper are used to help filtration and avoid breakthrough.

Vacuum is produced by means of a water pump (aspirator) available from chemical laboratory suppliers. Plastic, not metal pumps should be used, as the acid fumes from aqua regia filtering rapidly reduce the pumping ability of a metal pump. For the same reason mechanical vacuum pumps are not recommended unless provided with efficient acid vapor traps that are regularly maintained. See following sketches for filter set up and details of the aspirator.

It is convenient to connect the aspirator to the city water system. Much use will result in high water costs. A following photo and sketch shows how a plastic drum and a plastic pump can be set up to circulate water through the aspirator(s) creating vacuum without high water costs. The water should be buffered with a few scoops of soda ash to avoid acidity.

The filtrate is usually clean and clear. If, however, some solids come through at first the filter should be stopped after a little while and the liquid poured back for refiltering. Usually the liquid will then be clear and clean.

If lead or tin is present filtering will be slow. Tin is an unlikely contaminant unless some tin alloy, such as some bronzes or if soft solder are part of the scrap. Lead is a more likely contaminant if lead center buffs were part of the scrap. Sulfuric acid is helpful in forming a lead sulfate with better filtering characteristics. <u>Hoke</u> in various parts of her book discusses these metals.

Filtering proceeds more rapidly if the clearest part of the aqua regia is decanted onto the filter first. When the sludge and solids get into the filter the process usually slows. All of the solids should be washed into the filter with a small stream of water. A wash bottle is useful for this operation. A small hose with a small nozzle connected to the water system and controlled by an electric solenoid valve and a foot switch gives a larger volume of water and frees both hands for the work. The following sketch diagrams this device. When the filtering is complete the paper and the sludge should be washed with repeated small streams of water. This is to wash all gold chloride solution out of the filter and sludge and into the liquid.

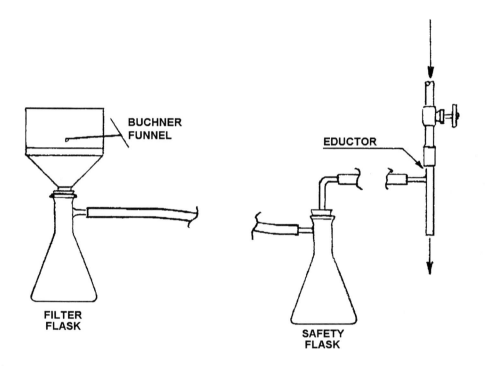

VACUUM FILTERING SYSTEM

Vacuum Filtering System

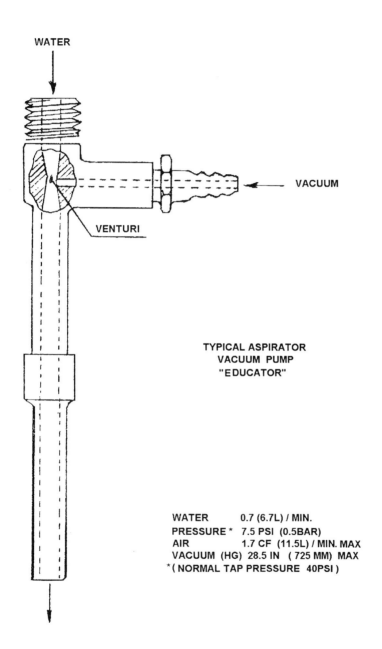

Aspirator (Eductor) Vacuum Pump

Water Saving Vacuum System

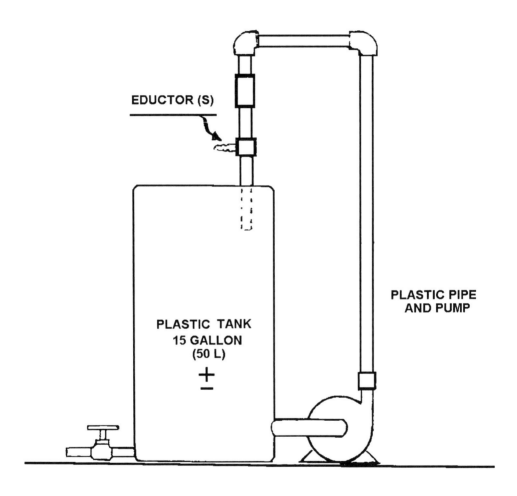

Water Saving Vacuum System

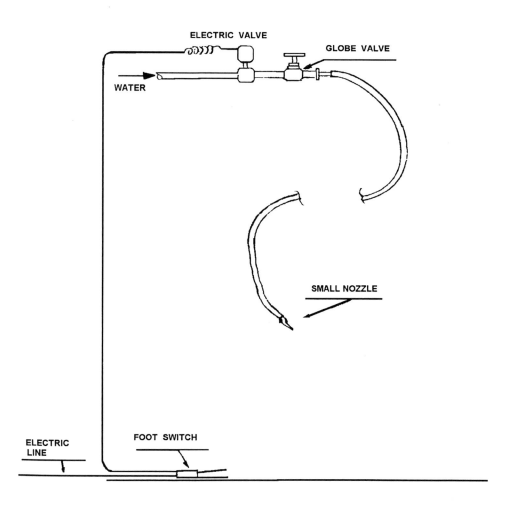

Wash Water System

The filter paper now contains the unwanted material and also the silver chloride. It is recommended that this should be saved until at least a 30 gallon drumful is accumulated. The silver and any residual gold can be recovered separately or the material sent to a sweeps refiner.

The filtered liquid is usually a rather handsome clear green color, due to nickel and copper. If only gold chloride were present, it would be yellowish.

If the filtering work has been rather slow, the presence of lead is a possibility and if even fractional percentages of lead go through to the final melt, the gold will be brittle and make very poor castings. Even though sulfuric acid was added previously we find that when refining very dirty scrap from sweeps it is helpful to again add sulfuric acid to the liquid in small amounts of perhaps half a cup per gallon. Since lead sulfate is rather insoluble in dilute solutions, the pregnant liquid should be diluted with 1 or 2 equal volumes of water and refiltered. It is convenient to let this stand for some hours or overnight and then decant all but the bottom few inches with a siphon. Any lead sulfate will be at the bottom and is then filtered through paper.

The white precipitate may be silver chloride (also less soluble in dilute acids) or it may be lead sulfate or both. Lead sulfate shows a crystalline sheen we've never seen in silver chloride. A refiner of electronic scrap (that may contain much lead) says he has seen tree-like crystals which we believe are lead sulfate.

The filtered solution is poured into a plastic container (plastic 5 gallon pails are suitable) for the next steps of eliminating excess nitric acid and precipitating the gold.

NITRIC ACID ELIMINATION

The excess aqua regia that was added to insure complete solution of all gold is, of course, still in the solution at this stage and must be eliminated to allow the gold to be precipitated.

The classic procedure for nitric acid elimination is repeated boiling to near dryness with the addition of hydrochloric acid with some sulfuric acid near the end. This is a lengthy and patience-trying process, not often used to-day.

There are a number of chemical methods of eliminating nitric acid. These have been considered and after extensive experimentation the use of urea has been selected as the most practical for the type of process described here. Urea is much used as a fertilizer and is also known as carbamide. Our usual supply comes from a farm supply store. It will probably be marked 46% which refers to the percent nitrogen content. Our material comes in the form of small pellets. We add it as the solid and we add it very carefully. The products of reaction are volumes of gases and a boil over of valuable liquid is a danger. A lid on the container, while this gassy reaction goes on, will avoid any loss as mist. There is no sharp end point when it has destroyed the aqua regia, but the bubbling reaction gets fairly quiet. It is good to allow some time, say 30 minutes, and numerous small additions to finish this step. Dilution of the solution with several volumes of water is helpful. However, if dilution has been done earlier it need not be done again.

PRECIPITATING THE GOLD

The classic method of reducing gold chloride in solution to solid gold is to add "copperas" to the solution. "Copperas" is an ancient name for ferrous sulphate, a rather cheap chemical. A number of other chemicals will also reduce the gold chloride. One potentially useful chemical is hydroquinone that does not reduce the cupric chloride. It has disadvantages and our use was only experimental.

We have used formaldehyde (a rude and nasty chemical), oxalic acid, sulfur dioxide gas, hydrazine. There are others. Some of these require heat some are very gassy and tend to boil over, some make a very fluffy precipitate and require large gold filters.

We often use sulfur dioxide gas and the following sketch shows the set up we like.

For many years we used a solution of sodium bisulfite ($NaHSO_3$) as the reducing agent as well as the material to eliminate excess aqua regia. A solution of 35-40% strength is convenient. Maximum solubility is about 44%. Much stirring is required to get the bisulfite dissolved. It must not be added to the gold solution quickly or in large amounts. It is easy to overshoot the amount needed and an excess turns the soluble cupric chloride to an insoluble cuprous chloride that causes trouble. Addition from a small tank or a pail on a higher shelf is convenient. A small laboratory sized hose, a stop cock and a plastic or glass nozzle to limit the flow rate works well. Addition rate should be about 250-300 ml per minute or less. A hole in the nozzle about the size of lead in a wooden pencil seems about right. A following sketch shows a valve system and a siphon system for adding the bisulfite.

When the scrap contains platinum in sufficient amounts to make platinum recovery and refining worth while the gold should be precipitated with copperas

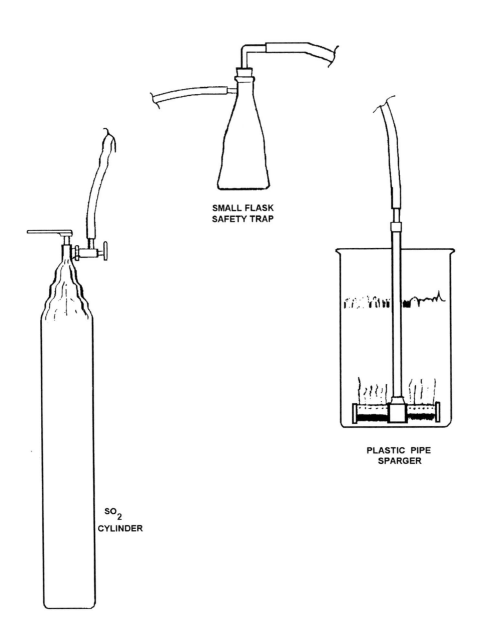

Sulfur Dioxide Equipment

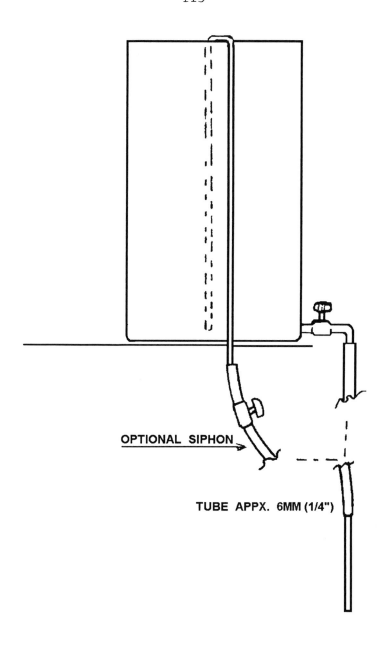

Sulfite Feed Tank

(ferrous sulfate). Mix the fresh green copperas with warm water (a ratio of about a pound to a quart of water is okay). When mixed add a little hydrochloric acid to make a clear green solution. This can be added with a small hose as described in the preceding paragraph.

The reason for using copperas is that it is a less aggressive reducer and thereby leaves the platinum in a chemical state easily changed to an insoluble condition. Sulfur dioxide and the sulfites tend to reduce the platinum compound to later soluble state.

Metabisulfite is the frequently used name for what we use as sodium bisulfite. It is the same except for the lack of a molecule of water (H_2O) and when dissolved in water is really sodium bisulfite. There are other aspects in the use of metabisulfite. See discussion in the Technical section of this chapter.

The precipitation of gold can be seen as a 'cloud' of particles in the solution. The end point of the precipitation is difficult to see, some clues may be noted in the density of the 'cloud' of gold particles. The solution will be clearer and noticeably less yellowish, especially if a drop is viewed on a white chinaware surface. This is because the yellow gold chloride is gone and the green of the other chlorides remains. Deliberate care during this gold precipitation work is advised. Observe the signs and test the solution frequently to avoid excesses of precipitant. Sometimes the solution seems darker.

If bisulfite is used the strong burning sulfur odor of SO_2 indicates the end has been reached and excess precipitant is being added. Frequent test with the test solution next described help reach an accurate end point.

The end point is accurately determined by a test for the presence of dissolved gold. For this you will need test material:

20 or 30 grams of stannous chloride crystals
20 or 30 grams of pure tin metal - physical shape not important
A little hydrochloric acid
A spot plate, i.e., white porcelain plate with small cavities or similar device
A dropping bottle about 30 to 50 ml. This has a groove in the glass stopper to let liquid out a drop at a time.

Put 1 or 2 grams of stannous chloride crystals into the dropping bottle and add one or two grams of the tin metal. Fill about 3/4 full of water and add about 3 drops of hydrochloric acid.

There will be a milky liquid and it is ready to use. The tin dissolves slowly and keeps the solution in condition. The solution does have a limited life of perhaps a few months but it is well worth the trouble of keeping on hand.

Check this solution very regularly with a small bottle of gold solution. A very small piece of gold (say 0.2 to 0.5 grams) is dissolved in a tiny amount of aqua regia and washed into a small bottle with a few ml of water. This is used as a standard known solution to be sure the stannous chloride has not become ineffective.

The stannous chloride test is made by dipping a glass or plastic rod into the solution to be tested and transferring one or two drops into one of the cavities in the spot plate.

Using the dropping bottle, a drop of stannous chloride test solution is put on to the sample in the cavity. If there is gold present there will be a prompt change to a very dark color. A slight darkening indicates some gold. If there is no gold there will be no change other than that caused by the mutual dilution of the two liquids. This is a very sensitive test and will detect about 1 or 2 parts per million.

The following photograph shows this equipment.

Good practice is that when the first test of the day shows "no gold" it is always checked by testing with a drop of standard gold solution. A dark color then shows the stannous chloride is okay and no color means the test solution is dead.

Discarding gold solution that has been tested "no gold" by old and used-up test solution can be very costly.

It will take extra time but it is possible and desirable to reach the end point of gold precipitation by repeated spot tests near the end. Just before the end the spot will darken more slowly and be somewhat lighter in color. At this time very little additional precipitant will complete the work.

If an excess has been added and cuprous chloride is formed, it can be removed later.

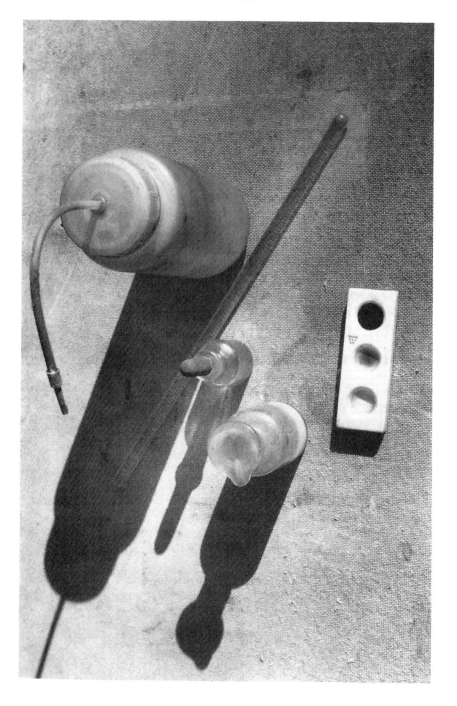

Gold Test Equipment

FILTRATION

When the solution has been cleared of gold it should be allowed to stand, preferably overnight. Although gold is heavy and most of it settles quickly, some particles are very small and require time to go to the bottom.

Before doing any filtering the solution is again tested with stannous chloride to be sure no gold remains in solution. On rare occasions gold has been redissolved or a previous spot test was in error and this simple quick retest is good insurance for loss prevention.

In the interest of reducing the time and aggravation of much filtering the clear upper portion of the barren solution can be decanted and only the few inches near the bottom put into the filter. An easy way is to construct a U tube that can be used as a siphon. This should be of a length that will leave several inches of solution over the gold. When this siphon is started we always quickly take a spot test to be sure there is no dissolved gold at the bottom. On rare occasions, the solution in the top of the container is barren but there is gold dissolved in the bottom part. Such a test is quick, cheap insurance. The following sketch diagrams a siphon decanting barren solution.

CUPROUS CHLORIDE

If sodium bisulfite, sodium sulfite or sulfur dioxide gas or other strong reducers were used it is possible a little too much was used and some cupric chloride ($CuCl_2$) was changed to cuprous chloride ($CuCl$). The cuprous chloride is soluble in strong hydrochloric acid or strong salt brine but insoluble in weak acids and in water.

When water is used to wash the gold into the filter any cuprous chloride precipitates and inhabits the gold. One way to avoid this is to wash the gold into the filter with an acid or brine stream. Another is to repeatedly wash the gold in the precipitation pail with strong acid or brine and finally transfer into the filter.

Dissolving any cuprous chloride out of the gold once it is in the filter is inefficient because contact with the acid in a filter is uncertain. It usually forms channels when it goes through the bed of gold and thus does a poor job of removing cuprous chloride.

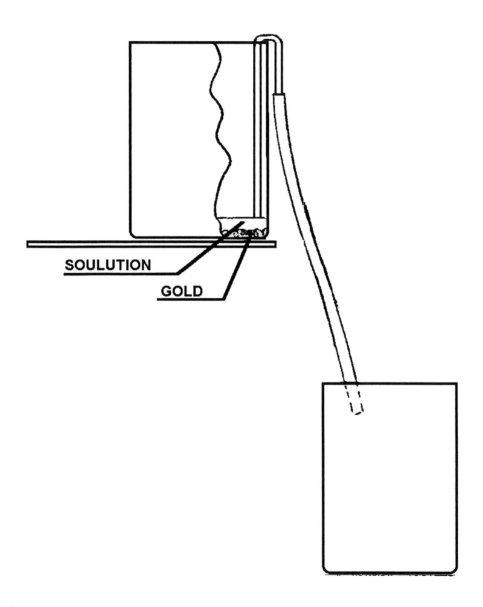

Siphon To Decant Barren Solution

WASHING THE GOLD

The preferred method is to set up the small filter and carefully pour the liquid through the filter with as little gold as possible. When all the liquid is gone add enough strong hydrochloric acid to generously cover the gold. Put a lid on the container (the acid fumes strongly) and agitate thoroughly. Let settle and again pour the liquid through the filter. This is done under the hood because of fumes.

After about 3 such acid treatments the filtered acidic liquid is put into the cementation tank with the other barren solution. Several inches of water is put into the filter flask and another acid treatment is made and poured through the filter. If cuprous chloride has been removed by previous washes the water will remain clear. If cuprous chloride is still being dissolved by the hydrochloric acid the water will be milky. This is because the diluted acid cannot keep the cuprous chloride in solution. If it is milky repeat acid washes and water tests until the diluted solution remains clear.

Then repeat this treatment of the gold with clear water to remove the hydrochloric acid. About three washes are usually enough.

We then use strong ammonia (NH_4OH) for another two or three washes. This is a rude material and working under a hood is the only way to be comfortable.

A final 2 or 3 water washes are made transferring all the gold into the filter. The container is scrubbed with a stiff brush so all the gold can be transferred to the filter.

EXPLOSIVE GOLD

Ammonia and gold metal present no special hazards. However, mixing ammonia with gold chloride can be dangerous. A fulminating gold (Explosive) can be formed. Be sure ammonia and gold in chemical combination do not mix. These can be unstable enough to explode even when wet. If acid conditions are maintained this fulminate is destroyed and there is no danger.

BARREN SOLUTION

The solution from which the gold has been precipitated and the solution obtained when the gold is filtered, is retained and given additional treatment. There are several reasons for this. It is very, very acidic and in almost all locations unfit and likely illegal to dispose of as is. It contains copper and possibly traces of other metals that may have toxic properties. It probably contains small amounts of gold and silver that may make any simple recovery work worthwhile.

This barren solution is poured into a small tank or pail which we call a cementation tank. Here we suspend a small bar or plate of copper. We stir this well and let the solution settle overnight. The solution is decanted by a siphon or small pump and sent to the effluent treatment system where it is treated as described in the section on Pollution.

The solids that accumulate in the bottom of the cementation tank are occasionally removed and added to the material treated for silver recovery. See the section on Silver.

MELTING THE GOLD

Any gas or electric furnace normally used for gold melting or alloy production may be used for melting the precipitated gold.

Crucible material is not critical and may be selected to suit the melting furnace. Crucibles, however, should be clean and kept solely for melting pure gold.

The filter paper and its load of gold is put into the crucible. When the gold is being melted the filter paper will burn and leave any adhering gold in the crucible. It usually burns quite slowly because the furnace flame at gold melting temperature does not have excess oxygen. With time it will burn away. This can be accelerated by reducing the gas so there is excess oxygen in the flame or the filter paper can be burned out very quickly by adding a small amount (say, 1/4 teaspoon or less) of sodium nitrate. When this is added to a hot crucible the paper burns with an eye-dazzling flame. Even though fluxes are not a definite need we sometimes use a little borax or mixed flux. A mixture of half boric acid and half borax is a good gold melting flux.

The mold must be warm and dry before gold is poured. A cold mold may have traces of moisture and molten metal poured onto traces of moisture can create the most amazing, costly and potentially painful eruptions. Smoky acetylene flame makes a good mold coating.

It is helpful to stir the melt when it has become liquid. This brings up any bits of paper for oxidation by flux or air. A small 1/8" or 3/16" diameter gouging rod is used. These are available at welding supply shops. The copper coating should be removed by immersion in aqua regia, washing in water and careful drying before use. A gouging rod is graphite. Graphite stirring rods are available from casting supply shops.

The gold and any slag are poured into a mold together. The slag separates easily when cold. Dilute sulfuric acid or dilute nitric acid removes traces of adhering slag. If pure gold shot is desired it is our habit to melt the gold bar with a welder's oxy-acetylene torch into a pail of water. This produces a minimum of fine shot and that makes it easier for the jeweler.

To make large amounts of shot we melt the metal in a crucible and then pour the molten metal into a jet of water. We use a 10 gallon aluminum cooking pot (a larger one is even better). Do not use a galvanized pot or a plastic vessel. Sometimes the metal particles reach the bottom still partly melted and then will stick to galvanized metal or burn through plastic.

Our "shot pail" is filled with water and a flat nozzle (home made) shoots water across the pail about 1 inch (2.5cm) under the surface. A garden hose is the water supply. (See sketch, Sweeps Chapter). A partial cover opposite the jet prevents water overflow and washing gold over the edge at that point.

The molten gold is poured slowly into the flowing water and falls to the bottom as pellets or flakes. The stronger the jet, the smaller the particles.

If a karat gold alloy is required we do not make fine gold shot. A fine gold bar is poured and cleaned and weighed. We do not try to make the alloying metal (we call it "alloy") for karat gold but buy it as needed from a supplier that produces a good master alloy.

The arithmetic we use to make up, say 14 karat plumb is as follows:

$$\frac{14 \text{ k}}{24 \text{ k (pure)}} = 0.5834 \text{ or } 58.34\% \text{ gold in this alloy}$$

It is our practice to use 0.585 as the gold content. Then in general terms:

$$\frac{\text{weight of the fine gold}}{0.585} = \text{weight of 14 k produced}$$

Weight of 14 k - weight of fine = weight of alloy to add. As a for instance, let us assume we have 152.3 grams of fine.

$$\frac{152.3 \text{ grams of fine}}{0.585} = 260.3 \text{ grams } 14 \text{ k}$$
260.3 - 152.3 = 108.0 grams alloy to add.

If you weigh in T/oz or pennyweights, the same procedure applies; just use the same scale for all the weights.

The same arithmetic is used for 10 k which is 10/24 gold;
18 k which is 18/24, or any other karatage desired.

The alloying metals used for making karat gold vary for yellow, white, green, red golds, etc. A good alloying mixture is not simple. We know of a very fine casting alloy that contains 6 metals. Of these zinc, a very often used and desirable part of most karat alloys has a boiling temperature below the melting temperature of copper and gold. Getting zinc into this melt is a task requiring special skills and techniques.

The alloy used to make karat gold should be purchased, mixed and melted and ready for use. There are some very poor and some very good already mixed master alloys available. Our experience is with already mixed master alloys. (see references). There are others of good quality but outside our specific experience.

When making karat gold, flux is not used. Extensive stirring with a graphite rod to be sure of a uniform melt is necessary. The karat gold can be poured to shot or poured to plates, rods or an ingot that is torch melted to shot.

GOLD CHEMISTRY

Aqua regia is a mixture of hydrochloric and nitric acids. According to <u>Rose</u> p 17 the dissolution of gold is:

$$Au + HNO_3 + 4HCl = H_2O + NO + HAuCl_4$$

They correspond to one part by weight of nitric acid specific gravity 1.42 (approximately 70 % HNO_3) and four parts by weight of hydrochloric acid specific gravity 1.2 (approximately 37 %). By volume the ratio is 1 to 4.7.

An equation for the formation of aqua regia or nitrosylchloride in chemical nomenclature according to <u>Mellor</u> Vol. VIII p 619:

$$HNO_3 + 3HCl = 2H_2O + Cl_2 + NOCl$$

This reaction is reversible in a closed system. At 21°C the pressure is 5.1 atm. In our experience the chlorine evolves for several days showing the reaction to be quite slow. We suspect it may not go to completion.

<u>Rose</u> p 17 says that the reaction he gives (first one above) and the proportions given are the most economical. Because of chlorine evolution this economy could be realized only if mixing and gold dissolution were done at the same time and not with premixed aqua regia. Some refiners do this by having the metal in hydrochloric acid and adding nitric acid.

Directions are often written to use a <u>volume</u> mixture of 1 to 3. Because of the presence of water in these acid solutions this becomes a molecular ratio of 2 nitric to 3 hydrochloric acid. This quite readily dissolves gold. In fact we think of aqua regia as a successful gold dissolver that can be applied to a rather broad ratio of nitric-hydrochloric mixtures.

A reference we found in the London Patent Library (exact name now lost) made the statement that a 2 to 3 ratio was unstable and gave the following equations:

$$2HNO_3 + 3HCl + 2H_2O = Cl_2 + NOCl + HNO_3$$

$$NOCl + H_2O = HNO_2 + HCl$$

$$HNO_3 + HNO_2 = N_2O_4 + H_2O$$

An algebraic addition (i.e., cancellation of the intermediate terms on opposite sides of the equations) gives the following final result:

$$2HNO_3 + 3HCl = N_2O_4 + 2H_2O + HCl + Cl_2$$

This reaction too is slow and we believe completion may be a matter of weeks or more.

The reaction with nitrosyl chloride:

$$3NOCl + Au = AuCl_3 + 3NO$$

Note that here we show the gold chloride as $AuCl_3$. The form $HAuCl_4$ seems to be the accepted solid condition. It would require another molecule of HCl in the above equation. In refining we deal with gold chloride solutions and $AuCl_3$ is probably the entity. In any case the entire system is not rigidly dependent upon chemical theory. The presence of other metals use the acids in their own ways and in varying amounts. These are usually quite soluble.

The standard electrode potentials for the half reactions with gold are:

$$Au \pm Au^{3+} = 3e^- \qquad E = +1.50 \text{ volts}$$
$$Au + 4Cl^- = AuCl_4^- + 3e^- \qquad E = +1.00 \text{ volts}$$

According to these potentials the reaction would not proceed. However the presence of chloride ions for the formation of stable complex ions and the resulting increase in reduction strength of the metal may be the reason it works, Sisler p 494.

Silver in gold scrap presents a different activity because of its insolubility.

$$Ag + NOCl = AgCl + NO$$

The silver chloride is a very insoluble material and if present in amounts more than perhaps 8-12 %, it forms a silver chloride surface on the gold and quite effectively stops dissolution.

Although very insoluble in water silver chloride is somewhat more soluble in hydrochloric acid and chloride salt solutions. Seidell p 605 shows solubility in water at 25°C as 0.00172 grams AgCl per liter of water. Solubility in hydrochloric acid (p 608) is from 0.035 to 0.56 grams AgCl per liter depending upon acid strength. It is also temperature variable. A similar range of solubility is given in various chloride salt solutions.

We can therefore depend upon some silver chloride going through the filter with the solution. Fabian and Ryan in a recent paper advocate the use of SO_2 reduction of gold chloride to produce high quality (999.99) gold. They state that the silver in the solution during SO_2 reduction forms silver sulfite (Ag_2SO_3). Lange's "Handbook of Chemistry" shows silver sulfite to be soluble in NH_4OH and slightly soluble in cold water.

As mentioned earlier with lower grade scraps (watch bands are an example) aqua regia usually dissolves gold only at the very last part of a considerable number of acid additions. This is caused by the presence of a large amount of base metal in such scrap. Base metals are chemically more active than gold and combine with aqua regia more easily than gold. They can also replace gold already in solution.

This chemical activity has been measured and a simple version of this reactivity made up in an Electromotive Series. It is so called because the measurement of reactivity is made with electrical apparatus. Such an electromotive series follows. The least reactive are at the bottom and reactivity increases to the top. The metals at the top are so active that reaction with water is explosive.

ELECTROMOTIVE SERIES

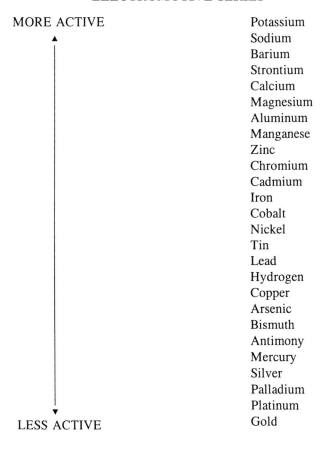

MORE ACTIVE ▲

Potassium
Sodium
Barium
Strontium
Calcium
Magnesium
Aluminum
Manganese
Zinc
Chromium
Cadmium
Iron
Cobalt
Nickel
Tin
Lead
Hydrogen
Copper
Arsenic
Bismuth
Antimony
Mercury
Silver
Palladium
Platinum
Gold

▼ LESS ACTIVE

Often during the dissolution of low grade scrap some small amounts of gold will dissolve and a stannous chloride test will show dissolved gold. When reaction has subsided and some time has elapsed the same solution shows no gold in solution. A reaction has occurred whereby some undissolved base metals trade places with the dissolved gold. This puts more base metals in solution and gold is precipitated.

Occasionally the precipitated gold does not drop to the bottom of the vessel. Physical and chemical conditions result in reverting the gold chloride to gold metal in particle sizes too small to settle out. Such suspensions are known as colloids. The addition of aqua regia with agitation dissolves such colloids.

This was demonstrated to us when we had a very dark solution testing "no gold" with stannous chloride. The addition of aqua regia resulted in a reaction and the production of nitrogen oxide fumes. The solution became green showing that the dark material had dissolved. The solution now gave a positive gold test.

Usually such solutions do not change color because of the presence of dark metal compounds, perhaps iron.

Colloids are very persistent. Faraday made a gold colloid in 1857 that was in suspension until destroyed in the bombing of England in World War II.

LEAD CONTAMINATION

The presence of lead in gold metal is a serious matter. Rose p 3 says that more than 0.005 % lead makes gold brittle. The addition of sulfuric acid is suggested by Hoke p 72 as a part of the original aqua regia.

Lead nitrate, a possible entity during aqua regia reaction, is quite soluble in water but less so in nitric acid. Lead sulfate however is quite insoluble. Seidell p 364 lists the solubility of lead sulfate ($PbSO_4$) as 0.003 grams Pb per liter of water and up to 0.088 grams lead (Pb) per liter of HCl depending upon strength and 0.029 grams lead per liter of HNO_3 also depending on strength. Dilute solutions dissolved less.

GOLD PRECIPITATION

The precipitation of gold from the clear filtered solution is chemically called reduction. Reduction is chemically the opposite of oxidation which is what the aqua regia did in the first place.

During gold dissolution some excess aqua regia was used and this excess is there ready to react. If the excess is small, it can be destroyed by diluting the solution with water so the gold reducer can first destroy this excess and then precipitate gold.

Foo investigated this matter and developed a chart showing the needed dilution factor. This chart is given on the following page. Our experience is that for a moderate excess of aqua regia a dilution of 2 to 3 times works with a sulfite reducer as well as with a copperas reducer. This chart does not apply if a large excess of aqua regia is present.

Larger excesses require much more dilution and an easy alternate method is the use of urea. Urea is a rather common material used in considerable amounts as a fertilizer. Urea reacts to destroy aqua regia (or nitrous acid also). Mazia quotes James Frinkbone as saying that urea probably works according to the following:

$$(NH_2)2CO + 2NOCl = 2N_2 + H_2O + CO_2 + 2HCl$$

and

$$4(NH_2)_2CO + 6NO_2 = 7N_2 + 8H_2O + 4CO_2$$

The reaction is gassy and we are sure it sometimes follows other paths. We once in a while see a red gas above the solution, probably NO_2.

Cementation with zinc (useful in cyanide processes) does not work here, nor will aluminum or iron because they will also precipitate copper and make a gold-copper mixture. The classic material for gold reduction is copperas, an antique name for ferrous sulfate. The reaction is:

$$3FeSO_4 \cdot 7H_2O + AuCl_3 = Fe_2(SO_4)_3 + FeCl_3 + Au + 7H_2O$$

In this reaction as well as the others that reduce gold chloride to gold metal there is an exchange of electrons. In this case the copperas is the donor of electrons or the reducer. The iron in three molecules of ferrous sulfate each donate one electron to the gold in the gold chloride. Supplied with these three electrons it ceases its life as part of a gold compound and becomes a metal atom. The gold is the oxidizer, the acceptor of electrons.

The iron which was deficient two electrons each in its ferrous state is now deficient three electrons each and rearranges itself with the sulfate and chloride parts of the chemicals.

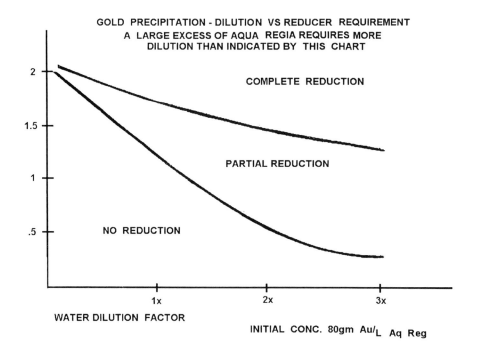

Chart - Gold Pptn.-Dilution Factor

Such reactions are called redox, a short term for reduction-oxidation reactions. A similar type of reaction is what occurred with gold and aqua regia. The very powerful oxidation potential of aqua regia was able to dissolve the gold.

There are other reducers capable of reducing the gold chloride to gold. We have used oxalic acid, formaldehyde, hydroquinone, hydrazine, sulfur dioxide gas, sodium bisulfite and sodium sulfite. There are numerous others. Gold is quite easily reduced and many chemicals work.

We use sulfur dioxide in one form or another and the chemistry of these materials follows.

Sulfur dioxide, a gas:

$$3SO_2 + 2AuCl_3 + 3H_2O = 3SO_3 + 6HCl + 2AU$$

The SO_3 promptly combines with water to form sulfuric acid:

$$SO_3 + H_2O = H_2SO_4$$

It is possible that at least part of the reaction could be the formation of sulfurous acid:

$$SO_2 + H_2O = H_2SO_3$$

This reacts to reduce the gold chloride:

$$3H_2SO_3 + 2AuCl_3 + 3H_2O = 2Au + 3H_2SO_4 + 6HCl$$

A good source of sulfur dioxide that does not involve a pressurized gas is sodium bisulfite ($NaHSO_3$). It is often purchased under the name metabisulfite ($Na_2S_2O_5$). This is actually two molecules of bisulfite with a molecule of water removed. When dissolved for use it reacts to bisulfite:

$$Na_2S_2O_5 + H_2O = 2NaHSO_3$$

The reaction that precipitates the gold is essentially the same as with SO_2 gas:

$$3NaHSO_3 + 2AuCl_3 + 3H_2O = 3NaHSO_4 + 6HCl + 2Au$$

The bisulfite changes to a bisulfate. Again the gold has been presented with three electrons and as before the sulfur is the donor.

The reaction of sodium metabisulfite with water to form sodium bisulfite is not necessarily as neat and complete as shown above. <u>Eilbeck</u> page 179 says that some tests made several years ago indicate the dimerization is not complete and that some metabisulfite remains. Most of the material is in the bisulfite form, probably more then 90%.

We have looked into <u>Antelman</u> p 179 and it is possible that the metabisulfite form is a somewhat stronger reducer than the bisulfite. Our own plant use of several forms has shown us no obvious differences but we have reports from others indicating a difference.

Sulfur dioxide gas in solution is reported by <u>Eilbeck</u> to be a weaker reducer than solutions of sulfites. This may help alleviate some of the problems of cupric chloride reduction that are discussed below. In our experience it will not prevent reduction of Cu II to Cu I.

<u>Eilbeck</u>, Chapter 4, pp 177-201, discussed reduction and various reducers and their use. Specific reference to gold is not made but the information given easily applies. A statement that bisulfite is not available except as solution apparently does not apply in the United States. We find numerous suppliers listed.

We also use sodium sulfite (Na_2SO_3). The reaction is the same. There are two sodium atoms and no hydrogen (the acidic portion of bisulfite). The amounts are small but a very little less acid needs to be neutralized during water treatment later if the sodium sulfite is used.

An undesirable feature of sulfite reduction is that if an excess is used the sulfite will react with the copper chloride that is usually present. The reaction is:

$$Na_2SO_3 + 2CuCl_2 + H_2O = Na_2SO_4 + 2CuCl + 2HCl$$

The cupric chloride ($CuCL_2$) has been reduced to cuprous chloride (CuCl). This is not immediately apparent. Both of these copper chlorides are soluble in strong acids but the cuprous chloride (CuCl) is not soluble in water or in weak acids.

If cuprous chloride is present it will remain in solution as long as the liquid is strongly acidic. When the gold "sand" is washed it will precipitate as a white powder. If there are large amounts and the gold sand is melted the resulting furnace emits dense clouds of acrid smoke so unpleasant that, as one writer said, it effectively empties the furnace room.

The gold that contains cuprous chloride usually has a red color after it is melted. This may be caused by a reaction with air to make basic cupric chloride ($CuCl_2 \bullet 2CuO \bullet 4H_2O$). Butts p 787 mentions this formation in solutions of hydrochloric acid. Perhaps more likely is the formation of red hydrated cuprous oxide which forms quickly in hot water. The gold to be melted is wet and this could occur.

Washing thoroughly with hydrochloric acid to dissolve and wash away any cuprous chloride removes this material. An ammonia wash is, we believe, also helpful. Be sure all gold chloride has been precipitated to gold metal (use stannous chloride test). Also be sure the filter flask contains acid to prevent the formation of fulminating gold.

Hydrazine (N_2H_4) is a good reducer and in regular use by some refiners. Hydrazine produces a gas and the reduction reaction is probably:

$$3N_2H_4 + 4AuCl_3 = 12HCl + 3N_2 + 4Au$$

It is easy to use. The product gold is very fluffy and uses more crucible space. It has a reputation as a carcinogen, is somewhat volatile even at dilution to 10 % strength. This and the fluffy nature of the gold caused us to stop its regular use.

Hydroquinone is a chemical much used as a developer for black and white photography. It was suggested to us as a gold chloride reducer that would not reduce cupric chloride to cuprous chloride. Our tests show this is true. We have used hyroquinone briefly. It often produced a very fine, difficult to filter, gold precipitate. A nitric acid treatment of the precipitated gold was somewhat troublesome and if not done quite right resulted in melting problems later. It was not very useful in a production shop. There are other related materials of possible interest. Methyl, dimethyl, ethyl and butyl hydroquinone have come to our attention, also chlorohydroqinone. We have no experience with them.

SILVER

In our gold refining operation, we are occasionally offered material that is high in silver but contains valuable amounts of gold. The usual "parting" operation for such material is quite simple but the processing of the silver to a reasonable purity has never been pleasant or consistently satisfactory.

The "parting" method uses nitric acid to dissolve the silver and any copper and other base metals. Gold, not soluble in nitric acid, remains as a sludge or slime and is separated by filtration.

The clear solution containing the silver and base metals is mixed with salt brine thereby making the very insoluble silver chloride but leaving the base metals dissolved. When the silver chloride is separated from the dissolved base metals it must be converted to silver metal.

Silver is a fairly reactive metal. There are numerous silver chemicals and the reduction of silver compounds to silver metal can be done in a number of ways. Consideration needs to be given to the quality of raw scrap and its physical and chemical condition, disposal of by-products (pollution problems), suitability for batch or continuous operation, all aspects of cost, time and size. Methods were explored by literature search and by practical tests on small lots of silver scrap. The methods investigated included:

1. Electrolytic refining (Thum cell) of the original silver bar.
2. Reduction of silver nitrate with caustic and formaldehyde.
3. Cementation from solution.
4. Melt reduction (crucible furnace) of silver chloride with soda ash.
5. Sodium borohydride reduction of silver chloride.
6. Solid phase reduction of silver chloride with soda ash (500°C max - Kunda method).
7. Cementation of silver chloride (solid phase in trays).
8. Sodium dithionite ($Na_2S_2O_4$) reduction.
9. Dextrose (sugar) reduction.

The usual electrolytic cell refining is not suited to batch operation, especially on a small scale. The classic fire reduction of silver chloride with soda ash is rather wasteful with losses in slag and in smoke. We lacked suitable equipment for the

Kunda method of doing silver chloride reduction at lower temperature in the solid state.

The use of formaldehyde and caustic soda to obtain silver from silver nitrate was tried but formaldehyde is obnoxious, possibly a carcinogen and the project was never pursued to the point of determining silver purity.

Our decision to pursue the last of the above list was based on several things. One was the possibility of using simple equipment and fairly common materials. Our success in the early experiments (where we used corn syrup) and our early ability to produce good quality silver metal was a real encouragement.

The advantages of this process are that it is suited to individual lots, it uses common chemicals, common equipment and can purify low grade silver scrap.

A minor disadvantage of the recommended process is the need to wash the material so many times. However this requires only occasional attention by the operator. The use of hot water washes acidified with nitric acid promotes rapid settling of silver chloride and the washing proceeds at a reasonable pace.

Some consideration for safety is required. Silver dissolution in nitric acid produces fumes that need a chemical fume hood. The use of salt brine and dextrose (a food) are without hazard. The use of caustic soda needs at least eye protection and rubber gloves and deliberate care to avoid boil-over. Sulfuric acid is used in one wash procedure and the melting of the silver "sand" needs the usual care for furnace and hot metal work.

OUTLINE OF THE PROCESS

1. Scrap silver is dissolved in dilute nitric acid. Most coins and all sterling will dissolve completely. If gold is present it will remain as a sludge.

2. The solution is filtered.

3. A clean salt solution (brine) is made with ordinary table salt.

4. Brine is added to the clear, filtered silver nitrate solution and a white precipitate of silver chloride forms. This is allowed to settle.

5. The solution (which contains the impurities and is usually green due to copper) is decanted (removed) by means of a simple siphon.

6. Hot water acidified with nitric acid is added with vigorous stirring and the silver chloride is again allowed to settle.

7. Steps 5 and 6 are repeated until the wash water is quite clear and then a test is made for the completeness of the washing.

8. After the last wash (usually after 12 to 15 washes) the silver chloride with a small amount of residual water is stirred up with dextrose, although other forms of sugar may possibly be used.

9. Flake caustic soda (lye) is added with caution. The material gets very hot and the silver chloride changes to silver metal. After standing overnight it is tested for completion of the reaction.

10. A water washing procedure as described above is repeated with the silver. A 10% sulfuric acid wash is used after about seven or eight water washes.

11. After tests show the silver to be free from impurities (copper) three or four further washes are given.

12. The silver is dewatered on a filter, dried, melted and poured into an ingot mold.

SAFETY

The statements concerning safe workmanship given in the previous chapter on gold are of equal importance for silver work. Some of the chemicals used for gold are also used here. The recommendation for the use of eye protection, safety showers, and the precautions when melting are exactly the same.

EXPLOSIVE SILVER COMPOUNDS

When using ammonium hydroxide to test the reaction from silver chloride to silver metal, one should know that the specified procedure should be followed. Any solution containing ammonia should be acidified with hydrochloric acid or another mineral acid like sulfuric acid. IN NO CASE ALLOW AMMONIACAL SOLU-

TIONS TO DRY OUT. At high pH (above 10), under some conditions, ammonia and silver chloride will form fulminating compounds (i.e., explosive).

The melting of the silver powder should be done with normal prudence to avoid burns. Heat-resistant mittens and eye protection are basic, as are decent shoes and clothing. The melting area should be uncluttered and orderly. Crucibles and ingot molds must be preheated and dry. Wet silver should be dried before melting. Any contact between dampness and molten metal will most likely result in eruptions of dynamic force.

It is prudent to dry the silver in an oven or compress into blocks in a press and then dry them before melting.

Melting should be done with a block of charcoal in the crucible to give a reducing atmosphere. Fine silver will absorb great volumes of oxygen unless protected in this way.

The nitric acid used to dissolve the scrap silver produces the same noxious fumes that emanate from aqua regia action. A fume hood is needed. The caustic soda (NaOH or lye) used to change the silver chloride to silver oxide is an aggressive material. When dissolved in water it becomes very dangerous to human skin and flesh. When hot this peril is increased.

The use of dextrose (a sugar) results in a second heat producing reaction and very careful addition while wearing eye protection and rubber gloves is necessary. We have seen temperatures of these concentrated solutions approach 120°C (248°F) and actual eruptions occur unless additions are careful and deliberate. In our opinion, a hot caustic burn is worse than the damage from a great many acids.

LIST OF MATERIALS

1. Nitric acid 42° Bé (BAUMÉ)-(HNO_3)
    This liquid is about 70% nitric acid and about 30% water. It fumes slightly, but very little when further diluted with water. It differs from other acids in that it is a strong oxidizing agent.

2. Hydrochloric acid-(HCl)
    This liquid is about 37% acid and the rest water. It fumes readily from open containers, but much less when diluted. It is also known as muriatic acid. Here used in rather small amounts

for testing silver content of solutions.

3. Salt(sodium chloride)-(NaCl)

    The well-known household salt or pickling salt. Do not use "rock salt" which can be contaminated and dirty.

4. Sulfuric acid-(H_2SO_4)

    A heavy liquid, 93% sulfuric acid and 7% water. Here used in a diluted form. When diluting sulfuric acid ALWAYS POUR THE ACID INTO THE WATER which then becomes quite warm. When done the other way, this heating effect can be so local and so strong that acid is thrown out into the room.

5. Caustic soda(Lye)-(NaOH)

    Here used as solid flakes or solid pellets. Flakes are preferred, but not essential. It strongly reacts with moisture and containers must be closed tightly. It is a strong base (the opposite of acid). Lye has a slippery soapy feel and should be washed away promptly if it contacts the skin. It burns skin and flesh and can be as uncomfortable as acid burns. Strongly attacks aluminum. Rubber gloves are a necessary precaution when using caustic.

6. Ammonium hydroxide-(NH_4OH)

    A liquid that fumes easily when containers are opened. It has a strong (rude) odor. It, like lye, is a base. Here used in small amounts for testing solutions for copper. As mentioned earlier is capable of forming explosive compounds with silver. Used solutions must be promptly acidified. Do not allow to stand.

7. Dextrose

    A white powder (made from starch) with a sweet sugary taste. Major use is as a food additive. Also known by the name d-glucose, grape sugar, corn sugar, honey sugar, starch sugar. Corn syrup (Karo) contains about 75% dextrose (USA) and can be used as a substitute by suitably increasing the amount. Most confectionery sugar works well.

DIRECTIONS FOR DOING THIS WORK

Dissolving the scrap silver

Silver scrap in the form of wire, sheet, coins or other smallish pieces will dissolve quite rapidly in diluted nitric acid. Ingots, heavy casting scrap and other lumpy scrap dissolve slowly and we prefer to melt and make shot. We pour such molten scrap into a large aluminum cooking pot, or a small stainless steel pail filled with water. A strong cross-flow jet of water near the surface helps make small shot. (See description in the chapter on gold.)

Commercial nitric acid comes as the concentrated 42° Be (Baume) material which is roughly 70% acid and 30% water. This acid will dissolve silver only slowly, if at all. At 40% or 50% strength the action is vigorous and produces copious brown fumes. At lower concentrations the reaction is slower, but brown fumes are greatly reduced and possibly can be eliminated entirely. Theoretically brown fumes stop at 27 or 28% strength. However under actual working conditions there are always some fumes. They may be quite dilute and not easily seen but nevertheless present.

We normally dilute the as-received concentrated acid with three to four parts of water to reduce fume emission and still maintain a reasonable dissolving rate. This is done in chemical glassware or plastic under a suitable hood. This acid will dissolve silver and most impurities found in scrap. By-product silver from gold refuse work may contain traces of gold. Gold will not dissolve in nitric acid and will remain in the sludge in the reaction vessel or, subsequently, on the filter. This gold may then be refined as previously described.

If gold is present in amounts much greater than 25% it will "protect" the silver and may completely stop the action of the nitric acid. In such case melting the silver with additional silver or scrap of a higher silver content is necessary. if silver is not available, copper can be used but of course this must later be removed and discarded.

The nitric acid is added to the scrap metal with some caution. There may be quite vigorous action and boil-over is possible. When the reaction vessel is reasonably full and reaction has stopped, the solution is filtered through chemical filter paper or through paper coffee filters. A Buchner filter funnel and vacuum assist is strongly advised. The solution must be clear. If not, it should be refiltered. The presence of copper and other metals give color to the solution - usually blue-green.

We use a siphon to transfer the solution from the dissolving vessel to the filter as this leaves the undissolved scrap and sludge (and a small residue of solution) undisturbed. More acid is added for further dissolution and further filtration until all dissolvable scrap is removed. If gold was present in the scrap, the sludge (and filter) is aqua regia processed for gold recovery.

MAKING SILVER CHLORIDE

A clean brine of good quality is made by dissolving sodium chloride (table salt) in water using 200g or 250g of salt per liter (about 1/2 lb. per quart). Heating is not needed as cold water dissolves a sufficiency of salt. Rock salt is usually too dirty to use. Pickling salt is clean and works well. The brine should be filtered if it is not clear and clean. Add the brine to the silver nitrate solution while stirring <u>vigorously</u>. A very noticeable white precipitate forms. This is silver chloride and it is quite insoluble. Copper and other metals remain in solution.

It is not easy to see when enough brine has been added but a small excess is not harmful. Stirring should be very strong and vigorous. Strangely this causes the silver chloride to settle quite rapidly when stirring ceases.

A simple test for sufficiency of brine is to stop stirring. When the top of the solution clears a little (it will do this quickly) drop some more brine into the solution. A white precipitate shows more brine is needed. No precipitate shows the reaction is complete. The use of a little hydrochloric acid rather than brine for this test makes it easier to see.

WASHING THE SILVER CHLORIDE

The copper and other metal compounds are now separated from the silver chloride by repeated water washes. If these water washes are hot and acidified the silver chloride will continue to settle out very rapidly, usually within 15 or 20 minutes.

Decanting with a siphon is our simple way of removing the water after the silver chloride has settled. The liquor is removed with a siphon leaving about an inch of liquid above the white silver chloride so no silver is lost.

The exact depth of this silver chloride layer may vary from one wash to another so it is prudent to insert the suction to just above the silver chloride layer. The first discharge of the siphon is put into a special pail and if silver chloride appears this portion can be returned to the next wash.

When the liquid has been siphoned away we add hot water from a household hot water heater. The silver chloride is thoroughly stirred during this time. We use a stainless steel pipe to inject the water into the bottom of the vessel. Our container is about 75 liters (20 gallons) and we add about 1/4 to 1/2 a liter (approx. 1 pint) of concentrated nitric acid while adding the hot water.

Our reason for the use of nitric acid is that it seems to help maintain the quick settling characteristics of the silver chloride. We also have a theory that it may help remove base metal compounds from the silver chloride which is a notorious co-precipitator of other, normally soluble materials. Nitric acid does not dissolve any appreciable amount of silver chloride.

The wash and decant cycle is repeated until the wash seems quite clear, perhaps 10 to 12 washes. At this time take a sample of the liquid in a clear glass beaker and add enough ammonium hydroxide (NH_4OH) solution to make it definitely ammoniacal. A very cautious sniff will tell. Take a second sample in another similar glass beaker set up side by side and compare color against a white background. Copper with ammonia will turn blue so any, even faint, blue tint shows that more washes are needed. We find that usually some 15 washes are required.

Be sure to use only clear solution for this ammonia test. Acidify the solutions after the tests have been made.

CHANGING SILVER CHLORIDE TO SILVER METAL

When the washing is done the silver chloride is left with about 1" (3 or 4cm) of water above it. To this slurry we will add caustic soda and dextrose.

The amount of caustic and dextrose to use is not critical except that enough must be used to handle all of the silver chloride. A great excess is a waste.

If the silver content of the scrap is known it is easy to estimate the caustic and dextrose amounts to use -

Fine silver content of the scrap x 0.33 = wgt. of dextrose
Fine silver content of the scrap x 0.56 = wgt. of caustic

This is more than chemical theory says is needed but an excess is better than silver loss. Weight units must be the same, i.e., if the fine silver is known in troy ounces, the chemicals needed are in troy ounces. Use of grams, kilos, pounds, etc., is in order if such scales are used.

In the more prevalent instance where the silver content is not known, we estimate the requirements from the <u>volume</u> of the silver chloride. For those who seldom deal with such dimensions or such arithmetic we give the following example.

Assume that we have a cylindrical container 30cm (approx. 12") diameter and that we have measured the depth of the silver chloride which is 10cm (approx. 4").

The formula for volume of a cylinder is

$$\text{Radius}^2 \times \pi \times \text{depth} = \text{volume or } (\pi R^2 D) \qquad \pi = 3.14$$

In the above we have

15cm x 15cm x 3.14 x 10 = 7065ml   1 liter = 1000 ml

So $\frac{7065}{1000}$ = 7.065 liters (say 7)

If this were measured and calculated in inches the same calculation would be made using the inch measurements and the result would be cubic inches. Then multiply this by 0.0164 to get the equivalent volume in liters. The caustic and dextrose to use is then calculated:

Liters of silver chloride x .15 = kilos of dextrose
Liters of silver chloride x .30 = kilos of caustic

If you weigh in pounds multiply the kilos x 2.2 to get equivalent pounds.

Dextrose is a benevolent material (a food) and little care is needed in handling; however caustic soda must be treated with respect. Wear gloves and eye protection as caustic burns can be painful and as bad or worse than acid burns. Close caustic containers tightly. It absorbs water from the air until it cakes into lumps and finally becomes liquid.

Caustic added to silver chloride changes the silver chloride to silver oxide (there is a very definite color change). Next the addition of dextrose to hot silver oxide will convert the silver oxide to silver metal.

We do not need to heat the solutions since solid caustic soda added to water gets quite hot and does this for us. Also the very considerable heat of reaction between dextrose and silver oxide (and caustic) brings the temperature to boiling and is sufficiently reactive to require prudence when adding these materials.

Plastic containers can be used for smaller lots, say 5 gallons (20 liters), if done with care. The temperature easily exceeds the boiling point of water (212°F or 100°C) so thin walled plastic may sag and deform. Large plastic containers may collapse. Water cooling can be helpful.

The reaction sequence indicates one should add the caustic to the chloride sludge (with care, with gloves and with eye protection) and then, whilst the sludge of silver oxide is quite hot, add (with care) the dextrose. However, the reaction also works well (or perhaps better) by adding the dextrose first and then the caustic. We prefer the latter and do as follows:

The entire amount of dextrose is dumped into the silver chloride sludge and well stirred. The mixture becomes somewhat more liquid. There is little, if any, temperature change.

We believe the dextrose tends to defloc the silver chloride and thereby aids the reaction with caustic soda when it is added.

Then with deliberate care we add the caustic soda, usually one or two small scoopfuls at a time. The sludge is vigorously stirred by hand, mechanically or with an air jet. Face protection or at least eye protection is essential. We stir each addition of caustic into the mixture leaving no chance of having undissolved pockets of caustic. The temperature rises rather quickly, the reaction is apparent in the dark colors produced and in the foam and steam that are released.

We find that the temperature often comes to boiling and it is sometimes expedient to leave it for a while or to add a little cold water and then proceed with more caustic. The entire addition and its reactions can usually be done in less than a half an hour for 5 to 6 kilos of scrap (10-15 lb.). Very fast addition can result in boiling over and even eruption to the ceiling. A very undesirable action with costly and hot, dangerous, materials.

Toward the end, the solids will change character. Usually they will be a grey color and, if stirred by hand, will seem to be heavier.

TEST FOR COMPLETE CONVERSION

The heat and the activity of the reaction would make one think it is quickly completed. We find this is often not so. Cover the vessel and let it stand for some hours or preferably overnight.

Test for completeness of the reaction by removing some of the solid silver material from several places in the container. Rubber gloves and a spoon or ladle are used. This sample is well mixed and all but about 10ml (several teaspoons full) is returned to the container.

The 10ml of solids are washed 7 or 8 times by adding water, stirring, settling and pouring off until the water is quite clear. After the last wash add 4 or 5 ml of ammonium hydroxide and stir. Then dilute to 100ml and let the solids settle. Pour about 30-50ml of the liquid into another beaker and add hydrochloric acid. Be sure it is quite acid. If no change occurs the reactions are complete.

However, if a white cloud forms more caustic and dextrose must be used to finish the conversion. The white cloud is silver oxide or silver chloride that has been dissolved by the ammonia and reverted to white silver chloride by the hydrochloric acid.

When using ammonium hydroxide to test the reaction from silver chloride to silver metal, one should know that the specified procedure should be followed. The metal particle sample should be washed until the wash water is clear and the pH down to pH 8 or 9. When the test is complete, any solution containing ammonia should be acidified. IN NO CASE ALLOW AMMONIACAL SOLUTIONS TO DRY OUT. At high pH (above 10), under some conditions, ammonia and silver chloride will form fulminating compounds (i.e., explosive). The solution of silver chloride in ammonia is regularly done in many laboratories, but the materials are not allowed to dry out and are promptly neutralized with acid.

ANOTHER TEST METHOD

Sodium thiosulfate (photographic hypo) can be used to test for the presence of silver chloride. Photographic fixer solutions are usually acidic and have about 24 parts hypo per 100 parts of water by weight. The other ingredients in photo fixer are not needed for this test.

Make up a hypo solution of about 24 parts of hypo to 100 parts of water by weight. Take a small sample of the solids that may contain silver chloride (or silver oxide) and wash until clear and most of the lye or other basic material is washed away. Add a few drops of dilute sulfuric acid so that the test sample is somewhat acidic.

Stir well and transfer a small amount of the solids into a small beaker with some of the hypo solution. Stir well and let it settle. Pour the clear solution into a separate beaker and add hydrochloric acid.

If silver chloride or silver oxide is present in the hypo solution it will now slowly form a turbidity that is silver chloride. This turbidity is less intense than that formed when ammonium hydroxide is used. There is little or no explosion hazard and the rude odor of ammonium hydroxide is avoided.

HYDRAZINE

Recently we have tested the use of hydrazine as a reductant for silver chloride. Our experience is that it is somewhat easier to use than dextrose and lye. See Simpson for some general information.

Perhaps the most generally known feature of hydrazine is the use of the very concentrated form as a "rocket fuel" component. At such strength it is very dangerous.

Hydrazine as we buy it comes as a 30 or 35% solution. We dilute it to about 10% with water. This is done in good ventilation under a chemical hood. We wear rubber gloves and eye protection. Hydrazine is a fuming material and as the 30% strength fumes about as much as strong hydrochloric acid although the fumes are not acrid like the acid. The fumes however are carcinogenic and to be avoided with care.

The 10% dilute also fumes but less. Contact with the skin must be avoided. If this occurs, promptly wash with water.

When we use hydrazine to reduce silver chloride we follow the procedure described previously to the point of using dextrose and lye. We have the washed silver chloride with an inch or two (approximately 25 to 50ml) of water over the silver chloride. To this we add soda ash (sodium carbonate) to make a basic solution.

Stir well and test with pH paper to be sure it has a pH of about 11 or 12. Hydrazine works better in basic than in acid solutions.

Then the 10% hydrazine is added slowly with careful stirring. It does not boil like lye and dextrose but foams and evolves gas. The amount to be used is relatively small because hydrazine can reduce up to 14 times its weight of silver. The approximate amount required can be estimated from the known or estimated amount of silver chloride and the strength of the hydrazine being used. Silver chloride is about 75% silver.

The reaction may be quite rapid at first but time is needed to finish and we find it wise to let stand overnight. We can estimate completion by testing to see if excess hydrazine is left. Or one may test for the presence of unreacted silver chloride with ammonium hydroxide as described above.

The test for hydrazine is a spot plate test and uses the following indicators according to Ashcraft.

A solution is made of paradimethyl amino benzaldehyde (a solid) available from chemical supply houses. This is mixed (2%) with 1 normal sulfuric acid (about 50 grams of acid in 1 liter of water or approximately 30ml of concentrated sulfuric acid in 1 liter of water) or an equivalent smaller amount.

For convenience put this solution in a dropping bottle. A drop of solution from the silver work is put in a spot plate and a drop of the above test solution added. An orange color shows the presence of hydrazine. It is sensitive to about 0.1 parts per million. If excess hydrazine is present after standing overnight the reaction to silver is probably complete.

The precipitated silver should be washed in a series of washes and then dewatered in a filter.

Excess hydrazine should be destroyed before the water is released. Use hypochlorite (household Clorox is an example). Swimming pool hypochlorites will probably work also. Add this at a pH of 10 or above. The above test shows when the solution is safe for disposal. Releasing untreated hydrazine to a sewer is probably illegal.

WASHING THE SILVER METAL

The excess materials of the conversion process must be washed away. The solution is very black and considerable washing (up to 12 or 15 washes) with vigorous stirring is needed.

Plain water is used for the first 5 to 7 washes. Then we added some sulfuric acid to each wash water to make some definitely acidic washes.

The reason for this is that the conversion work changes any base metal compounds that may still be present into their respective oxides or hydroxides which are quite insoluble and would not be removed in those final washes. Acidic washes help dissolve any remaining traces of base metals.

Be sure that acid is mixed by pouring <u>acid into water</u>. The heat of dilution of sulfuric acid is large and pouring a little water into this acid creates a local and very hot spot that blows hot acid around the premises.

After a total of some 10 or eleven washes, or when the wash water seems clear, take a wash water sample and add ammonia. Over a white background compare color with wash water of equal amount in a similar container.

Sometimes a very slight bluish color indicates the presence of copper and more acid washing is then needed.

A very high purity silver product depends largely on great care and a large number of acid washes at both stages of washing. On small lots with great care we have produced silver that assayed 999.99.

We make no regular effort for such quality as we do not receive a bonus for very high purity.

FILTERING

The silver is now filtered in a vacuum Buchner funnel filter through paper. This is the same as the gold filtration work except there is no acid treatment, only a few washes with water. The quantity of silver will normally be quite large comparatively and a large filter and a large paper coffee filter will be needed.

MELTING

Melting work requires a clean crucible that has been dedicated to this work. The quantity of silver will usually require a larger crucible and furnace than is used for gold.

Often it is necessary to fill the crucible as completely as possible and then add more silver as heating proceeds. It is best to dry the silver completely so additions can be made safely as melting proceeds. The use of a quite large crucible and furnace that will hold the entire lot of wet silver is safe.

Wet silver in contact with molten silver causes steam explosions that are costly, noisy and very dangerous. Because the wet silver shrivels so much as it melts there is a fairly strong urge to add more as this shrinkage proceeds.

If you insist on melting in this fashion we add these precautions.

Watch the melting with great care. Do not depart to do other things. The wet silver will dry and shrink. Before any molten silver appears small amounts of wet silver are added with care and this repeated as drying and shrinking proceed. If the crucible contains any molten silver, wet material must not be added. Even a little damp silver touching molten silver will result in some interesting, very active, dangerous and costly eruptions.

Molten fine silver will absorb large volumes of oxygen from the air. When this is cooled in the ingot mold, this oxygen spews out making small volcanoes and some loss of silver. To prevent this a small piece of charcoal or graphite should be put into the furnace with the silver.

When the silver is poured into the ingot mold, the charcoal can be held back in the mold with a small piece of wood or it can be picked off the top of the mold with a stick or tongs.

The usual precaution of having the ingot mold quite warm (therefore, dry) and coating the mold with a mold wash or a smoky flame is necessary.

Flux is not needed or desirable.

HYDROQUINONE

While this volume was being written another method of reducing silver chloride to metallic silver has been given some experimental tests. Hydroquinone is a well known developing agent for black and white photography. It is a somewhat fluffy white powder about 6% soluble in cold water.

Our work with hydroquinone reduction is very limited and our only occasional silver work means that further experience will be slow. We believe that its use has the possibility of distinct advantages and that the disadvantages can be solved.

With this in mind we outline our process in its present incompletely developed state. Some theoretical aspects are given at the last of this chapter where we comment on ideas, probable problems and possible solutions for making this a viable technique.

Outline of Our Work with Hydroquinone

The silver chloride was washed as previously described. After the final wash about 1 or 2 inches (2.5-5cm) of water was left above the silver chloride layer. Sodium carbonate (soda ash) was added to make this distinctly basic (pH approx. 10). We used solid soda ash, stirred thoroughly until dissolved and then tested for pH. We then added hydroquinone as the solid powder. The use of a solution may or may not have advantages. Stirred thoroughly and let stand overnight.

A sample of the solid material was taken and tested for the presence of silver chloride using ammonium hydroxide as described above. Previously mentioned precautions with ammonia were used. When the test showed no silver chloride we washed the silver by water addition and decanting. This may be somewhat ineffective. The reaction products of hydroquinone with silver chloride is quinone that is quite insoluble.

Melting the silver in a crucible proceeded quite well but can produce clouds of smoke. However we have been able to eliminate that by starting the melt with a mixture of about 75% soda ash and 25% sodium nitrate in the crucible and then the silver.

We speculate that the smoke may be organic material that sublimes but with nitrate it is oxidized (burned).

More experience is needed before we can present a definite work procedure.

SILVER CHEMISTRY

Our refining of silver is limited to the recovery of the silver chloride in the filter paper scrap from aqua regia filtrations. As earlier mentioned this trash is burned and the ashes are then mixed with a high soda ash flux and melted. The reaction between silver chloride and soda ash is:

$$2AgCl + Na_2CO_3 = Ag_2CO_3 + 2NaCl$$
$$Ag_2CO_3 = Ag_2O + CO_2$$
$$2Ag_2O = 4Ag + O_2$$

This is a classic but messy method. The furnace temperatures are far above those required for these reactions. It is fast, very gassy and a bad smoke producer. Boil overs in the furnace are a problem. Our present technique is to reduce the silver chloride in the ashes with caustic and dextrose or with hydrazine (see equations below). Then the metal ash mixture is fluxed and melted.

The metal from this melting operation contains mostly silver, some gold and some other metals. This metal is dissolved in nitric acid to make silver nitrate, <u>Butts and Coxe</u> p 221:

$$4Ag + 6HNO_3 = 4AgNO_3 + NO + NO_2 + 3H_2O$$

The undissolved portion contains gold and is dissolved in aqua regia for refining.

The filtered silver nitrate solution is mixed with sodium chloride, table salt:

$$AgNO_3 + NaCl = AgCl + NaNO_3$$

The silver chloride is very insoluble and is repeatedly washed and then reduced to silver metal. A watery slurry of silver chloride is mixed with caustic soda and dextrose. Dextrose is also known as d-glucose, grape sugar, corn sugar, etc. Karo syrup is said to contain about 75 % dextrose.

When the caustic is added the heat of the solution is enough to get the reactions going. The first:

$$2NaOH + 2AgCl = Ag_2O + 2NaCl + H_2O$$

The silver oxide is then reduced to silver metal with the dextrose which chemical formula we shorten to RCHO:

$$RCHO + Ag_2O + NAOH = 2Ag + RCHONa + H_2O$$

Silver oxide will also decompose by heating in a crucible to produce silver metal. Silver oxide is a good starter for making silver nitrate. The silver oxide is dissolved in nitric acid. We suggest care when this reaction is initiated as these are both very reactive materials. The production of NOx is minimal.

Silver oxide is a powerful oxidizer. Wear protective gloves and shields when handling it. It can react explosively with combustible and organic materials. Prompt reduction to metallic silver is a wise precaution.

A more direct reduction can be done with hydrazine. We prefer this because it is less trouble. However this needs to be done under a hood to avoid the fumes of hydrazine. Any residual hydrazine must be destroyed after the silver has been precipitated and filtered.

The reduction reaction is:

$$4AgCl + N_2H_4 = 4Ag + 4HCl + N_2$$

Simpson gives a redox potential of +1.16v in alkaline conditions and only +0.23v in acidic conditions. This is our experience. We add enough soda ash to raise the pH before adding hydrazine.

The test for completion is to stand overnight and test for excess hydrazine with the hydrazine spot test.

Destruction of excess hydrazine is done with hypochlorite (bleach) or a similar source of chlorine. Swimming pool bleaches are easily available and have higher available chlorine.

An interesting reaction of silver that may be of minor importance to a small refiner but could be important to a silver refinery is the reaction of silver with strong oxidizers. An example is manganese dioxide and silver at furnace temperatures:

$$MNO_2 + 2Ag = Ag_2O + MNO$$

A similar reaction may be possible with sodium nitrate:

$$NaNO_3 + 2Ag = Ag_2O + Na_2O + 2NO_2$$

We regularly find that slags will contain minor amounts of gold (a metal pellet we think) but also even more silver than gold. Since the ratio of gold and silver in jewelers karat gold must be about 7 to 1 we believe it is likely that the oxidation reactions above have made enough silver oxide to materially increase the silver in slag. Such silver will be present as a compound and not as an element.

HYDROQUINONE

Hydroquinone is a much used developing agent for black and white photography. The chemical formula is: $C_6H_4(OH)_2$ and a little basic information about it is given in Langes Handbook of Chemistry 10th Ed. No. 2314 Physical Constants of Organic Compounds. The chemical name there is Dihydroxybenzene. It is the six carbon benzene ring with an (OH) at opposite ends of the ring, the para position.

During reaction it goes to quinhydrone loses one H of the two (OH) above and then to para quinone where both Hs are removed. The simple quinone formula can be written:

$$CO\,(CH:CH)_2\,CO$$

See Langes Handbook 10 Ed. organic compound #5535 and 5542 for some more information about these two compounds.

Photographic developers are basic and in darkroom work when development has reached the desired level an acid stop bath is used to stop the developing reaction. For this reason we add sodium carbonate to our silver chloride to make a basic solution.

Developing solutions contains a number of chemicals some of which are there, we believe, to limit the reduction reaction to the silver compounds that have been exposed to light. Without these and with sufficient time (we are letting stand overnight) all the silver chloride should be reduced. This action may vary with a weak solution (6% maximum solubility of hydroquinone) compared to a strong situation where solid hydroquinone is available. We believe that stirring will help the reaction.

Complete reduction means that all silver chloride has been changed to silver metal. Our test for this consists of treating the solids with ammonium hydroxide which will dissolve silver chloride but not silver metal. When this is acidified with hydrochloric acid any dissolved silver chloride ammonia compound is destroyed and becomes easily visible silver chloride again. (This also works for silver oxide.)

The very dark color of the quinone compounds make this difficult to see so the acidified test solution must be filtered to see if silver chloride is present.

Silver chloride is also soluble in sodium thiosufite (hypo). It is possible that this can be substituted for ammonium hydroxide.

SILVER CHLORIDE

The reduction of silver chloride to silver metal by melting with soda ash is a classic process. It is often disliked because it boils violently and tends to be smoky. Considerable silver loss is attributed to this smoke.

Earlier in this chapter we have outlined other reduction methods which we devised partly to remove base metals and partly to avoid the use of soda ash.

Very recently we have returned to the use of soda ash. The technique we have developed is a great improvement over our earlier methods. There is little smoke and boiling is easily controlled.

The silver chloride is dried and weighed. A flux is calculated as follows:

Weight of dry silver chloride X 0.5 = weight of soda ash to use. The theoretical amount is 0.37 so this is an excess of about 35%.

Five MOL Borax in an amount equal to the soda ash is also used. The silver chloride, soda ash and borax are mixed. This mixture is melted in a crucible furnace starting with a half full crucible. At low temperatures the melting and the reaction is so quiet that filling the crucible to perhaps three forths full may be possible.

The most important matter in this method is temperature control. Crucible furnaces are quite capable of 2500°F (1400°C) temperature. The reduction of silver chloride with soda ash only requires 932°F (500°C) and proceeds rapidly at temperatures below the melting point of silver.

The temperature of the furnace is kept low, enough to melt the mix and not much more. If full furnace temperature is used the reaction is essentially out of control.

When all of the mixture has been added it is normal to find a lump of sintered but unmelted silver in the bottom of the crucible. The temperature is then increased.

When we can no longer feel such a lump with an iron stirring rod we run the furnace about 10 minutes longer and then pour the crucible into a mold.

The slag is very, very liquid and when cold separates easily from the silver.

We find this to be a vast improvement over the very hot furnace process that is so often used.

This was developed according to information given by Schneller in "Silver Chloride." The first reaction is chemical. Silver chloride and soda ash form silver carbonate and salt:

$$4AgCl + 2Na_2CO_3 = 2Ag_2CO_3 + 4NaCl$$

The second reaction is thermal decomposition of the silver carbonate to silver oxide and carbon dioxide gas:

$$2Ag_2CO_3 = 2Ag_2O + 2CO_2$$

In a final thermal decomposition the silver oxide breaks down into silver metal and oxygen gas:

$$2Ag_2O = 4Ag + O_2$$

If these reactions are added algebraically so that those compounds that are created and destroyed during the several steps are eliminated we have the overall reaction:

$$4AgCl + 2Na_2CO_3 = 4Ag + 4NaCl + 2Co_2 + O_2$$

An elevated temperature is required to make these reactions go but this is far below the temperature available in a standard crucible furnace. Wasyl Kunda has demonstrated that this reaction starts at about 400°C (752°F) and is complete at 500°C (932°F). This is well below the melting point of silver.

Schneller gives the following information:

Silver carbonate is decomposed at 225°C (437°F)
Silver oxide is decomposed at 340°C (644°F)

Handbook data (Langé) gives the following melting temperatures:

Silver chloride - M.P.	455°C	(851°F)
Soda Ash - M.P.	851°C	(1564°F)
Silver - M.P.	960.8°C	(1761°F)

We are fairly confident that our gas fired crucible furnace can reach 1400°C (approximately 2500-2600°F). It has been our habit to melt the silver chloride - soda ash mixture at full available furnace temperature.

It is a general rule of thumb that each 7° rise in temperature doubles a chemical reaction. If we assume this reaction can go to completion at 500°C and that we run the furnace at 1100°C (about 2000°F) we have a 600°C excess temperature or reaction rates about 85 times higher than absolutely necessary.

The reactions produce gases and at high temperatures very rapidly and also at an expanded volume.

With this data in mind we decided to try a silver chloride-soda ash reduction at a very reduced temperature. We were not sure of the exact silver chloride content of our test batch so we used an excess of soda ash. It turned out that the excess was about 35%.

We also hoped to make a thinner slag to help reduce boiling and foaming over the top of the crucible. For that reason we added some 5 MOL Borax and a little fluorspar. We now believe the fluorspar is unnecessary.

The mix going into the furnace was:
Silver Chloride containing material	58%
Borax 5 MOL	21%
Soda Ash	19%
Fluorspar	2%

The procedure for this test was essentially what was described in the first part of this section. Boiling was active but not out of control. Smoke production light and intermittent.

We do very little work with silver, however, we have made certain observations. Salt (sodium chloride) has been pointed to as the culprit responsible for the strong evolution of smoke at high temperatures. A test where we melted salt in crucible to the highest temperature we could get produced no smoke. The boiling temperature is given as 1413°C (2575°F) by Lange. A combination of salt with other chemicals, (perhaps silver chloride) may result in a lower boiling mixture and may help explain the 5 to 7% silver loss sometimes reported. Other materials may be a part of this smoky boil.

We believe that the use of borax and an excess of soda ash may give a rather low melting mixture that promotes the chemical reaction at a relatively low temperature. The very liquid nature of this slag permits the gases to escape with less chance of foaming and boil over. Fortunately when cold this slag also separates from the silver ingot very easily.

However, further tests where soda ash (Na_2CO_3) was added to very hot molten salt (NaCl) immediately produced large amounts of smoke. This indicates that the boiling temperature of this mixture is lower than the boiling point of salt.

The boiling temperatures of sodium chloride and silver chloride are 2574°F (1212°C) and 2822°F (1550°C) respectively. We have not tested the effect of silver chloride in such a mixture but we believe it's reasonable to expect a similar boiling point reduction and a loss of silver chloride and this may explain the 5 to 7% silver loss reported for soda ash reduction of silver chloride.

It is possible that the 7 or 8 volumes of phase diagrams published by the American Ceramic Society would give melting points information. We know of no similar boiling point data.

See Mishra for some more information.

PLATINUM AND PALLADIUM

The platinum group metals consist of platinum, palladium, rhodium, iridium, osmium and ruthenium. The chemistry of these six metals has been described as among the most complex inorganic chemistry in regular practice today.

Platinum and palladium are two metals of this group that are used in dentistry and jewelry work and small amounts can be occasionally found in the scrap. A fairly simple method of recovering platinum and palladium is given in Hoke. We use her method for these metals.

Rhodium plating solutions are useful to the jeweler and we have been offered such scraps once or twice in our many years of refining work. We know of no reasonable small scale method for dealing with this material and it should be sent to specialists in the platinum group metals business.

A possible recovery method for Rhodium from rhodium plating solutions is recovery by cementation. Zinc powder used in a small excess could replace the rhodium and the excess zinc removed by acid.

This is a speculation based on the published characteristics of these materials. We have no hands-on experience with rhodium recovery.

The recovery of platinum and palladium is fairly simple as we know and do it. However, separation of these two metals may not be complete. The recovery of platinum and also palladium is less than complete. Hoke suggests that 95% is possible. We believe it is often less.

Sometimes the gold scrap that comes to the shop contains platinum and/or palladium. This is most likely in the case of dental scrap. Platinum jewelry should be separated from gold jewelry. We think that it should then be sold as unrefined scrap platinum jewelry.

Gold jewelry with platinum settings or other platinum parts that cannot be removed by clipping or sawing should be separated and this material run in a separate small lot. The separation and recovery of platinum and palladium is in the form of ammonium chloride salts and is incomplete because they are not entirely insoluble. A small amount of these salts in a large volume of refining liquids thus becomes a larger loss of the platinum and/or palladium.

OUTLINE OF THE METHOD

The recovery process for these two metals as we occasionally do it is according to the descriptions in several chapters of the book by Hoke. The method consists of dissolving the scrap in aqua regia and filtering the solution through paper. The precious metal pregnant solution is boiled to remove any excess nitric acid. The gold can be removed by precipitation (as previously described) at this time or later after platinum and palladium have been removed. In our rather limited experience we have done it both ways. We do not have any reliable advice about the best way if there is indeed a best way.

The use of potassium chloride instead of ammonium chloride has been recommended to us by Genco manager of a New York refinery. We have not used it in our work but we believe its use would be an improvement. In the procedures here described potassium chloride can be used as a substitute for ammonium chloride. We are told that the potassium platinum/palladium compounds are a little less soluble than the corresponding ammonium compounds with better recovery of the metals.

Its use also allows one to do the gold recovery as a last step after platinum and palladium are out. The reason for removing gold first is that the presence of ammonia in a solution containing gold creates the possibility although perhaps somewhat remote of making a detonating ammonia gold compound. A serious explosive hazard under some conditions.

Ammonium chloride is added to precipitate a colored powder of ammonium chloropalatinate. This palatinate is removed by filtration and the solution is then treated with sodium chlorate to change any palladium from the ammonium chloropallidite to ammonium chloropallidate, the insoluble form.

This pallidate is removed by filtration and the solution is treated with sodium bisulfite to remove gold. Actually the gold can be removed first and then the described procedure used to remove platinum and palladium.

The brightly colored powders of platinum or palladium are heated slowly for a period of hours to drive off the ammonium chloride. The black powders remaining are platinum or palladium that can then be melted to metal buttons.

THE REFINING PROCESS

The scrap material is dissolved in aqua regia. If it is largely platinum or palladium dissolution will probably be slow compared to gold. A gentle heat may be necessary. Do not boil because boiling drives off aqua regia. We like to think of 140°F (60°C) as a good temperature for speedier dissolution.

The crude pregnant solution should be allowed to cool and then filtered through paper in the manner and with the equipment described under gold refining. When dissolution is complete and filtering finished the clear pregnant solution must be cleared of nitric acid and nitric material.

This we do in the classic and lengthy boil down procedure. The reason for this is that platinum group metals seem to have a very definite ability to form nitrogen compounds. The reduction of nitric acid (e.g., aqua regia) by chemical means may well not eliminate the nitrogen but merely reduce it to a lower oxidation state that then does not redissolve gold. It has been suggested to us by experienced refiners that these lower nitrogen compounds may interfere with platinum-palladium recovery and result in losses. Others who work specifically in platinum-palladium processing were not sure it would be troublesome but we got no for-sure answers. We do know that the addition of urea can result in the appearance of a red precipitate.

For these reasons we boil the pregnant solutions slowly to drive out nitrogen compounds. The boiling is done until the solution is thick and syrupy but not dry. If it gets to the dry state some metal may be precipitated. In this case a solution of sodium chlorate is carefully added. Reaction may be very very active so caution is needed. This will redissolve metal.

Sodium chlorate is a powerful oxidizer and can react with organic and combustible materials sometimes with enough vigor to start a fire. Store in closed containers, wash away spills and treat it with respect.

When the solution is quite thick and viscous add a little hydrochloric acid to re-establish liquidity. Also cautiously add a small amount of sulfuric acid. This helps drive out the nitrates as will be seen by a cloud of brown fumes.

Repeat the boil down and the addition of hydrochloric and sulfuric acid until brown fumes are not seen when the acid is added. Add water until the syrupy material is dissolved.

The gold can now be removed by precipitation with sodium bisulfite or sulfur dioxide (see chapter on Gold) and then the platinum and palladium recovered as described below. The sequence we describe here is to remove the gold first. We prefer this approach.

The precipitation of gold if done first before removing platinum/palladium should be done with copperas (ferrous sulfate), Genco. The reason is that sulfur dioxide (or sulfite, bisulfite) precipitant's are very strong and can reduce the platinum chloride to a lower state making them soluble when treated with ammonium chloride. Copperas is less active and does not change the platinum.

RECOVERING PLATINUM

When the gold has been precipitated and removed by filtration we add some ammonium chloride, a white powder. This can be done as the powder or as a solution. Any platinum present will form a yellow precipitate of ammonium chloro palatinate which is quite insoluble. An excess of ammonium chloride is not harmful and is useful in the next step. To determine if enough has been added we set up a small paper filter and filter some yellow material out of the solution. Then we add some ammonium chloride to the clear liquid. If no more yellow powder forms we have added enough ammonium chloride.

Then the liquid is filtered leaving the yellow powder on the filter. A solution of about 85% water and 15% ammonium chloride is made up into a small container. A laboratory squirting type wash bottle is useful. Wash the yellow powder several times with this solution. The yellow powder is fairly insoluble in this solution but water will dissolve some and increase losses.

The filter paper and the yellow powder are now dried in a gentle heat. A drying oven is useful. We do not have one and usually use an ordinary heat lamp set up about half a meter (18") above the wet material. Use care not to char the paper.

RECOVERING PALLADIUM

The clear solution from the previous work should be warmed a little and some sodium chlorate carefully added by sprinkling the powder into the solution. The solution may boil and foam. If there is enough excess ammonium chloride from the previous work with platinum and if palladium is present a very handsome red powder of ammonium chloro pallidate is precipitated. It is quite likely that any excess ammonium chloride had already formed some ammonium chloro pallidite but this is soluble and therefore unseen. The addition of sodium chlorate changes this to the pallidate form which the chemist calls a higher oxidation state. This happens to be largely insoluble.

All of the palladium will be precipitated as the red powder only if enough ammonium chloride has been added to react with the palladium and enough chlorate to change such material from the soluble "ite" form to the insoluble "ate" form. See the section on chemistry at the last of this chapter for details of these forms.

We test this by filtering a small amount of the solution. The clear liquid we divide into two small portions. We add ammonium chloride to one. If a red precipitate forms we need more ammonium chloride. If no change is seen we add some sodium chlorate. If a precipitate forms we need more chlorate and perhaps more ammonium chloride. To the second small sample we now add only chlorate. If a precipitate forms it shows we are in need of more chlorate only.

When these tests show no further precipitation, no more additions are needed. An exact end point is not important because an excess is not harmful but an insufficiency results in the loss of valuable metal.

The solution is now filtered, the red powder is washed with 15% ammonium chloride solution and dried like the platinum powder.

GOLD

If the gold has not been removed as a first step the solution can now be treated with sodium bisulfite to remove the gold.

RECOVERY OF PLATINUM AND PALLADIUM FROM COLORED POWDERS

If the washing of the colored powders was done carefully and if the drying is complete, the colored powders can be brushed into a porcelain dish with a soft brush and almost no material will adhere to the paper. Do not put pieces of paper into the colored powders. Carbon from the paper will form undesirable compounds with platinum and palladium.

The colored powders must now be slowly decomposed and the procedure is the same for both. These powders are quite volatile and if heated rapidly will effervesce into the air and there will be considerable loss. Slow heating avoids losses.

We use a small kiln and heat the colored powder in a ceramic dish slowly, starting at a low temperature - a little above boiling (100°C) and go to nearly red heat, about 800°F - 900°F (450-500°C) in a period of about 8 hours. This slow heating also reduces the visibility of any ammonium chloride fumes.

The black metallic powders of platinum and palladium are then melted. The melting temperature of these metals is high, palladium 1550°C (2822°F), platinum 1769°C (3216°F). A gas fired or electric gold melting furnace will not melt them. The ideal furnace is an electric induction furnace. Melting can also be done with a welders torch using oxygen and acetylene.

We use such a torch and it is adequate for small amounts if a large torch tip is used. We transfer the powder into a platinum melting dish which is a high temperature white ceramic melting dish and has a higher wall on one side. Jewelers supply shops usually have them.

We dampen the powders so that the blast of the flame is less likely to blow away valuable powder. We use a No. 8 welding tip and start with a rather bushy fairly cool flame and hold the torch high directly above the dish and then warm the wet powder. It is our intent to use a non-violent flame to hopefully sinter the powder a little to prevent loss.

Then we carefully increase gas and oxygen flow and lower the torch and begin to really heat and melt the metal.

This _must_ be done with goggles that are suitable for gas welding work. The temperatures are so high and the flame so bright that eyes can be damaged.

Palladium is noticeably easier to melt as its melting temperature is lower. Platinum melting may require much more time and patience and the highest temperature available from the torch. The amount meltable by a torch is probably limited to 5 or 10 troy ounces (T/oz).

These metals tend to absorb gases.

When the torch is taken away and the metal cools the surface may be rough due to the evolution of gases while cooling. Such a button can usually be made smooth by removing the torch slowly. Lift the torch up and allow the metal to cool more slowly. Sometimes we raise and lower the torch a number of times to remelt and slowly cool it to get the gases out. Occasionally we must turn over the solidified button and repeat it on the other side.

We recommend that those who wish to follow this process for these metals obtain a copy of Hoke. She gives many suggestions that we do not repeat in this short procedure.

The fact that these platinum and palladium ammonium compounds are somewhat soluble (in the order of 5%) and also that they may not separate the metals with full efficiency makes this a less efficient process than the one for refining gold.

We suggest that solutions left over from this work be saved in what Hoke calls a "stock pot". The reuse of this solution would likely increase long term recovery.

GENERAL NOTES

A batch of scrap containing gold and probably palladium was received in our shop. After the gold had been removed some additional work was done. The following paragraphs are our notes made at the time.

After aqua regia recovery of gold from the scrap the gold barren solution was routinely tested with stannous chloride. The spot slowly turned brown in a way typical for the presence of platinum or palladium.

The gold barren solution was treated with 10% hydrazine and a precipitate formed. After settling and decanting the material was filtered. The precipitate was dissolved in nitric acid. (Palladium is soluble in nitric acid.) It all dissolved and then hydrochloric acid was added.

We then added urea (as a nitrate remover) and a dense red precipitate formed which we assumed to be ammonium chloro pallidate. With a further addition of urea some of the red material seemed to redissolve.

We then added sodium chlorate and ammonium chloride and proceeded in the way described above for palladium.

The dry red powder was weighed and the palladium content calculated. The original scrap was a dental alloy of a known palladium content. The recovery was in the range of 90-95%.

We later learned that urea will form complexes with palladium so we are unsure of what we had after urea addition.

This concludes the description of our hands-on experience with platinum group metals. However there has been much written about these metals. Some of this includes information about refining techniques and chemistry. We will give a few references.

Amman has written about refining techniques. Much of his small book concerns chemistry and electron theory not really needed to do a refining job, however, refining directions are given.

Some years ago Epstein wrote a twelve page description of the chemical reactions in refining platinum group metals. This does not give directions but does describe much of the work.

Some of these platinum group metal (PGM) chemicals are not pleasant. Refining the entire six PGM's must be done with real care. For instance osmium in one of its forms reacts strongly with tissue. It is volatile and has been known to coat the eye with an osmium film and cause blindness. In some forms it is quite toxic.

Leary in a short article outlines refining in a laymens terms. He includes lists of supplies needed and gives a flow chart of the work.

Kirk-Othmer, 3rd Ed. Vol., pp 228-277 gives considerable information and an extensive bibliography.

Lundy, in a two part article, describes mining and refining in South Africa.

Other sources of information that have come to our attention:

The Encyclopedia Britannica, Vol. XIX, 9th Edition: This early edition has more information than more recent ones.

Hartley writes about the complexes of platinum and palladium. Dennis chapter 19 gives a general review.

Jha and Hill has a section on PGM's. Harris has several articles starting page 201 through 244. International Precious Metals Institute has had several meetings devoted to PGM's and proceedings have been published. The 1983 proceedings edited by Lundy and Zysk and the 1985 sessions by Zysk Platinum Group Metals and the Quality of Life was published by IPMI in 1989. Altogether IPMI has published more than 15 proceedings and much information is given in these volumes.

Kudryk, Corrigan and Liang, p 463, gives a paper on recovery from automobile catalysts.

Recovery from automobile catalysts we think is not for the small shop. The very small precious metal content of this material requires a very sizeable plant and tonnage thruput to be successful. There are numerous ideas (perhaps almost a dozen) about techniques for recovery. A real problem in this kind of recovery is the matter of getting a steady supply of used mufflers to keep a plant going once an efficient process is set up. The catalytic material must be gathered from here and there, removed from the muffler shell and often transported impressive distances to keep a recovery plant going.

We know of recovery systems that are chemical in nature and we understand that the alum by-product is an important part of financial success. The trend is to use less aluminum oxide beads and more honeycomb which is a different chemical entity.

We think that pyrometallurgical recovery is perhaps the most successful and know of one plant using plasma arc furnaces in the process. Rao, p 217, presents an article about this technique and Zysk and Bonucci, p 157, give an article by James Saville describing the operation of a plasma arc plant in some detail.

Recovery of PGM's from auto catalysts can be a side line in a copper refinery. The catalyst can be fed into the incoming "ore" stream and the PGM's later report to the tank house slimes with gold, and silver.

In a recent conversation with a copper refiner from Belgium we were told the main problems were sampling, a rather long hold up in process and sometimes a need to modify furnace slags.

The recovery of PGM's from ore is being steadily improved. A South African film recently showed the use of a plasma arc furnace instead of the traditional electric carbon-arc furnace. The refining processes are developing in the direction of liquid-liquid extraction to separate various precious metals.

This means that the traditional methods described are obsolete or being replaced by newer technology.

PLATINUM AND PALLADIUM CHEMISTRY

Both platinum and palladium will dissolve in aqua regia. Palladium will dissolve in nitric acid. Reactions are similar to gold and aqua regia. A simple equation for platinum:

$$Pt + 4NOCl = PtCl_4 + 4NO$$

For Palladium:

$$Pd + 2NOCl = PdCl_2 + 2NO$$

However a list of chemical reactions gives:

$$Pd + 3HCl + HNO_3 = PdCl_2 + NO + 2H_2O$$

By whatever complexity of reaction the usual product is $PtCl_4$ the platinic form of platinum but palladium goes to the palladous form, $PdCl_2$.

When ammonium chloride is added to a solution of these chlorides we have:

$$PtCl_4 + 2NH_4Cl = (NH_4)_2PtCl_6$$

This is a relatively insoluble red colored material and most of it can be recovered by filtration.

The palladium reacts in a similar way:

$$PdCl_2 + 2NH_4Cl = (NH_4)_2PdCl_4$$

This is the palladous form and very soluble.

The addition of an oxidizer (Hoke specifies sodium chlorate) the quite insoluble ammonium chloro pallidate is formed.

This reaction is likely:

$$2(NH_4)_2PdCl_4 + 4NaClO_3 = 2(NH_4)_2PdCl_6 + 2Na_2O + 5O_2$$

This colored solid can be recovered by filtering.

For those interested in some basic chemical facts about chlorates ($NaClO_3$ is one of a series) college chemistry texts usually have information <u>Nebergall</u> p 516-525 gives fundamental information.

As mentioned earlier, because these ammonium compounds are somewhat soluble, separation and recovery is not complete. For occasional single batch work there are losses. For regular platinum and palladium refining work the solutions are saved and reused and over the long term, recovery is improved.

These red powders are heated and the reaction is a simple thermal decomposition:

$$(NH_4)_2PdCl_6 + heat = 2NH_4Cl + Pd + 2Cl_2$$

OTHER REFINING METHODS

Recovery Methods that do not Refine

Probably the oldest recovery work depends upon gravity and the heaviness of gold to obtain the metal. Fleeces and rag plants, gold pans, riffles, sluice boxes; tables and jigs are mechanical ways of doing gravity separation.

As mentioned before the mere recovery and separation of gold from its "as found" conditions usually does little to improve the quality of the gold itself.

Mercury because it alloys with gold and silver (and other metals) was long used to increase the recovery of gold and to retrieve it from a very finely divided natural condition. This often required crushing of the ore.

Cyanide since the turn of the century has to a large degree replaced mercury as a recoverer of finely divided gold particles. It is usually more efficient, and although toxic is probably less of a health threat then mercury, especially since there are effective antidotes for cyanide poisoning.

Thiourea has been studied during recent years as a non-toxic substitute for cyanide. The chemistry of thiourea is quite different from cyanide chemistry and all problems have not been entirely solved.

Bromine once used for gold recovery is receiving some attention again. Both bromine and thiourea are presently more costly than the methods now in use.

Quality Improvement or Semi Refining

A very ancient method of quite materially improving gold quality is given by Pliny in the 1st Century A.D. He describes the use of brick dust and salt mixed with impure gold in a crucible that is heated, usually for days. At the elevated temperature of the furnace the chlorine of the salt reacts with the silver (and with base metals) to form chlorides. Quite possibly the silver chloride tended to volatilize and condense out at the top or cooler parts of the vessel. The unreactive gold separates from these compounds as purer metal. Although not as effective as present methods it should probably qualify as a refining process.

Cupellation or the gathering of metals (precious and base) in molten lead is a long used quality improvement procedure. It is the basis of the fire assaying system of precious metal analysis.

Once the base metals are dissolved by the molten metallic lead, air is used to oxidize the lead to litharge. At the same time base metals are also oxidized. The precious metals do not oxidize and remain metallic. The oxides are a slag which will not mix with or dissolve in metals. These oxides can be absorbed in a porous crucible often made of bone ash, a magnesium compound or cement. Another way is to add fluxes so that they can be skimmed away. In either case a separation of precious and base metals occurs.

This can be done on a fairly large scale and is sometimes used to advantage as one step of refining. Stanley, pp. 648-650, describes a cupellation system. JHA and Hill, pp. 465-473, describe a new furnace for this work. Cupellation produces a bullion containing precious metals and very little if any base metals.

Refining

Miller Chlorine System

A much used refining method is the Miller chlorine process. This was done by Lewis Thompson in 1838 and by F. B. Miller in 1867 (see Int. Prec. Metals meeting report London 1982, pp. 173-4). It consists of sparging gaseous chlorine into molten bullion. The chlorine reacts with base metals such as copper to form chlorides and also with silver to make a silver chloride. A flux cover on the molten bullion gathers these chlorides which are periodically skimmed.

When the base metals and silver are essentially all removed the chlorine begins to react with the gold. It is reported that a good operator can detect this as a purple color in the vapor above the furnace. At this time, a final slag skim is made and the gold is poured.

It is prudent and customary to have a recovery system in the off-gas ducts of chlorination furnaces to recover any gold chloride vapors as well as any metallic gold spheres that are carried by the escaping gas. We have seen a small refinery that depends upon settling chambers to recover such gold. In one German refinery we saw a bag house in use for this work. Perhaps the most common and efficient gold recovery is with electrostatic precipitators.

The Rand refinery in South Africa describes their use of the chlorination process. The Canadian mint chlorinates as one step in their refinery. It is often used by scrap recovery refineries. Stanley, pp. 621-623 describes the process as done in the Rand refinery.

Wohlwill Cell

Very high purity gold can be produced by the electrolytic treatment of gold bullion in a hydrochloric acid solution.

It is a costly method because the amount of gold that is "in-process" as anodes, cathodes and solution is quite high.

However, it is used by some secondary refineries, also by the South African refineries when high purity is required and by the Canadian mint for all refining.

This system was devised by Charles Watt in 1863 and by E. Wohlwill in 1878, see Rose p. 481, and is known as the Wohlwill Cell for the man who devised and used it in Germany. It was also used and probably independently worked out in Philadelphia in 1902 (Rose p. 481).

The Wohlwill Cell is an acid proof container (open top box) perhaps 12" or 18" (30 or 45cm) on a side containing a solution of hydrochloric acid and gold chloride. A thin sheet(s) of pure gold forms the negative terminal(s) or cathode(s). A bar (or bars) of impure gold is the positive terminal(s) or anode(s). A direct current voltage of perhaps 3-5 volts is applied. At the anode the positive voltage removes electrons from the metals and thereby forms positively charged metallic ions which are soluble.

Copper ions remain in solution as long as the amount of copper is kept below certain limits. Silver ions react with the chlorine of the hydrochloric acid to form insoluble silver chloride. The gold ions migrate to the cathode where they very willingly accept electrons and thereby revert from the ionic to the metallic state and plate onto the cathode.

Eventually the copper and base metal will build up in the solution to the point where they also plate onto the cathode. Before this point is reached the electrolyte must be treated. During all of this the electric current is solubilizing all metals but depositing only the gold. The difference between anode and cathode activity is made up by depositing some of the gold chloride that was a part of the original solution. So while the solution gains base metals it also loses gold.

Solution maintenance usually consists of a regular removal of electrolyte and replacement with a new electrolyte that contains fresh pure gold chloride. This pure gold chloride can be made chemically, often with aqua regia, or it can be made electrolytically in a "fizzer" cell, or by chlorine gas and hydrochloric acid dissolution.

A sketch of a Wohlwill cell follows.

Fizzer Cell

The fizzer cell is quite similar to a Wohlwill Cell. But the anode is a very pure gold bar and the cathode is an inert material, perhaps graphite. This cathode is suspended in a porous pot so that it is separated from the anode compartment. The walls of this porous pot form a membrane that will permit the flow of current and the passage of small ions such as hydrogen. It does not permit gold to reach the cathode.

A traditional semi porous membrane is an unglazed ceramic container.

Fizzer Cell

The fizzer cell (see following sketch) is a Wohlwill cell with a semiporous wall to prevent gold from plating onto the cathode. Its use for making high purity gold chloride involves the same anode electrochemistry as the Wohlwill cell. The anode is high purity gold and impurities are not present to be dissolved.

The semiporous wall permits passage of current and migration of hydrogen. The reaction at the cathode is:

$$2H^+ + 2e = H_2$$

The hydrogen gas leaves the cathode with a fizzing sound.

An uncommon use of the fizzer cell is to dissolve impure anodes to make gold and base metal chlorides without plating metals on the cathode. The anode reactions are the same as a Wohlwill cell and the cathode reaction is of course the evolution of hydrogen.

The impure electrolyte is removed from the cell and filtered and the gold precipitated. The fizzer cell replaces aqua regia with an electrolytic device.

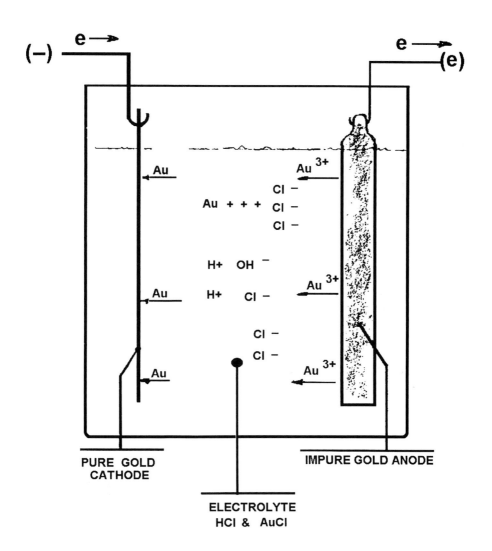

Wohlwill Gold Cell

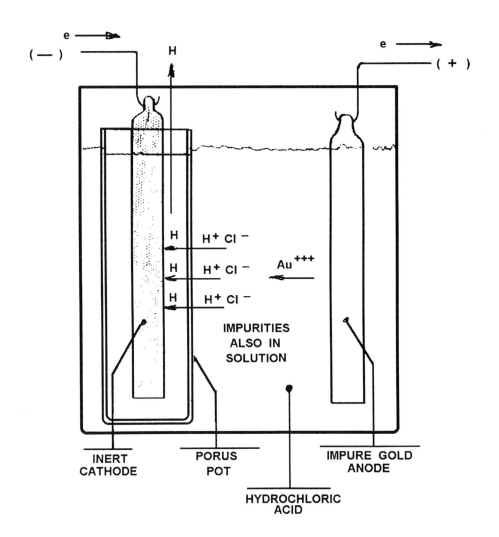

Fizzer Cell

Salt Cell

The salt cell is a fizzer cell that uses sodium chloride rather than hydrochloric acid in the electrolyte.

The dissolution of metals is the same as in a fizzer cell except the dissolved species is sodium chloroaurate. This behaves much like gold chloride. The source of chloride to form the metal chlorides is the Cl⁻ ion of salt (NaCl). These salt cells are described in a patent by Peter Shor. The kits sold for this work include a proprietary additive that is a buffer to control Ph. In the salt cell solution we have salt that when dissolved is mostly present as Na^+ & Cl^- ions. Much of the water is present as H^+ & OH^- ions.

We can think of this reaction in two steps.

$$2Au - 6e^- + 6NaCl + 6H_2O \rightarrow 2AuCl_3 + 6NaOH + 6H^+$$

$$6H^+ + 6e^- = 3H_2$$

These reactions actually occur simultaneously and the effect is to create gold chloride and sodium hydroxide. The buffer helps alleviate the bad effect of the hydroxide.

Chlorine and hydrochloric acid will dissolve gold because chlorine is an oxidizer. In other words a de-electronizer. We made a few tests with strong hydrochloric acid and gaseous chlorine at summer ambient temperatures. The reaction was slower than aqua regia. The reaction we believe is:

$$2Au + 2Cl_2 + 2HCl = 2HAuCl_4$$

Hydrogen peroxide and hydrochloric acid will dissolve gold. This is used as a solvent in several refineries. One refiner reported that the recovery of platinum group metals was much improved when hydrogen peroxide rather than nitric acid was the oxidizer. The known affinity of platinum and palladium for nitrogen compounds makes this a believable conclusion. Unless extended boiling of solutions to remove nitrogen compounds is done it is quite possible that some forms of nitrogen could combine and hold platinum group metals.

We have no experience with hydrogen peroxide oxidation. The use of the 50% grade is reported. We speculate that the metal is in hydrochloric acid solution and is treated by adding the H_2O_2. Because hydrogen peroxide is an unstable material considerable care in its use is needed. The stream of peroxide should not be introduced under the solution because of the chance of draw back to the supply tank. There the metals present will likely catalyze peroxide decomposition which can be explosive.

Hydrogen peroxide is a very reactive chemical. It also decomposes and a product of decomposition is a gas (oxygen). In low concentration and with a stabilizer this decomposition is slow. At high concentrations and/or in the presence of a catalyst (many metals are such catalysts) this decomposition goes at explosive rates. Damage can be severe.

A thorough education in the characteristics of hydrogen peroxide must proceed any work with this material. The manufacturers of hydrogen peroxide can usually give considerable information and advice.

The dissolution reaction is probably:

$$2Au + 3H_2O_2 + 6HCl = 2AuCl_3 + 6H_2O$$

Parting is very simply the dissolution of silver and base metals in nitric acid. Gold is not soluble in nitric acid. A simple chemical equation for a mixture of gold, silver and copper where copper can be considered as representative of all base metals is:

$$HNO_3 + Au + Ag + Cu = Au + AgNO_3 + Cu(NO_3)_2$$

The purity of the gold in this simple one step process depends on the physical availability of silver and base metals to the action of the nitric acid. An excess of gold either in the gross amount of the crude metal or in local spots will prevent complete dissolution of silver and base metals.

Silver refining is mostly done by electrolysis of silver in a silver nitrate-nitric acid - copper nitrate electrolyte. The process is described in texts that concern non-ferrous metallurgy. See Butts & Coxe, Thompson, Liddel, Creighton & Koehler, etc.

The reactions in terms of electron transfers are at the anode:

$$Ag - 1e = Ag^+$$

If we use copper, a common base metal in silver dore', as representative:

$$Cu - 2e = Cu^{2+}$$

As compounds these can be thought of as

$$AgNO_3 \text{ \& } Cu(NO_3)_2 \text{ in solution.}$$

At the cathode the silver is deposited:

$$Ag^+ + 1e = Ag$$

The current density and the electrolyte strength is maintained so that only silver deposits at the cathode. The copper (base metals) remain in solution and the quantity builds up. When the copper content approaches a concentration that begins to favor co-deposition on the cathode old electrolyte is removed and fresh electrolyte replaced.

The "foul" electrolyte that was removed is treated for silver recovery. This can be precipitated with sodium chloride to form insoluble silver chloride. Silver chloride can be cemented with a more active metal to produce a silver metal.

Silver chloride can be reverted to silver as earlier described under silver. A cementation reduction from silver chloride to silver metal is done with iron bars by a small refiner in England. The wet silver chloride is placed in a flat pan with iron bars on a 2" (5cm) spacing. This spacing is horizontal but if large amounts are involved can be also so spaced vertically. Enough dilute sulfuric acid is used to wet the entire bed of silver chloride. The purpose of this acid is to make an electrically conductive bed i.e. it acts as an electrolyte so that electrons from the iron can migrate to all of the silver in the pan.

This reaction is:

$$Fe - 3e + Ag^+ = 3Ag + Fe^{3-}$$

or possibly

$$3Fe - 2e + 6Ag^+ = 6Ag + 3Fe^{2-}$$

This is an electrolytic half reaction showing that the electrons from the iron fill the lack of electrons in the silver ion.

The reaction at the anode of the fizzer cell is like that at the anode of the Wohlwill Cell. The positive current removes electrons from the gold and the gold becomes soluble ionic gold and with the presence of hydrochloric acid can be considered a solution of gold chloride. In this case very pure gold chloride solution because a very pure gold anode is used.

The gold however, cannot reach the cathode because of the membrane so it stays in solution thereby producing a pure gold chloride solution useful for maintaining Wohlwill Cell solution or for other chemical needs.

The membrane however, passes electricity so the cell works. The negative potential at the cathode puts electrons onto the positively charged hydrogen ion present in abundance due to the presence of hydrochloric acid. The hydrogen collects on the cathode and passes out with a distinct fizzing sound.

Fizzer Cell-a substitute for Aqua Regia

Gold and the impurities in bullion and impure or scrap gold can be put into solution electrically by using a fizzer cell. The impure gold is cast into anodes and the set up is as described above. The membrane keeps these metals in solution in the anode section of the cell and hydrogen fizzes out at the cathode.

The advantage is the elimination of the brown fumes that aqua regia dissolution produces. There is a small acidic spray at the cathode, a minor matter compared to aqua regia.

A disadvantage is the need to melt metal and make anodes and the need to remelt the anode ends that cannot be entirely dissolved.

If silver content is above about 8 or 10% the anode is passivated by the formation of an adherent layer of silver chloride. This effectively prevents gold dissolution and current flow may be curtailed, stopped, or it may produce chlorine at the anode.

Wohlwill found that the superimposition of an alternating current onto the direct current so that there was a reverse component of about 20-25% would dislodge this silver chloride layer. He found that a silver content of about 20% could then be tolerated.

The application of reverse a.c. means that the forward and reverse components are limited to 100th of a second for 50 cycle and 120th of a second for 60 cycle current. The smaller reverse portion must then be a lower voltage and smaller amperes.

Recently the author made the suggestion that the submicroscopic electrolytic surface chemistry at the anode might respond more favorably to longer or shorter pulses of power and perhaps full reverse or even excess reverse voltage. Modern electronic switching devices are quite capable of producing "square waves" of controllably different duration both forward and reverse.

A company in Rhode Island has made a thoughtful and thoro investigation of such equipment in their fizzer cell. A verbal communication reports improved results with square waves over a.c. waves in small scale tests. At this writing a larger production unit is to be installed in that plant.

Aqua regia is also ineffective when gold has 10% or more silver. In this case the gold must be remelted with copper to dilute the silver to less than 8 or 10%. This is an occasional problem with the aqua regia process.

Efficiency of Electrolysis

There are two forms of gold chloride. The usual one is gold trichloride ($AuCl_3$) which is quite stable. A less common form is gold monochloride (AuCl) and this is much less stable. Both can be formed at the anodes of Wohlwill and fizzer cells. The gold mono chloride goes through a reaction whereby three atoms of gold mono chloride become one atom of gold trichloride and the two gold atoms settle out of solution as metallic gold.

Therefore, the bottom slimes of both Wohlwill and fizzer cells usually contain small amounts of such gold. These slimes must be treated for gold as well as silver recovery.

Some control over the amount of monochloride of gold produced can be exercised. A very low ampere loading produces much gold monochloride and at a high ampere loading is much less. However, it seems that gold monochloride cannot be completely avoided.

Pollution by Fizzer Cell

The solution produced by the fizzer cell is much the same as that produced by aqua regia except for the absence of excess aqua regia. Final filtering and gold precipitation and recovery are similar. (Water pollution problems are about the same).

It is not a batch process and discrete batches cannot be kept separate. Fizzer cells as described are not used much in commercial refining.

The Salt Cell

A variation of the fizzer cell is the salt cell. A patent issued to Peter Shor describes the process. In this fizzer cell the electrolyte is a salt brine (ordinary table salt) and a proprietary additive. We are quite sure this additive is a chemical "buffer." A buffer is a pH or acid-base controller. Without a buffer this solution would become more basic during the cell operation. There are a number of possible buffers that might be useful in the pH range of this cell. The salt (sodium chloride) provides the chlorine ion for gold dissolution.

Small salt system refining units have been offered for sale recently. They are aimed toward jewelers and very small refiners and are rated at 5 and 20 T/oz.

We have no experience with these units nor any knowledge of details of chemistry, power loading or other matters. We think the major advantage would be the use of a brine that is less corrosive than acid.

Chlorine Dissolution

Gaseous chlorine is a rather strong oxidizer and is capable of oxidizing gold. We have investigated this technique with several small tests. We granulated scrap and put the granules in a tube so there was a relatively deep bed of metal. This was filled, well above the bed of metal, with strong hydrochloric acid. Chlorine from a cylinder was introduced at the bottom bubbled through the metal and solution.

The scrap dissolved but at a slower rate than aqua regia. However, it was not heated and a warm or hot solution may well increase reaction rates. Cold aqua regia is also slow. Some chlorine passed out the top of the tube and was lost. We understand however that chlorine fumes can be completely scrubbed.

The method is not really suitable for our work and we made only a few test runs. Although chlorine in cylinders is very widely used it should be used only with the proper equipment and safety devices. Adamson, pp. 320-325, discusses chlorine as once used for ore and also mentions its use for metals.

Parting

A technique that dissolves silver and base metals and not the gold is called parting. It is sometimes used as a "refining" procedure. The gold content of the scrap must be 25% or lower.

Nitric acid is used to dissolve the metals that are not gold. Normally this would be copper, silver and small amounts of other metals. If the gold content is higher than about 20-25% the gold protects the other metals from the nitric acid. It is then necessary to remelt the scrap and add copper or silver to dilute the scrap to 20-25% gold content (therefore called inquartation). This metal will then dissolve in nitric acid. A 50% dilution is best. A strong nitric acid may work slowly or not at all. The gold does not dissolve in nitric acid and remains as a sludge (sometimes called gold sand). It is usually dark brown.

This gold is filtered, washed and melted. As a reliable refining method it is somewhat iffy. Should the dissolution of the other metals be less than complete gold quality would be low. We know of no reliable test for complete dissolution. If inquartation is not thorough i.e. if not completely mixed some copper or silver particles could resist solution and remain in the gold to reduce its quality. The normal product only assays in the high eighties or low nineties on a production basis. If washed and parted a second or third time with hot fresh nitric acid the assay may reach the mid or high nineties. (Schneller-private communication).

Parting is a good and often necessary step in some refining work. We know of one in-house refinery that has considerable silver in their gold scrap that routinely does parting before using aqua regia to finish refining the gold. This consistently produces high grade gold of 9995 quality or above.

Rose pp. 363-365 describes parting with strong boiling sulfuric acid. This process in not free of fumes as sulfur dioxide gas (SO_2) is emitted.

In our refinery we do not use the parting technique except in our occasional work of retrieving silver from the filters used during gold refining. Any gold that may be present is finished by aqua regia.

OTHER METHODS

Gold refining is described by a number of authors. Information is given by Rose, by Schnabel, pp. 936-1138, Gowland, pp. 248-423 to mention several that we know.

Some years ago <u>Rimmer</u> wrote a paper about the separation of gold and palladium by liquid-liquid extraction. <u>Barnes and Edwards</u> give information in a more recent paper. <u>Lashley</u> gives some similar information also concerning the dibutylcarbitol extractant.

Inco has done further work involving platinum group metals. We have seen some of this in their Acton (London) refinery but the details are proprietary. Liquid-liquid extraction may be useful in specific situations even for the small refiner. Some years ago <u>Lagowski</u> published some information about the solubility of gold in ammonia (NH_3). Ammonia is a gas at ordinary temperatures and pressures but it occurs to me that a refining process may possibly be devised to use pressurized ammonia. At that time I saw a few mentions of super critical solubility. I find this has been applied with carbon dioxide (CO_2). <u>Tolley and Tester</u> of the U S Bureau of Mines did some work on this. Other information is apparently available but mostly on carbon dioxide systems. Possibly a super critical ammonia system would be useful to a refinery that has the funds for such equipment.

SILVER

Sources of silver are numerous. Although silver ores produce much of the worlds silver, the recovery of silver as a by product of the mining and refining of other metals is a very important and worthwhile source. <u>Butts and Coxe</u>, in Chapter 4 outline many extractive processes including historical methods and amalgamation, cyanidation, flotation, smelting, desilverizing lead by the Parkes process, by the Pattison method, cupellation, electrolytic lead and electrolytic copper processes. Recovery of silver from secondary sources is included.

In Chapter 5 refining methods are given with an outline of slimes treatment, dore' furnacing and electrolytic refining. Chapter 6 is devoted to a description of treatment and refining of a specific plant. Considerable detail is given.

These chapters give a good general description of the usual silver processes. The electrolytic refining for final purity seems to be a standard method that has been in use for many years and continues to be the most cost effective and efficient method to-day.

Electrolytic refining is also described in texts of non-ferrous metallurgy. Some of the older ones are <u>Liddell</u>, Chapter XXVII, <u>Bray</u>, pp. 433-435, <u>Schnabel</u>, pp. 604-933, <u>Gowland</u>, pp. 373-423, <u>Thompson</u>, pp. 257-261 and <u>Creighton and Koehler</u>, pp. 175-179.

The electrolytic system widely used for refining silver to high purity is simple in concept but requires attention to specific details.

Silver Electrolysis

Silver electrolytic cells use a solution of silver nitrate, copper nitrate and some nitric acid. An impure anode (positive connection) is immersed in this electrolyte and an insoluble cathode (negative connection) receives the silver when the electric current dissolves the anode.

Two kinds of cells are in general use. One uses anodes and cathodes that are suspended in the electrolyte from hangers at the top of the cell. The other holds the anode in a horizontal tray in the upper portion of the cell and the silver is deposited on a cathode at the bottom of the cell. Each has advantages and disadvantages.

Metals insoluble in nitric acid are retained in cloth anode bags. Nitric acid soluble metals (often copper) remain in solution. When these reach levels that lead to their codepositing on the cathode with silver new electrolyte must be added and old (foul) electrolyte removed and treated for silver recovery.

When the silver content of this anode is high and impurities are low the cells may run for a week or so before electrolyte becomes foul. However sterling silver anodes with a 7 1/2% copper content make electrolyte treatment a need every few days.

Recovery of the silver from foul electrolyte can be a real nuisance. The removal of the copper by liquid-liquid extraction and reuse of the purified silver electrolyte was once practiced by Brookside Metal Co., Watford, England. A report by Hunter discusses this process in considerable detail. His paper, "The Use of Solvent Extraction for Purification of Silver Nitrate Electrolyte" was presented at the 1978 conference of the International Precious Metals Institute but not printed.

We ran laboratory scale tests with several extractant compounds used by the copper industry for copper retrieval. Our experience indicated that the nitric acid environment slowly deteriorated the organic extractant. We never put this into use on a production basis. It is very successful and extensively used in recovering copper when the solutions are sulfuric acid.

Often the foul silver cell electrolyte is treated with salt brine to make silver chloride. The silver chloride is then processed for silver recovery.

Another method is to cement out the silver with copper. A silver nitrate - copper nitrate solution in contact with metallic copper results in precipitation of silver metal and dissolution of a chemical equivalent of copper.

Copper recovery could be done with Dietzel cells. These are slowly rotating copper cylinders we understand once much used for high copper scrap. Essentially a Dietzel cell has a bottom anode and a rotating cathode at the top. This cathode is an open ended horizontal cylinder at the top. This copper cylinder is partially submerged in the upper part of the cell.

The electrolyte is a nitrate solution and the gold collects as an insoluble mud near the bottom anode. The silver copper solution is removed a little higher in the cell and sent to a separate cementation vessel where copper is used to displace the silver.

The copper rich solution is then returned to the cell at the rotating cathodes where copper is plated out. The dendritic copper is scraped away.

We saw one such plant in operation in Pforzheim, Germany. There were hundreds of such cells and apparently need little operator attention. We believe that careful adjustment of solution flow positions and rates together with a very steady rate of operation is required. Dietzel cells in a form somewhat different than the ones in present use were once much used but seem to have been replaced by other methods in most refineries.

<u>Other Methods</u>

Mercury and gold and silver do not react to make a chemical compound. They make an alloy just as gold and copper or silver and copper dissolve in one another and make alloys. Mercury having a very low melting point can be quite easily driven out of an alloy (called an amalgam to specify the presence of mercury) by heat. The mercury boils out as a vapor leaving gold and silver behind. Mercury is toxic and accumulates in the body. This is a dangerous process.

Cyanidation of gold and silver is a chemical process and is discussed under mining.

Thiourea combines with gold and silver and has had considerable attention from those who want a substitute for cyanide. It is not now in industrial use. Combinations of thiourea and thiosulfate have also been tested.

Bromine has had considerable use about 90 or 100 years ago. When the cyanide process was developed recovery with bromine was dropped. There has been some recent experimentation and promotional work and a few patents. Again a substitute for cyanide is the cause for interest in bromine.

The description of gold refining by Pliny (ca, 4OAD) using brick dust, salt and extended furnacing is interesting in that it was truly a method of removing silver from gold there by increasing purity. To write a chemical equation for what really occurred in this process requires some assumptions. Ours are that the chlorine in the salt combined with the silver to form silver chloride. The sodium in the salt likely combined with some component(s) in the brick dust. If we write these assumptions as an equation:

$$Ag + NaCl + X = AgCl + NaX$$

Where X is the mixture of various things in brick dust. In this X we can surely expect silica or some silicate of an acid nature or an aluminum compound that can assume an acidic nature. In all likelihood there is no great problem for these to take up the basic sodium. The silver chloride would leave the molten gold and enter the nonmetallic slag portion of the melt or volatilize and condense in cooler portions of the crucible.

Cupellation or the separation of precious metals from base metals by means of lead and lead compounds involves some interesting chemistry.

The fire assayer uses a lead oxide, litharge, to collect the small and disseminated particles of precious metals from his sample. Metallic lead has a strong ability to make alloys with a considerable number of metals.

The assayer mixes his finely ground up ore with finely ground up litharge and flour which contains the carbon needed for his first reaction. There are other materials (fluxes) to liquefy the sample so that the chemical reaction can occur;

$$PbO + C = Pb + CO$$

The litharge is reduced to metallic lead by the carbon in the flour. The intimate mixture of materials much increases the chances of the lead to be in contact with precious and base metals. The lead alloy of these metals sinks and can, when cool, be separated from the slag. For purposes of illustration let us use copper as the base metal that is typical of many others. Let us designate gold, silver, palladium as PMs.

The lead button is then melted and air allowed to contact the lead. A reaction occurs fairly rapidly:

$$Pb + Cu \text{ (Base Metals)} + PM_s + O_2 = PbO + CuO(\text{etc}) + PM_s$$

The oxygen of the air has oxidized the lead back to litharge and the base metals to their oxides. These are a slag. The PMs (not oxidizable by air) remain as metals and are separate from the slag.

In the case of an assayers cupel the oxides sink into the porous crucible leaving the precious metals as a small sphere.

In a large cupelling furnace the steps are somewhat different. An impure dore' is put into a shallow furnace with lead and the materials are melted. The lead takes up the metals. Air sweeps over the molten mass and the lead and base metals are oxidized and form a floating slag. More lead and dore' is added. The slag is removed by skimming or by running out through a notch high in the furnace. When metal reaches the notch the last of the slag is skimmed and the metal poured out. The metal has had base metals removed but there is still a mixture of precious metals. Quality is improved but more refining is required.

The following sketch is a diagrammatic representation of a cupel furnace. These can be of various sizes but we understand they can be as large as 4 to 6 feet by 4 to 6 feet and perhaps 2 or 3 feet bottom to top.

A somewhat different method is used to recover values from very low grade refinery or gold mill by products. It is really a large scale fire assay system. The low grade scrap is melted with litharge and carbon sometimes using an electric arc furnace.

Gold and silver containing lead is taken from the melt and put into a large version of a regular laboratory assay furnace. Very large cupels (crucibles) are used to absorb the litharge leaving precious metals behind.

In all cases extensive pollution control is needed to contain the toxic lead fumes.

The Miller chlorine process is an effective and much used refining procedure. According to Stanley this chlorination process consistedly produces 996 or a little above. The dore' is melted and a ceramic tube inserted to carry gaseous chlorine into the crucible. The chlorine bubbles through the metal and reacts with base metals and

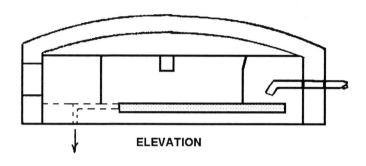

ELEVATION

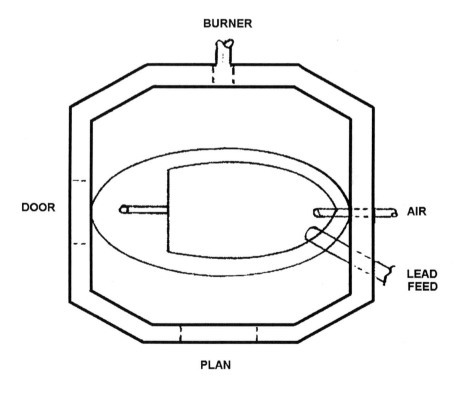

PLAN

Cupel Furnace

silver to make their chlorides. Using silver as an example:

$$2 \text{ Ag} + \text{Cl}_2 = 2 \text{ AgCl}$$

A slag layer accumulates these chlorides. Gold reacts with chlorine reluctantly and the process is stopped before gold chlorination is a problem.

The Wohlwill cell is an electrolytic device to dissolve gold. Early in the development of chemistry it was found that certain solutions would conduct current. The reason is that some chemicals when dissolved in water dissociate themselves to some degree. For instance let us look at hydrochloric acid known to be HCl. Chemical theory states that in water the hydrogen will be present as H+, hydrogen lacking one electron and therefore carrying a positive electrical charge. The chlorine present as Cl-, chlorine with an extra electron and therefore negative electrically.

In solution these are all together so these charges are not apparent. When electrodes are placed in the solution and a direct current applied, hydrogen appears at the negative terminal (cathode) and chlorine at the positive terminal (the anode).

The Wohlwill cell (See previous sketch) has a positive terminal of impure gold, the negative cathode is a thin piece of pure gold. The electrolyte is hydrochloric acid and gold chloride in water solution.

When a voltage is applied electrons are removed from the gold and other metals at the anode. They then become ions which is what these charged atoms are called. They go into solution.

The reaction at the anode can be written:

$$\text{Au} - 3e = \text{Au}^{3+}$$
$$\text{Cu} - 2e = \text{Cu}^{2+} \text{ (or other base metals)}$$

The electrons removed <u>are forced by the power equipment</u> through the wires to the cathode which is thereby filled with electrons and is thus negative. Here electrons are applied to any positive ions at the cathode surface. Since the electrolyte contains some gold ions and since gold is the metal that most readily accepts electrons the action can be written:

$$\text{Au}^{3+} + 3e = \text{Au}$$

See Wohlwill cell illustration.

The metallic gold deposits itself on the surface of the pure gold cathode. Base metal ions accept electrons with more reluctance so gold is preferentially plated out unless the amount of base metals becomes large. This is a diffusion controlled process so agitation is needed.

The silver ion does not remain as an ion because it combines with the chloride to form insoluble silver chloride and ceases to be a part of the electrolyte.

Several matters need attention however, one is that the amount of current at cathode and anode is the same. However, at the anode this current dissolves gold, and base metals and makes insoluble silver chloride. At the cathode this same amount of current plates out only gold. This gradually depletes the solution of the gold that was in the electrolyte at the start.

The solution must be regularly maintained to add more gold chloride and to remove base metals that are in solution but were not plated out. If this is done properly the net effect is, an improved (refined) gold cathode.

Very early Wohlwill found that when the silver in the anode reached 8 or 10% the surface of the anode was covered with an adherent and poorly conductive layer of silver chloride. This caused the flow of current to stop or sometimes it produces chlorine at the anode. He found that by superimposing an alternating current on the DC he was able to dissolve anodes with up to 20% silver content. This reverse component is reported to be 20-25% of the DC.

Another situation early noted in the operation of these cells was the appearance of metallic gold in unexpected places in the cell, especially in the silver chloride and other material in the bottom. It was determined that an anode reaction that produced gold mono chloride also took place:

$$Au - 1e^- = Au+$$

This could be written AuCl. This is unstable and has a life of perhaps a few hours. The instability gives this result:

$$3AuCl = AuCl_3 + 2Au$$

McMillan pp. 359-382 reports the experience and conclusions of Wohlwill with his electrolytic process and his conclusions about the production of aurous chloride, chlorine and the method of reducing the production of these undesirable materials.

The production of chlorine at the anode is avoided by keeping up the strength of the hydrochloric acid in the electrolyte. The undesirable effects of chlorine production are of course the nasty character of chlorine but also the waste of power. Electrons that release chlorine do not solubilize gold.

The production of undesirable aurous gold (Au^{1+}) can be reduced by using a strong current. In other words a high anode current density makes more of the desirable auric gold of a +3 valence (Au^{3+}).

These reactions and cell conditions have been studied by others. Milazzo p. 460 states that anode passivation results in chlorine production. On p. 463 he says the periodic reverse current must be greater than 10% and makes a higher current density possible thus diminishing the production of aurous gold.

Schalch and Nicol concluded that aurous gold production is reduced by 1. Low stirring intensity 2. High anode current density 3. Low temperature 4. Low chloride concentration. (This is the opposite of Wohlwill's idea).

Nicol also says the problem of possible passivation at the anode places an upper limit on current density. Some stirring is needed to prevent stratification but stirring can be small. Low hydrochloric acid concentration helps but a very much reduced Cl⁻ may result in passivation. The use of sodium or potassium chloride rather than hydrochloric acid is not helpful.

Schaler reports that ultrasonic agitation of the tank by a sidemounted transducer was effective in removing silver chloride from the anode.

It has been the opinion of this author that electrolytic action should be thought of as diffusion, the chemistry of an extremely thin film at the surface of the electrode. Interrupted or periodic reverse current would allow the chemical action to stabilize or "catch up" in the surface layer.

Pulsed forward and reverse "square wave" current is now quite easily produced and could have the advantage of control of time in each mode. Imposition of standard AC (50 or 60 cycles) must use voltage to control the amount of reverse and time cannot be controlled. Pitocco has done extensive testing of "square-wave" pulsed forward and reverse composed to superimposed 60 Hertz AC. Conclusions based on tests were that a forward 57 milliseconds pulse followed by a 11 milliseconds reverse would probably give best results. This is approximately 20% reverse power and not too different than that given for AC reverse. Silver chloride removal was deemed more efficient than for AC reversal. This work was done in a "Fizzer" cell a modification of the Wohlwill cell. (See next section).

It has been suggested that anode passivation may (sometimes) be due to the formation of gold oxide. The reaction at the surface of the anode could be:

$$2Au - 6e = 2Au^{3+}$$

The gold ion in this case could react with $3O^{2-}$ of water:

$$2Au^{3-} + 3O^{2-} = Au_2O_3$$

Another reaction with hydrochloric acid then could be:

$$Au_2O_3 + 8HCl = 2\ HAuCl_4 + 3H_2O$$

Such reactions we think surely occur in a very, very thin layer at the electrode surface. It is an opinion that such reactions become troublesome only with excess current or a deficiency of HCl.

POLLUTION - AIR AND WATER

The refiner of precious metals by whatever process we know and especially the refining done with aqua regia has the responsibility for not contaminating both air and water. In the development of our small refinery from a hobby to a very small backyard garage operation we made an effort to scrub out noxious fumes and to precipitate metals from our effluent water.

When we combined wet chemical work with furnace work in a more spacious and suitable building we made specific arrangements for an air scrubber and for water treatment. This was done without constraints from authorities or neighbors. When after a time we were visited by pollution control authorities we were in reasonably good standing and our relations have been amicable.

We have some background of experience in air pollution work but in an unrelated industrial situation. A background in chemical engineering was helpful in at least understanding the problems. We are not however experts in the rather complex field of pollution control. We will describe what we are doing but we believe more sophisticated approaches will be needed in many other locations. As time goes the standards for effluents will almost certainly be more stringent and greater care will be required.

Air Pollution

Burning sweeps can be a source of smoke and odor. Our way of burning sweeps is to burn slowly which means to limit the amount of air. This tends to be smoky and we use an afterburner in a ceramic lined pipe to deal with this. It is modestly successful. We are told that a very hot afterburner is the secret of success. A very good gas burning jet is required to accomplish this. We suggest that the design of a crematory furnace be studied with the thought that these probably have a very effective afterburner.

Burning more aggressively with gas jets in the main body of the fumes followed by settling chambers bag houses or electrostatic precipitation for recovery of valuable dust is common in the refining industry.

We have made no systematic study of possible ways to burn sweeps effectively without loss and without pollution. The use of a water spray chamber may be good although we know of none in use. Incinerators may be subject to severe legal restrictions.

Ash Melting

The liquefaction of the sweeps ashes with suitable fluxes in a crucible furnace is in our experience a relatively smoke free operation. Excessive use of sodium nitrate can result in some impressive clouds of white smoke. The reduction of silver chloride with soda ash smokes at higher temperatures. We have gone to considerable trouble to convert all silver chloride (even that in rough scrap) to silver metal before the scrap goes to the furnace. See comments about silver chloride in the chapter on silver.

The size of a crucible furnace that may be legally operated without dust collection equipment may be very small perhaps only the size of a jewelers crucible furnace. A bag house or a wet scrubber may be required for crucible furnaces.

We do not consider the melting and liquefaction of the ash-flux mixture to slag and molten metal as more than liquefaction and gravity separation of the heavy metal from lighter slag.

We refer to this as sweeps melting as there is no smelting action to remove metals from chemical combination as is done in the smelting of ores. Smelters may be smoky and chemically polluting or both and are often subject to extensive and stringent controls.

Refining

Aqua regia dissolution of metals and nitric acid dissolution of silver both produce nitrogen oxides (NO_x) that are acidic and somewhat toxic. The brown pall that hangs over large cities is to a large degree the result of nitrogen oxides from internal combustion engines, material chemically similar to that from aqua regia reactions.

This NO_x reacts readily with basic solutions (i.e. high pH) if good contact between the air containing the NO_x and the solution can be achieved. A standard device extensively used in the chemical industry for this purpose is known as a "packed tower". These consist of a tower, essentially a pipe, which is filled with saddle shaped objects or other suitable packing. This packing is so designed that it takes up the least possible amount of the tower space so that the gas (air) can flow upward through this packing with the least possible resistance. It is also shaped so that the scrubbing solution is not allowed to form channels as it falls through the tower but remains distributed throughout the tower. A photograph of a plastic saddle follows.

Tower Packing

The characteristics of such scrubbers are to a large degree well known and the design of scrubbing towers is quite straight forward. The chemical reactions of many materials in such towers are well known and scrubbing efficiency can be predicted.

In the case of NO_x scrubbed with water the efficiency is quite limited because of a series of reactions and re-reactions with the oxygen of the air. With a caustic solution in the scrubber the efficiency is improved.

Scrubber Description

Our scrubber, though homemade, was built according to accepted engineering design. It is a square tower. Round pipe would be better but too costly for us at that time. It has a cross section of 4 square feet (0.37 sq meters). It is 16 feet (5.4 meters) high. The packed section is 10 1/2 feet deep and filled with 1" (2.54cm) plastic saddles. These rest on a plastic grid. The air from our hood enters the tower through this grid.

The bottom of the tower is set into a 50 gallon (190 liter) tank slightly larger than the 2' X 2' (60cm X 60cm) tower walls. The gases (mostly air) are drawn into and through the tower by means of a belt driven blower with a 13 1/2" (34cm) diameter wheel and a 3 HP motor. Wheel speed is about 2670 RPM, the pressure drop of the air through the scrubber is about 2.75" (7cm) of water. Fan characteristic curves gives this an estimated 1500 (43cm meters) cubic feet per minute of air movement.

The blower is very noisy so a home made muffler was attached. This is a plastic drum, about 50 gallons (180 liters) in size. The blower discharges into this drum near the bottom. Air is discharged through numerous slots in the top. The top is about 50%-60% slots. It effectively reduces the noise. See photo.

The chemical hood has a front opening that is 5 feet (1.5 meters) long and 2'-7" (.79 meters) high. The average velocity into this opening is about 115 linear feet (35 linear meters) per minute. Since the tower is at one end more air is drawn in near the tower than at the far end. However, fumes do not escape the hood at any part of its length. The fact that this hood is in a quiet air part of the room is a help in achieving good fume capture.

A simple test can be used to determine the approximate rate of flow of air. A smoke source is held at a point where the rate of movement is important. If the smoke moves toward the collecting area in a straight line without wavering the flow is about 100 feet (30 meters) per minute. This is often adequate. Wind and similar

Muffler

disturbances may require more.

The NO_x is heavier than air and a 2" (5cm) curb along the front prevents over the edge escape. The exit from the hood into the tower is low at the level of the hood floor. It was so designed to better capture the heavy NO_x.

A sketch of this hood and scrubber follows.

Scrubbing Liquid

The scrubbing liquid is a water solution of caustic soda (NaOH) or soda ash (sodium carbonate) (Na_2CO_3). It is maintained at a pH of +10 by a daily check with pH paper and additions of caustic or soda ash as needed.

Caustic soda is strong and very high pH values are possible. It is more costly than soda ash. The pH of a solution of soda ash usually measures less than that of caustic soda but it has proved to be quite satisfactory. This is probably due to its ability to maintain a specific and for us a safe pH, a characteristic called buffering. Furthermore the scrubbing load in terms of the quantity of acidic NO_x to be removed is modest.

The solution is pumped to the top of the tower where it is distributed across the top of the packing by a grid of perforated pipes. The pump and impeller are plastic, the intake opening 1" diameter the outlet pipe is 3/4" (1.9cm) diameter. Our measurements indicate it is circulating about 35 or 40 gallons (130-150 liters) per minute.

We found that an iron pump in this service did not survive, even though the pH might lead one to think it would be suitable.

There is considerable evaporation during scrubber operation and the pump will usually run dry in a few hours. Water level is maintained in the 50 gallon (190 liters) bottom tank by means of a float or more recently a simple outside feed tank that drops in some water whenever the scrubber tank level get low enough to provide the feed tank with air to release some of its water.

The hold up of water in the scrubber is quite large in the order of 20-25 gallons (15-95 liters). The scrubber tank level must be quite low when the pump is running or else it will over flow when the pump is shut down and the scrubber drains itself.

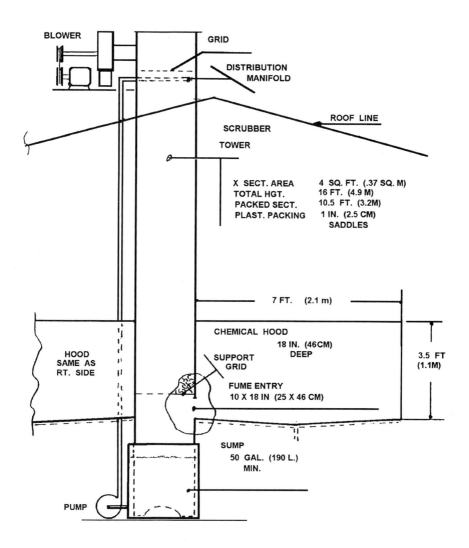

Scrubber and Hood

The solution is occasionally pumped out and made up new. The used scrubber water is utilized in the water treatment process to raise the pH of the very acidic effluent water from the refining work. This is done at intervals of many weeks.

Other Gases

The scrubber quite effectively handles the gases and acid odors that may come during filtration work, and the minor fumes if nitric acid is used. It is effective for the chlorine that is produced when aqua regia is mixed.

In our shop we have a similar hood on the opposite side of the centrally located scrubbing tower. The fumes (if any) from the work of precipitating and filtering go to the tower, at the opposite side of the scrubbing tower.

Possible Methods for Reducing Pollution Gases

Fizzer Cell

The electrolytic fizzer cell dissolves the metal without the production of NO_x fumes. Some acid spray is created at the cathode and fizzer cells should be operated under a hood or with suitable fume extraction. The salt cell would not have an acid spray. See Other Methods.

"Johnson" System

A closed system and the use of oxygen to completely oxidize the NO to nitric acid is extensively used in the dissolution of silver with nitric acid. We call it the "Johnson" system because of the patented process developed by Johnson & Sons Smelting Works in England. See Butts & Coxe, p. 222.

This basic idea also works for the NO that is emitted by aqua regia if the equipment is closed and is injected with oxygen.

Briefly the method consists of using a packed tower to make contact between a mixture of the effluent NO gas, oxygen and scrubbing water. Without the diluting effect of nitrogen, as would be the case if air were used, the reaction between NO, the oxygen (O_2) and water (H_2O) goes readily to completion making nitric acid (HNO_3). In other words this reaction must be done in an oxygen environment or it does not go to completion.

The scrubbing water accumulates the nitric acid. At a strength of about 50% this nitric acid can be re-used.

The system consists of a packed tower, an acid-water recirculating pump, a heat exchanger to cool this liquid, a catch tank, oxygen supply system and a simple bubbler at the top of the scrubber to visually show that a small excess of oxygen is being supplied.

A schematic diagram (following page) describes the system.

We have made several small tests using this for the nitrogen oxide that comes from aqua regia dissolution and it works quite well.

<u>Chlorine System</u>

A very similar system of equipment but using chlorine instead of oxygen may be more useful for aqua regia refining than the oxygen reaction.

We know of no refinery using this technique. Our experience is limited to about half a dozen small tests but our success prompts us to outline it here as a potentially useful technique.

The basis of our interest is the reaction between chlorine gas and the nitrogen oxide(NO) produced by aqua regia gold dissolution. This reaction is given in <u>Mellor</u>, p. 613.

$$2\ NO + Cl_2 = 2\ NOCl\ \text{(aqua regia)}$$

The equipment as we set it up for our simplest and most successful tests is very similar to that used for the oxygen reaction described above.

It is a closed system so that the NO gas from the aqua regia reaction goes to the bottom of a packed tower with a receiving tank below and a pump to recirculate water through the tower.

Also to the bottom of this tower or into the reaction vessel above the aqua regia is a chlorine duct to inject chlorine into the system.

Once the air has been purged from the system (we think chlorine gas may be the best material to use as a purge) the reaction is very rapid. In our experience often so

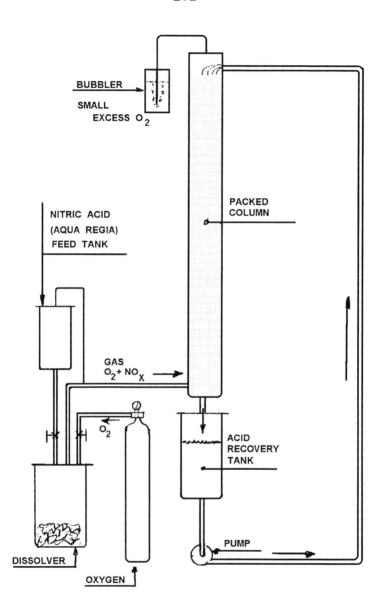

Nitric Acid Recovery

rapid that a fairly sizeable vacuum is created. For this reason a bubbler to atmosphere is not suitable. We found that a pressure measuring device in the form of a U tube was useful. We regulated the chlorine flow manually to maintain the system between a small pressure and small vacuum.

In a regularly used production system of this kind we believe a sensitive flow control device should be used on the chlorine supply. This would be similar to a good (perhaps 2 stage) oxygen cylinder regulator except constructed to withstand chlorine. These do not seem to exist but we are told can probably be rather easily made.

The reaction apparently does not change temperatures significantly. We ran one test with thermometers in the system at a number of important places and found little if any temperature changes.

We found that we could run the system and produce a red liquid with the appearance and specific gravity of the original aqua regia. This liquid dissolved the next batch of scrap gold in a normal way.

The advantages of this would be a limited amount of air pollution. A minor advantage could be the recovery of aqua regia.

Disadvantages are the cost and complexities of handling chlorine and a much more complex aqua regia dissolution system.

A diagram of our system is on the following page.

Water Pollution

When scrap metal is dissolved and the gold removed by selective reduction, the barren solution still contains the base metal salts. These, in the case of jewelers scrap, are largely copper but also any other metals that were in the gold alloy or in the scrap.

Copper compounds are toxic and cannot be legally dumped in any area of the U.S. Silver compounds are usually legally restricted to very low levels because of their undesirable action in sewage disposal plants. Other metals are also subject to limits, that may vary from place to place.

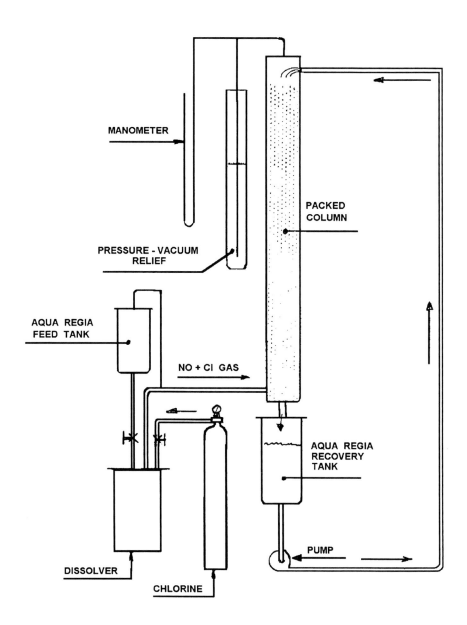

Aqua Regia Recovery

The treatment of the effluent liquids to meet required standards can be complex and costly. We are not expert in this field and any refiner should inform himself about the allowable limits for the metals in the liquid effluent. The limits of the moment may be temporary because they are regularly being lowered. The trend is toward stricter regulation of all metal waste discharges.

The chemical complexity of water treatment to remove the various metals is such that professionally expert advice is needed in most situations. The treatment involves pH control (acidity control), sludge removal, perhaps ion exchange resin treatment, etc.

In our small refinery where water disposal is a few gallons per day we treat the effluent in a very simple way. As time goes by we expect this to become more complex but we describe it as it now exists.

The most desirable, most costly and probably most difficult is to release only pure water. This may be the legal requirement in some locations now and should be planned for at all locations.

We know of one in-house refinery that precipitates essentially all metals by increasing the pH. Most metals form hydroxides-oxides at elevated pH that are quite insoluble. They are usually voluminous, gelatinous and difficult to filter or centrifuge or otherwise dewater. The sludges from such dewatering operations usually require drying before disposal. There are many sludge driers on the market. They tend to be agitated heaters of one design or another.

The action taken in the matter of water pollution will be very largely dictated by the laws of the location or federal law, whichever is stricter. Professional advice is necessary.

In the following pages we describe our rather simple treatment process. We do not expect to operate at this level for very long and expect to improve the technique in the near future.

Precious Metal Cementation

The barren solution from the work of filtering the precipitated gold as well as any acids and wash water from the washing of this precipitated gold is poured into a small plastic tank that we call the "cementation" tank. This is a plastic tank with a capacity of about 15-20 gallons (60-75 liters). A 1/2 inch (1.27cm) plastic pipe is connected to this tank about 6 inches (15cm) above the bottom. A plastic pump is used to pump this solution from the tank when the cementation treatment is complete.

When the cementation tank is full or nearly so a bar of copper is suspended in the liquid and allowed to stand with occasional stirring for some hours. There may be very small amounts of precious metals left in the solution and the copper metal displaces these. The settlings in this tank accumulate slowly and at intervals of many months we remove them to retrieve values.

Acidity Control

The liquid from the cementation tank is pumped into one of two plastic tanks that have a capacity of about 50 gallons (190 liters) each. We fill these to about 35 gallons (130 liters). When filled to this level we inject air to stir the solution and start to reduce the acidity by adding soda ash (sodium carbonate) (Na_2CO_3).

The reaction between soda ash and the very acidic solution releases a large amount of carbon dioxide gas so addition must be cautious to avoid boil-over. Stirring the solution is important to avoid unreacted pockets of soda ash. Recirculation with the pump is helpful but not completely effective. Stirring with a rod or wooden stick is good but requires operator attention.

We use air to stir because it is quite effective if an air lift type of injector is used. This is a simple homemade device and illustrated in the sketch-following page.

A small scoop of soda ash is added and the reaction allowed to go for say 10 minutes or so. When foaming subsides another scoopful is added. Foaming can be reduced somewhat by adding a little oily material. A few shots of charcoal starter fluid is helpful.

Soda ash addition fairly soon raises the pH from the zero or near zero level to 1 or 1.5. Then the solution accepts a rather large amount of soda ash before it goes much higher. When a pH of 2 or 2.5 is reached we add no more soda ash.

We used a small pocket pH meter during our learning time because we were taking a great many readings. A meter must be calibrated to a standard solution every few days.

By now we can judge progress by foaming rate and similar signs and we use pH paper. Above pH 3 an insoluble material forms. This can be seen as a turbidity. If

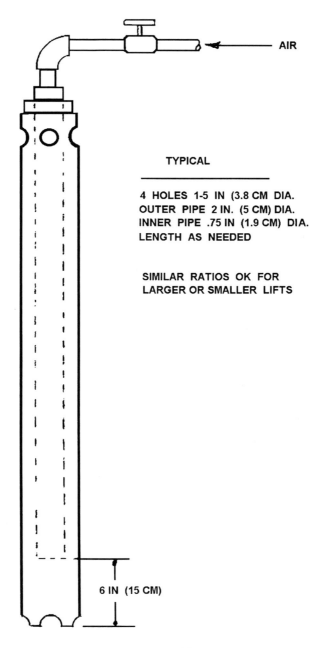

Air Lift

the pH is too high and this forms the addition of some untreated acidic, solution dissolves it but this may take considerable time.

This soda ash reaction work may take several hours but is done by occasional additions in between other work and does not require much labor.

Iron Tanks

When reaction is complete and the pH is stabilized in the 2.0-2.5 range the solution is pumped to two elevated plastic tanks. These hold about 50 gallons (190 liters) each.

When these are full a valve at the bottom is opened and a small stream perhaps half the diameter of a pencil is run into the first of the four "iron" tanks. These tanks are plastic and about 30 gallon (115 liters) in size. The size is of no great importance. Ours are this size because they were readily available drums. We use 4 tanks to insure good residence time for the liquid.

These tanks are filled with scrap iron. The solution flow is in at the bottom, out near the top, then through a pipe to the bottom of the next tank, etc. through the four tanks. Here another cementation reaction occurs but in this case the iron goes into solution and displaces the copper which plates out onto iron surfaces.

We are told that the addition of a few pinches of sodium thiosulfate (photo fixing chemical) in the acid tanks will help form a loosely adherent copper that can be more easily washed off of the iron so that iron surface is exposed and the reaction can continue.

Between every run of 100 to 150 gallons (380-570 liters) of solution we agitate the iron to remove as much copper as possible. Bulk iron is not as good as sheets and thin scrap because the surface area of sheet material is large for each unit weight of iron.

The final solution has a green tint due to the iron chloride content. The solution is so acidic that it continues to dissolve some iron. A final wash with large amounts of water or draining the iron tanks between runs conserves iron. At this time iron is not a problem in our effluent.

Copper Retrieval

At infrequent intervals (usually many months) we drain one or more of the iron tanks completely and remove all the larger iron pieces by hand. The fine sludge is mostly copper with some partially digested particles of iron. These we shovel onto a wire mesh screen with openings of approximately 1/8 inch (3mm). The copper sludge is washed through with a hose along with the very small bits of iron. The coarser particles of iron we discard.

The copper sludge is allowed to settle in plastic pails and after a time the water is poured off. Since filtering to further dewater this is very slow we now air dry this material. We have a metal pan about 2 feet (60cm) square and 4 inches (10cm) deep. We pour the watery sludge till this is full and let it stand in the sun for a week or two. A temporary cover is used if rain threatens. It loses moisture readily and the dry material is pulverent and dusty.

Although we have accumulated this copper for a few years the amount is rather small and we have not come to any firm conclusion about final treatment. At this time we find that this dry copper sludge melts fairly well usually without visible smoke especially if soda ash is used during the melt.

Treatment for Iron

The solution is at present sent to the drain however iron can be removed from the solution by raising the pH. The iron forms an insoluble sludge. This iron sludge settles poorly and filters so badly that this is not a reasonable method unless costly filter pumps and filter presses are used. Centrifuges are used by some but are not entirely satisfactory. Sludge driers are a possibility.

If magnesium hydroxide is used to raise the pH and precipitate the iron the resulting sludge settles quite well and filters at a reasonable rate based on reports by suppliers and the few small tests we have made.

Addition of magnesium hydroxide will not raise the pH above 9. It is easy to use too much magnesium hydroxide if one relies on pH measurements alone. The amount to use is easily determined, however, by making up a sodium hydroxide solution of known sodium hydroxide content.

A measured sample of the solution is then treated with a standard caustic solution until the pH reaches 9. Then from the known amount of sodium hydroxide and a ratio factor the required amount of magnesium hydroxide can be calculated and used.

This treatment will leave soluble materials in the water. This certainly includes some magnesium and probably sodium sulfate ion, chloride ion and nitrogen in some form. The general direction is toward standards that equal distilled water. Some standards for discharged water are more restrictive than for drinking water.

We will not comment on reasonableness or fairness of such laws. However it may be necessary for industrial water users to treat their discharges and then polish them with ion exchange resins and/or activated charcoal.

Other Methods

The refiner may adopt processes that do not produce much effluent. The Miller chlorine process may be useful. Techniques that reuse solutions could be required. A combination of electrolytic dissolution with a liquid-liquid extraction for gold recovery might be devised. Possibly the Dietzel cell would have new life in copper-silver-gold recovery.

The use of super critical pressure dissolution of metals may be a future possibility. It is reported that ammonia (not ammonium hydroxide) can rapidly dissolve gold. See Lagowski.

The activity of carbon dioxide at supercritical pressures has been studied and is in some commercial use in other fields. Other chemicals will probably be studied.

Air Pollution Chemistry

The NO gas produced when the aqua regia reacts with metals or when nitric acid reacts with silver, immediately reacts with oxygen in the air when it leaves the reactor. The reaction is:

$$2NO + O_2 = 2NO_2 \text{ (sometimes written } N_2O_4\text{)}$$

Here the nitrogen in the NO goes from a N^{2+} state to a N^{4+} by oxidation.

A packed tower scrubber is reported to be only 80% efficient. The reaction with water is:

$$3NO_2 + H_2O = 2HNO_3 + NO$$

Here the nitrogen in the nitric acid has gone to a N^{5+} valence by each losing an electron. The third nitrogen has taken these and gone from N^{4+} to N^{2+}. As the gases proceed through the scrubber the NO and oxygen (air) must repeat these reactions. The gases become quite dilute in O_2 and NO content and in a scrubber of reasonable size the reaction does not have time to finish.

A possible reaction of the NO with water to form nitrous acid does not work:

$$NO_2 + NO + H_2O = HNO_2$$

The chemical concentration and the characteristics of nitrous acid limit reaction if it does occur.

The scrubbing action of a caustic solution at elevated pH is more effective. Solutions of caustic soda absorb the nitrogen tetroxide to form nitrates and nitrites:

$$N_2O_4 + 2NaOH = NaNO_3 + NaNO_2 + H_2O$$

Sodium nitrate and sodium nitrite are both quite soluble. Caustic soda is more efficient than sodium carbonate which dissolves the compounds less vigorously. Some nitrous acid does escape this neutralization and decomposes with a loss of nitric oxide. Alkali concentration of about 1.5N (approx. 4-5% NaOH) gives best absorption. Higher concentrations are poorer, about equal to water for a 4 normal solution. Friend, p. 176.

Chlorine and the vapors of sulfuric and hydrochloric acids are quite efficiently absorbed in caustic solution.

Water Pollution Chemistry

The metals present in jewelers scrap are almost all dissolved by aqua regia. Silver is almost entirely precipitated as the chloride. Gold is almost entirely removed by reduction to the metal.

Karat gold usually contains considerable copper. Scrap may contain iron from saw blades and other iron not completely removed by magnets. Nickel will be present if white gold is refined. Casting alloys usually have small amounts of zinc. Depending upon the character of the scrap other metals may be present in small amounts. Copper is likely to be the major constituent in the solution.

The pH of the solution will be low often less than 1. It is a general characteristic of metals to be soluble in acids (metals are bases).

Characteristically metal hydroxides are insoluble. However different metal hydroxides are insoluble at different pH values. <u>Schrumb</u>, p. 592, gives the following list of pH values that are arbitrarily termed "precipitation pH" values. This is the pH at which a solution containing 0.001 g moles per liter of the metal can exist at room temperature.

pH Values at Which Various Metal Hydroxides Form a 0.001 Molar

Saturated Solution

Metal Hydroxide	"Precipitation pH"
$Fe(OH)_3$	2.5
$Al(OH)_3$	4.1
$Cr(OH)_3$	4.9
$Cu(OH)_2$	5.9
$Zn(OH)_2$	7.3
$Co(OH)_2$	7.6
$Pb(OH)_2$	7.7
$Fe(OH)_2$	8.1
$Mn(OH)_2$	8.4
$Ni(OH)_2$	8.6
$Mg(OH)_2$	9.9

Removing metals from solution by raising the pH is one technique for improving the quality of the liquid. At a pH of 12 precipitation is probably as complete as it can be. The metal hydroxides are usually non-crystalline and form gelatinous high volume precipitates that settle slowly and filter poorly.

Even after centrifuging or filtering the sludge retains large amounts of water and sludge driers are often used. The dried material may be (often is) subject to natural outdoor leaching and must be sent to a special dump.

The solution may still contain unacceptable traces of metals and may need a final polishing process to meet legal requirements. In any case the high pH solution will need acid addition to bring it down to a neutral pH.

Some very sophisticated treatment plants are now being used by some shops. These often use ion exchange resins and similar modern chemistry.

The use of magnesium hydroxide to precipitate metals seems to have some real advantages according to small tests we made. We found that the sludges precipitated by magnesium hydroxide settled and filtered quite well compared to that precipitated by calcium hydroxide or sodium hydroxide.

It is available from several companies and information about its use is available from the supplier. Our evaluation was that the use of magnesium hydroxide will be a not too costly improvement for metal precipitation and treatment.

Our method at the time of this writing is to first remove the copper which is a major containment and is also to some degree toxic as a chemical compound. The copper is displaced (cemented out) by iron. The more reactive (less noble) iron donates electrons to the copper ion whereby the iron becomes an ion and goes into solution. The copper becomes a metal and precipitates as a coating on the iron.

$$Cu^{2+} + Fe = Cu + Fe^{2+}$$

The copper coating must be occasionally removed and agitation of the iron is effective especially if a very small amount of sodium thiosulfate (photographic fixer) is added to the solution.

It is possible to do this over a rather wide range of acidity. It is desirable to do this at near neutrality because very acid solution will also attack the iron and dissolve it by acid reaction.

Jewelry shop scrap contains iron in the form of saw blades, etc. Magnetic separation does not remove all of this so the liquid waste contains some dissolved iron in the ferric state. When the liquid waste is treated to neutralize its acidity this iron precipitates at about pH 3. This iron precipitate causes problems in the flow through the iron tanks so we neutralize only to pH 2.5. The liquid then passes through the various tanks of scrap iron.

We suggest that <u>Eilbeck</u> gives useful information as this and other aspects of waste water treatment.

MINING PRECIOUS METALS

We feel that jewelers and the small refiner may have some interest in precious metal mining and mill operations. We have no experience with the actual mining of ore other then walking through several mines. For a very short time we ran a small cyanide plant in Mexico. We have visited several very large mills in the USA and Canada.

Most of what we think we know comes from convention papers, articles and books. We will try to present an outline of mining and recovery work and something of its history and its present form.

According to <u>Puddephat</u>, p. 1, the solar spectrum indicates gold in the sun is about 0.04 parts per million (ppm) but the earth's crust is about 0.004 ppm. The gold of interest to a miner must be present in much more concentrated form. Such concentration may have happened in several ways.

Gold is an unreactive metal and except for some that is found combined with tellurium or selenium it occurs in the metallic form. It is yellow, noticeable and attractive. The alluvial gold found in rivers is traditionally considered to be the result of the weathering of gold bearing rocks which caused the gold particles to be washed into stream beds. This is called placer gold.

PLACER GOLD

The great specific gravity of gold (19.3) compared to rocks at about 2.7 causes the gold to settle to the bottom of streams. Once discovered this specific gravity difference is used to separate nuggets and particles and "dust". The pan of the prospector is perhaps the simplest device used to make this gravity separation.

It seems probable that most gold of antiquity was placer gold and recovered by some gravity separation method. Jason's Golden Fleece of mythology is such a device. A sheep skin or fleece in a running stream of water in which there was gold would trap the particles of the heavy gold which would snuggle into the wool because of their weight.

There are modern plants using carpeting for the same task. Sometimes a sand and gravel operation can recover interesting amounts of gold by installing a "rag plant" on the downstream side of the sand and gravel washing area. This is a section where a wooly carpet lines the ducts that carry water and sand to screens or to storage piles. Gold is recovered by periodic "rag" replacement and burning the old one to recover valuable ashes. Indoor-outdoor carpeting can be vacuumed or washed and reused.

There are also sluice boxes that use a boxlike water duct with small cross bars in the bottom to trap gold. Rockers are another old time method of making a gravity separation. There are other methods such as jigs that mechanically thrash a mixture of water and ore in a vertical pulsation to bring gold to a bottom collection spot. The California Mining Journal is full of advertising for equipment to achieve this separation.

The great gold rushes of California in 1848, Australia in 1850 and the Yukon in 1896 were all placer or alluvial gold finds. The mountains of Russia also have placer gold. In many places placer gold is at the bottom of some rather deep streams and dredges have been and are used to bring the bottom material up to be separated and the waste discharged. Often such dredges also work the banks or depart from the present meander of the river and follow old river beds to recover gold left when the river changed its course.

There is work being done to search for long abandoned river beds often miles from present streams to see if dry placers of value can be found. These dry placers may be deep and the search can be costly. The large gold deposits of the Rand in South Africa are ancient placer deposits that concentrated in beach sand.

At one time very large jets of high pressure water were used to wash down entire hills of gold bearing earth. These large nozzles are now museum pieces in western mining areas because they have long been outlawed. However, a few such mining operations are still active. We know there was one in Alaska a few years ago.

A story told me in my youth was about the recovery of placer gold from the bottom of a river in Siberia. The work was done in the terrible cold of the Siberian winter.

A place on the thick winter ice of a river was chipped away almost through to the water. This thin ice would then freeze thick again. This would be thinned and again frozen thick as the depth of the hole in the ice increased over several days. Gradually an ice hole formed in the river. If this ice hole was deep the freezing at the bottom was quite slow. To speed freezing an ordinary oil burning lantern would be set in the bottom at the center. In quiet air a warm column of air would rise in the center and cold arctic air spill down along the sides and speed the freezing of the sides and bottom. In time an open hole with ice walls would reach the bottom and hopefully the gold in the bottom of the river. The miners could then work the sand and gravel deposits at the bottom of the hole.

VEIN GOLD

Much gold is locked up in ore. In South Africa it occurs as thin veins in quartz rocks. <u>Puddephat</u>, p. 2, tells how the gold can be dissolved and laid down elsewhere especially in hot or volcanic areas.

Such gold usually can not be detected visually and sometimes not easily under a microscope. We were told by a mill operator in Canada that in his ore he'd have to look at many thousands of particles under a microscope before he'd see a single particle of gold.

Such gold ore is crushed to release the gold. Early crushers were primitive. The Mexican aristra was built by setting up a quite large flat rock surface at about earth level. A central pole served as a pivot for an arm to which a mule could be hitched. A heavy stone was fastened to this pole near the central pivot. As the mule walked around in circles the stone was dragged over the flat surface. Ore thrown onto this device was ground down to release the gold.

Stamp mills were once used in great numbers. A stamp mill consists of a heavy flat piece of iron or stone set at about ground level. Above this rising about 8 feet (2 1/2 meters) is the stamp, a heavy piece of iron perhaps 12" by 12" (30 x 30cm) held upright by a suitable frame work and guides. A rotating cam lifted the stamp and then released it to fall onto an ore bed on the flat surface below.

Present day jaw crushers, cone crushers, rod mills and ball mills have long made museum pieces out of stamps.

MERCURY AMALGAMS

At one time much gold recovery was done with mercury. Mercury is a metal with a low melting temperature so that it is ordinarily a liquid and it has the useful characteristic of alloying with gold and silver and other metals. These alloys are called amalgams and are usually mushy semi-solid materials. The precious metals were amalgamated by having mercury in the sluice boxes, or on copper plates, in the stamp mills, etc., and then regularly harvesting the amalgam. This mushy amalgam can be squeezed through chamois skins to remove excess mercury. The amalgam is then heated in a tightly closed iron retort.

The retort has an exit for mercury gases that is a pipe that is usually bent over and down to dip into a container of water.

Enough heat is applied to make the mercury boil and the vapors condense in the water and mercury accumulates in the bottom of the water. Gold and silver and other metals remain in the retort to be later refined.

Some ores would "poison" the mercury so it would not amalgamate. This put some limit on the ores that could be so recovered.

Mercury is a hazardous material. It builds up in the body and what one inhales to-day may help kill you years later. One of the early symptoms of mercury poisoning is mental aberrations. The Mad Hatter of Alice in Wonderland was a victim of mercury poisoning. Mercury in those days was used to make felt from hair and wool and it was well known then that hatters were usually pretty dingy.

CYANIDATION

In the late 1800's and very early 1900's the long known affinity of gold and silver for cyanide was carefully studied and a workable gold recovery system devised.

In a relatively few years the cyanide system was used world wide and mercury largely displaced. We understand that recovery was materially improved by the use of cyanide. The health hazards of a cyanide plant are less than those in a mercury plant especially for long term daily exposure of the somewhat volatile mercury.

All mammals including humans have a natural mechanism for destroying small amounts of cyanide in the body. For this reason cyanide does not stay in the body. Also there are very effective antidotes for cyanide poisoning. Mercury, on the other hand, accumulates and small non-lethal amounts can build up to cause illness and death. This is also true of lead and other metals.

The cyanide in gold mill solutions is typically 2 lbs (1 kilo) per ton (1000 kilo) of water or 0.1%. A cyanide mill will usually smell strongly of cyanide but the actual amount in the air is far below the danger level and it does not accumulate in the body.

MODERN MILLS

Modern large gold mines and mills are rather amazing operations. Some mines are more than a mile deep. A hoist of one mile involves a cable that is capable of lifting 50 tons but the cable itself weighs 35 tons so the useful lift is only 15 tons. This cable is wound up onto a hoisting drum that is large enough to hold a mile of cable in a single layer. The maintenance and inspection of the cable, the drum and the drum shaft must be careful and regular.

At a 1 mile depth the rocks are very hot and costly man cooling equipment is needed. The mine faces are under great pressure and may occasionally burst with violence. Some gold mines have large secondary hoists underground and are working at depths below one mile.

The rather large pieces of ore, after being hoisted to the mill are crushed and this is done in jaw and gyratory primary crushers. The final grinding to the fine powder usually needed for gold extraction is done in large rotating cylinders filled with heavy iron rods (rod mills) and ball mills (filled with iron balls). The ball mills do the finest grind and are the last in the ore crushing system.

We have seen huge rod mills with motor drives of several thousand horsepower. The rods in these mills are enormous and our observation was that some ore went directly to these rod mills without preliminary jaw or gyratory crushers. This is possible when the ore is easy to crush. This milling is done in water and final ball mills were equipped with hydraulic cone classifiers to automatically return the coarse material to the mill.

Some mills add cyanide to the water in the crushers, others later. The maximum solubility of gold is in cyanide of about 0.25% strength. However, the usual mill "strong" cyanide is 0.1% sodium cyanide. It is essential to have chemical oxidizing conditions in the cyanide-ore slurry to make the gold dissolve. The oxygen in air can do this and is the least costly. The oxygen is added by agitating the tanks with air or with a combination of air and mechanical stirrers.

A traditional method of recovering the precious metals from the cyanide solution is to clarify the solution by letting the ore settle out and/or the use of large clarifiers, followed by filters to provide a clear solution of gold cyanide. This solution is then put into contact with zinc metal either in boxes containing zinc shavings or by injecting zinc powder into a moving stream of the pregnant solution. The zinc treatment must be preceded by a system of vacuum deaertion to remove the oxygen from the solution.

The zinc very quickly goes into solution and as it does the gold and silver fall out. A filter then removes the gold and silver and any excess zinc.

ACTIVATED CARBON

After the last World War, work was done (by the U S Bureau of Mines) on the recovery of gold and silver from cyanide solutions by activated carbon. Activated carbon was available from surplus military gas masks. A recovery method was successful and when the supply of gas masks was used up activated carbon was specifically produced to fill this need.

The best carbon seems to be made from coconut shells, using the shells left over from the production of copra and coconut oil. Coconut shell charcoal is made by incomplete combustion in brick lined pits. The charcoal is further processed to make the correct size particles and to activate it.

When activated carbon is used the clarified gold bearing cyanide solution is contacted with the carbon instead of zinc.

The activated carbon in a series of vertical towers removes gold and silver from the cyanide solution as it passes through the towers. Usually several towers in series are in use while a final one or two whose carbon is loaded are being stripped. A caustic (high pH) alcohol solution is usually used to remove the gold from the carbon. When stripped the tower is returned to the circuit and another is stripped.

The carbon must occasionally be reactivated, a heating process and an acid treatment of the carbon is necessary at intervals. Carbon that can not be reactivated is burned to recover the last traces of gold.

The strip alcohol solution usually goes to an electrolytic cell with an insoluble anode and usually a steel wool cathode. Steel wool in a suitable container connected to the negative terminal provides the very large surface area necessary for this electrolysis to work with useful efficiency. When the steel wool is loaded with silver and gold it is melted with a flux containing sodium nitrate (or sometimes manganese dioxide). These are oxidizing materials which turn the iron to iron oxide but do not affect the gold or silver. The iron oxide becomes part of the slag and the metal (bullion) is separated and refined.

Extraction Metallurgy 81, p. 128-137, outlines carbon processes and gives a list of references.

Most high grade ore had been worked out by the early 1900's. Gold mining gradually shifted to lower grade ores which were well suited to cyanide extraction as opposed to the gravity separation techniques of that were widely used in the 1800's.

We recently visited an open pit mine in the Carson City, Nevada area. While digging this large pit for their heap leaching recovery work they cut through and exposed a number of the mine tunnels from those early days.

Nearby was a tailings pile left over from the processing of the ore from those tunnels. These tailings contain more gold than the ore being mined from the pit.

CARBON IN PULP (CIP)

A recent development in the cyanide carbon system is known as carbon in pulp. Pulp is the slurry of fine ore and cyanide solution and the carbon particles are put directly into this pulp mixture. In this situation the cyanide removes gold from the ore and the carbon promptly absorbs the precious metal from the cyanide. This is done in a series of aerated and agitated tanks.

By means of screens or other separating devices a system of counter current flow is set up. This means that the pulp goes from tank to tank in one direction while the carbon proceeds from tank to tank in the opposite direction. This has real efficiency advantages in that new fresh carbon is put into a tank at the end of the series that has pulp that is mostly drained of valuable metal. As the carbon proceeds up stream from tank to tank (sometimes as many as 8) the carbon finally reaches the first tank nearly loaded with gold but in contact with new ore so that it will still remove some and fill up to best efficiency. The loaded carbon is stripped in separate tanks and the precious metals recovered in the usual manner.

Such mills may be modest in size but the very low grade of ore that is mined and processed (usually considerably less than 1/4 T/oz per ton) usually makes it the process of choice for very large mills handling many thousands of tons per day. Since one ton is the same as 29160 T/oz an ore with 0.13 T/oz per ton is a very very low 0.00034% gold.

TELLURIDES

Although gold normally occurs only as a metal it will react with tellurium and selenium to form natural ores known as tellurides and selenides. Of these the tellurides have commercial value and the techniques of pretreatment of tellurides so the gold can be recovered have been known since early in this century.

CONCENTRATION

It is sometimes worthwhile to improve the "quality" of the ore before the extraction is done. A common method is known as flotation. Flotation cells are normally fairly small tanks say 4 feet square by 6 feet deep. The properly milled ore and a solution of specialized chemicals are fed into these cells and frothed with air. Some components reject air and others attract air bubbles and are floated out over the top of the cells. This will often result in the rejection of portions of the ore that are injurious in the extraction work or are worthless.

Valuable parts of the ore are concentrated to a smaller weight and volume and extraction work is easier and cheaper. A concentration ratio of 10 or 20 to 1 is fairly common.

HEAP LEACHING

A recent development in the mining of gold is the result of U S Bureau of Mines work and research. This is called "Heap Leaching". In its basic form this consists of piling ore up in heaps and trickling cyanide solution through the heap to dissolve gold.

In practice a waterproof base or pad is prepared with clay, asphalt or plastic sheet. Crushed ore is piled onto this in a heap 12 to 20 feet thick. This has a flat top and steep sides and may contain thousands to hundreds of thousands of tons of ore that is known to be cyanidable.

The particle size of the ore that provides good recovery must be known. It is necessary to have an ore that will present its gold to contact with the cyanide. A heap consisting of very fine ore or material with a large proportion of fine ore will usually not be properly wetted by the cyanide solution. The solution will be diverted into isolated trickles and streams and much fine ore not wetted.

The Bureau of Mines has developed an agglomeration method whereby fine ore is mixed with ordinary Portland cement and put into rotating drums or similar devices and made into pellets or balls. The water for this is often a cyanide solution and such an ore-cement pellet is quite porous and leaches well.

At the other end of the scale we have heard of an unusual and apparently heavily veined ore that could be cyanided in football sized pieces.

In practice a series of lawn sprinkler type of sprays distribute the sodium cyanide solution to the top of the heap. Oxygen of the air provides the necessary oxidizer. The solution trickles through the heap and the slope of the base guides it to a gathering point where it goes to a recovery system which can be zinc precipitated or carbon absorbed as previously described. The cyanide is tested and its quality maintained and returned to the heap until the ore is depleted of value. This may take many months.

Then the spent ore is washed free of cyanide and removed or abandoned.

The ore that can be utilized for such work may be old tailings from previous mining work or new ore. Gold content may be very low, 0.008 T/oz to 0.12 T/oz per ton of ore has been successfully heap leached.

The advantages are that heap leaching requires much less equipment and operating expense and can utilize low grade ores. Disadvantages are that it is a summer time operation. Freezing weather stops heap leaching so it is not used in Canada. Heavy rains cause problems and a "rain lake" is usually a part of the system. Very dry desert conditions may create a water supply problem with considerable evaporation at the sprays. In every case the control of cyanide and the treatment of weak and spent solutions must be dealt with.

The recent increase in USA gold production is largely due to heap leaching and a large part of that is in Nevada. Much information about cyanidation plants is available in <u>McQuiston and Shoemaker.</u>

Silver can be recovered in a very similar way. However the value of silver requires a much higher grade ore to be worthwhile.

<u>Eisele</u> in a recent article reviews cyanide leaching since 1887 and describes recent developments.

BY-PRODUCT RECOVERY

The precious metals are often by-products of the recovery of other metals. INCO has mines in the Sudbury district of Canada for the recovery of nickel. However this ore contains all of the platinum group metals as well as gold and silver in small amounts. This material is sent from Canada to a refinery in Acton (West part of London, England) where these metals are refined. Acton people told me their raw material is one part per million of the Sudbury Canada material.

Copper mills also recover precious metals. One of the copper mill processes is electro-refining copper bars in a sulfuric acid bath. Impure bars are the anodes and are dissolved and pure copper plated onto the cathodes. Impurities either remain in solution or, if insoluble in sulfuric acid, fall to the bottom of the cells. This mud contains the precious metal that was in the copper and is regularly gathered and refined.

The mining of lead ores and the production of lead often results in the recovery of precious metals especially silver. A long used method is the Parkes process.

Large iron kettles equipped with mechanical stirrers are heated to melt the lead. When molten, powdered zinc is thrown into the kettles and the stirrers agitate the melt to thoroughly mix the zinc and the lead.

Silver is more soluble in zinc than in lead and is soon accumulated in the zinc. Zinc however is not soluble in lead and is lighter than lead. After a time the stirrers are stopped and the zinc rises to the surface where it is skimmed and sent to a silver recovery unit.

Here the zinc is distilled away as a zinc fume leaving the silver behind. The zinc fumes are cooled and solidified and then can be used again.

Rose p. 53, indicates that gold can also be recovered by The Parkes Process.

BIOLEACHING OF GOLD

The idea that placer gold came from a "mother lode", a vein of richer ore that was weathering away led to many searches up stream of rivers for the more valuable source. It was often not found. More recently the idea that alluvial gold may have an origin in chemical or biological transport is receiving attention.

Although gold is quite unreactive its slow dissolution by organic materials or by micro organisms is a probably not unreasonable idea. Such dissolution from host rocks and later deposition and accumulation in streams may explain at least some placers.

The bioleaching of metals has been studied in Russia and at least one English translation of a Russian book on this subject is available. This includes a little work on gold.

Useful bioleaching processes have been devised for a number of materials. Several very recent news items mention the use of a Thiobaccillus known as T. Ferrooxidans to remove sulfur from high sulfur gold bearing ores. These ores are known as refractory ores and may comprise about 30% of known gold ores. The sulfur is usually removed by costly acid pressure treatment or by highly polluting roasting. The bioleaching is beginning to replace these costly processes.

Giant Bay Resources of Canada reports that in July of '87 it recovered gold from refractory ore that had been treated for sulfur removal by T. Ferrooxidans. Warren Springs laboratory (near London) is working on a similar bacteria known as Sulfobus that functions at a higher temperature. We will probably see some extensive progress in this field of biological treatment of ore and recovery of gold by biochemical or bacterial methods.

OTHER METHODS

Other recovery chemistry is being studied and new materials tested. A material called thiourea was experimentally used in Russia and by laboratories in South Africa. Work has been done in the USA. We understand that at this time at least one extensive pilot plant has been used or is being used to investigate the practical aspects of thiourea. Apparently no industrial sized plant is in operation.

The interest in thiourea is as a replacement for cyanide. Thiourea is more costly than cyanide and the recovery of gold from the thiourea is more complex. See Salter, Wyslozil, & McDonald 259-279 and 359-379. There are numerous other reports. See IPMI publications.

We have heard almost as a rumor that certain bromide chemistry is useful in gold recovery. Bromine chemicals are costly and very special conditions only would warrant their use. Bromine was once in use as a recovery chemical but was displaced by cyanide.

The Bureau of Mines has published a report on the use of chlorine to recover gold from ores. It is a fairly high temperature process and involves a stream of chlorine gas passing over an iron compound and then gold ore. Gold chloride is made, volatilized and then precipitated for recovery. Chlorine processes of one kind or another are not new. There are quite a few fairly recent patents on ideas for the use of chlorine for gold recovery.

Wet chlorination was in use in the late 1800's and was tested in Australia and South Africa in the 1950's and 1960's. It is not presently in use in production.

As time goes on we can expect to see the development of new processes. We know that liquid ammonia has a high solubility for gold. The low temperature and/or high pressures required to maintain ammonia as a liquid probably make this uninteresting for gold recovery from ore.

PLATINUM AND PALLADIUM

The platinum group metals mostly originate in South Africa and Russia. Some comes from Canada and a mine has recently been opened in Montana. This is the Stillwater mine and the publication IPMI 1986 has a descriptive article. The ore contains much more palladium than platinum. Ore concentration is necessary to deal with these low grade ores and we hear that flotation is used. The concentrate is smelted and rather large electric furnaces are used to separate a crude metal that can then be refined.

Extraction Metallurgy p 20-34 gives a short outline of South African methods of ore processing and a further outline of solvent extraction processes that are probably fairly recent methods in use for PGM's.

Lundy as mentioned in the chapter Platinum and Palladium has written some descriptive articles.

GOLD CYANIDATION

The chemical technology of the most used processes in gold mills is essentially that of cyanide dissolution of gold. Rose p. 299 gives the equation:

$$4Au + 8KCN + O_2 + 2H_2O = 4KAu(CN)_2KOH$$

This is for potassium. Present practice is to use the less costly NaCN which substitutes quite exactly. Oxygen is a requirement for the reaction and the oxygen of air easily satisfies the need. Stronger oxidizing materials have been tried. Generally the improvement is small and costs are higher and they are seldom used.

The oxygen must be removed from solution if zinc precipitation is used and this is usually a vacuum deaeration in a tower.

Other recovery steps and methods are mostly physical or electrochemical in nature. Absorption on carbon and desorption followed by electroplating onto large surface areas (steel wool in Zadra cells) is an example.

Rose in later editions devotes many pages to a description of the cyanide process. The 1937 edition reprinted by Met-Chem has about 150 pages of cyanide information.

REFERENCES AND FURTHER READING

Adamson, R. J. <u>Gold Metallurgy in South Africa</u> 1972
    Chamber of Mines, Johannesburg

Agricola, Georgius <u>De Re Metallica</u> 1556
    translated by Herbert Clark Hoover and Lou Henry Hoover
    Reprint Dover Publications, Inc.
    180 Varick Street
    New York, NY 10014

Ammen, C. W. <u>Ammen on Platinum</u>
    P. O. Box 288C
    Manitoo Springs, Colo. 80829

Antelman, Marvin S. <u>The Encyclopedia of Chemical Electrode Potentials</u> 1982
    Plenum Press
    233 Spring Street
    New York, NY 10013

Ashcraft, Bill, Verbal communication

Badcock, William <u>A New Touch-stone for Gold and Silver Wares</u>
    2nd Ed. 1679
    Facsimile copy 1970
    Praeger Publishers, Inc.
    111 Fourth Ave.
    New York, NY 10003

Ballantyne, Bryan and Marrs, Timothy C. (Eds) <u>Clinical and Experimental Toxicology of the Cyanides</u> 1987
    IOP Publishing Ltd.
    Techno House, Redcliffway
    Bristol BS1 6NX
    England

Barnes, John E. and Edwards, Julian D. "Solvent Extraction at INCO's ACTON Precious Metal Refinery" <u>Chemistry and Industry</u> March 1982

Beamish, F. E. and VanLoon, J. C. <u>Analysis of the Noble Metals</u> 1977
    Academic Press, Inc.
    111 Fifth Avenue
    New York, NY 10003

Bell, Eddie, Private communication
    Rio Grande Jewelers Supply
    6901 Washington N E
    Albuquerque, NM 87109

Bergman, Torbet and Cullen, Edward <u>Physical and Chemical Assays</u> Vol. 11, 17
    London

Bray, John L. <u>Non Ferrous Production Metallurgy</u> 1947 p. 36
    John Wiley & Sons, Inc.

Browning, Myron E. & Corrigan, D.A. (Eds) <u>Sampling and Assaying of Precious Metals</u> 1978
    International Precious Metals Institute
    4905 Tilghman Street, Suite 160
    Allentown, PA 18104

Bugbee, Edward E. <u>A Textbook of Fire Assaying</u> 1922
    John Wiley & Sons, Inc.
    Available from:
    International Precious Metals Institute
    4905 Tilghman Street, Suite 160
    Allentown, PA 18104

Burke, Lawrence D. & McRann, Mary "Thick Oxide Growth on Gold in Base"
    <u>Journal of Electroanalytical Chemistry</u> 1981
    125 pp. 387-399

Butts, A. (Ed.) <u>Copper, the Metal & its Alloys</u> 1954
    Chapter 8 pp. 165-222
    Reinhold Publishing Co.

Butts, Allison and Coxe, Charles D. (Eds.) <u>Silver - Economics Metallurgy and Use</u>
    1967, D. Van Nostrand Co., Inc.

Calmanovici, B., Kerbel, H. and Gal-Or, L.
Gold Recovery from Cyanide Solutions
Center for Noble Metals
Israel Institute of Metals
Technion-Israel Institute of Technology
Haifa, Israel

Calmanovici, B., Kerbel, H. & Gal-Or, L. "Recovery of Gold"
Gold Bulletin April 1983 16 No. 2 pp. 44-45

Corrigan, Donald A. & Browning, Myron E. Sampling and Assaying of Precious Metals 1980
International Precious Metals Institute
4905 Tilghman Street, Suite 160
Allentown, PA 18104

Creighton, H. Jermain & Koehler, W. A. Principles and Applications of Electrochemistry 2nd Ed. Vol. II
Applications (by Koehler)

CRUCIBLE CHARLIE SAYS
Crucible information by
Crucible Manufacturers Association
271 North Ave.
New Rochelle, NY

De Jesus, A. S. M. "Authentication of Gold Products by Nuclear Methods"
Gold Bulletin Vol. 18 No. 4 October 1985

Deal, Robert J. "The Fire Assaying of Gold & Silver"
California Mining Journal June 1987 pp. 3-5

Dennis, W. H. Metallurgy of the Non-Ferrous Metals
Sir Isaac Pitman and Sons Ltd.
London

Demortier, G. "Analysis of Gold Jewelry Artifacts"
Gold Bulletin Vol. 17 No. 1 January 1984

Despic, A. R. & Pavlovic M. G. "Anodic Deposition of Colloidal Gold" <u>Journal of Electroanalytic Chemistry</u> 1984
    180 pp. 31-48

Devuyst, E. A., Conard, B. R., Vergunst, R. & Tandi, B.
    A Cyanide Removal Process Using Sulfur Dioxide and Air.
    <u>Journal of Metals</u>
    December 1989 Vol. 41 No. 12 pp. 43 & 44

Devuyst, E. A., Etiel, V.A.
    New Process for Treatment of Waste
    Waters Containing Cyanide and Related Species.
    <u>Society of Mining Engineers of AIME</u>
    Annual Meeting, Dallas, TX. February 1982
    Transactions Vol. 276 available as a reprint from:
    INCO Exploration and Technical Services, Inc.
    2060 Flavelle Blvd.
    Sheridan Park
    Mississauga, Ontario LSK129

Dillon, V. S. <u>Assay Practice on the Witwarsand</u> 1955
    Chamber of Mines South Africa
    Cape Times Ltd.

Eilbeck, W. J. and Mattuck, G. <u>Chemical Processes in Waste Water Treatment</u> 1987
    Ellis Horwood Ltd.
    Market Cross House, Cooper Street
    Chichester, West Sussux PO 191EB
    England
        or
    John Wiley and Sons
    605 Third Ave.
    New York, NY 10158

Eisele, J. A. "Gold Metallurgy - A Historical Perspective"
    <u>Canadian Metallurgical Quarterly</u> 1988
    Vol. 27 No. 4 pp. 287-291

Embleton, F. T. "New Gold Refining Facility"
    <u>Gold Bulletin</u> Vol. 14 #2 April 1981 pp. 65-68

Epstein, Peter <u>Chemical Reactions used in Analysis and Refining of Platinum Group Metals</u> A 12 page typed manuscript. Possibly available from:
Peter Epstein
Platina Laboratories, Inc.
4301 S. Clinton Ave.
S. Plainfield, NJ 07080

Ercker, Lazarus <u>Treatise on Ores and Assaying</u> 1541
Translated from the German by A. G. Sisco and C. S. Smith
University of Chicago Press 1951

<u>Extraction Metallurgy</u> 1981
The Institution of Mining and Metallurgy
44 Portland Place
London W1
England

Fabian, C. P. & Ryan, M. G. "Derivation of the Potential - pH Diagrams for the Au - Cl - H_2O Systems @ 25°C"
Golden West Refining Corp. Ltd.
P. O. Box 957
Cloverdale W A 6105
Australia

Fine, H. A. and Gaskell, D. R. <u>Metallurgical Slags and Fluxes</u> 1984
The Metallurgical Society
420 Commonwealth Dr.
Warrendale, PA 15086

Foo, George "Water Dilution Factor (Chart)"
Private communication
Western Electric Co.

Friend, J. Newton <u>A Text Book of Inorganic Chemistry</u> 1928
Chas Griffin & Co. Ltd.
42 Drury Lane W C 2
London, England

Gal-Or, Leah and Calmanovici, B. "Gold Recovery from Cyanide Solutions" Santa Fe
    Symposium on Jewelry Manufacturing Technology 1988
    Met-Chem Research, Inc.
    P. O. Box 3014 High Mar Station
    Boulder, Colo. 80307

Gaskell, D.R. et al Eds.
    The Reinhardt Schumann International Symposium
    The Metallurgical Society, Inc.
    420 Commonwealth Dr.
    Warrendale, PA 15086

Genco, A.J. Verbal Information
    Williams Advanced Materials
    2978 Main Street
    Buffalo, NY 14214-1099

Geyer, Rod, Verbal Information
    Du Pont Corp.

Gowland, William The Metallurgy of the Non-Ferrous Metals 1921
    Charles Griffin & Co.

Groshart, Earl "Waste Cyanide Control Processes"
    Metal Finishing November 1988

Harris, Bryn Precious Metals '89
    International Precious Metals Institute
    4905 Tilghman Street, Suite 160
    Allentown, PA 18104

Hartley, F. R. The Chemistry of Platinum and Palladium
    John Wiley & Sons

Hasenpuch, Dr. W. Verbal communication
    Degussa A G
    HANAU - Woldgang
    Postfach 1345
    6450 HANAU 1
    West Germany

Hoel, Robert F. "New Systems for Incinerating Jewelry Waste"
   <u>American Jewelry Manufacturer</u> April 1982 pp. 82-84

Hofman, H. O. and Mostowitsch, W. "The Behavior of Calcium Sulfate at Elevated Temperature with some Fluxes" <u>Transactions of the American Institute of Mining Engineers</u>
   Vol. 39 1909 pp. 628-653

Hofman, H. O. and Mostowitsch, W. "The Reduction of Calcium Sulfate by Carbon Monoxide and Carbon and the Oxidation of Calcium Sulfide" <u>Transactions of the American Institute of Mining Engineers</u> Vol. 41 1911 pp. 763-788

Hoke, C. M. <u>Refining Precious Metal Wastes</u> 1940
   Reprinted by Met-Chem Research
   P. O. Box 3014 High Mar Station
   Boulder, Colo. 80307

Hoke, C. M. <u>Testing Precious Metals</u> 1946
   The Jewelers Technical Advice Co.
   New York, NY.

Jacobson, C. A. <u>Encyclopedia of Chemical Reactions</u> 1949
   Reinhold Publishing Co.

Jha, M. C. and Hill, S. D. (Eds) "<u>Precious Metals '89</u>"
   The Minerals Metals and Materials Society
   420 Commonwealth Drive
   Warrendale, PA 15086

Koehler, W. A. <u>Principles and Applications of Electrochemistry</u>
   Vol. II Second Ed. 1944
   John Wiley and Sons
   New York, N.Y.

Kudryk, V., Corrigan, D.A. and Liang, W.W. Eds.
   <u>Precious Metals; Mining Extraction and Processing</u> 1984
   The Metallurgical Society of AIME
   420 Commonwealth Dr.
   Warrendale, PA 15086

Lagowski, J. J. "Anionic Gold" Gold Bulletin 1983, p. 16

Lange, N. A. Handbook of Chemistry Revised 10th Edition
McGraw-Hill Book Co.

Lashley, W. C. Refining Gold with Dibutyl Carbitol 1986 p. 14
American Society for Applied Technology
P. O. Box 1705
Silver City, NM 88062

Leary, Hal "Precious Metal Refining"
California Mining Journal Vol. 57 No. 1 September 1987
pp. 11-15

Lenahan, W. C. and Murray-Smith, R. del. Assay and Analytical Practice in the
South African Mining Industry 1986
Chamber of Mines of South Africa
P. O. Box 809
Johannesburg 2000

Levin, Ernest M., Robbins, Carl R. and McMurdie, Howard F. Phase Diagrams for
Ceramists 1964
The American Ceramic Society
4055 N. High Street
Columbus, Ohio 43214

The Ceramic Society has issued 8 more volumes to make a series of 10 or 11. Newer and more complete diagrams may be worthwhile and useful.

Liddell, Donald M. Handbook of Non-Ferrous Metallurgy Vol. II
1st Ed. 1926
McGraw Hill Book Co.
New York, N.Y.

Liddell, Donald M. The Metallurgists and Chemists Handbook 3rd Ed. 1930
McGraw Hill Book Co.
New York, N.Y.

Loewen, R. P. Small Scale Gold Refining 1980
    Goldsmiths Company, London
    Available from:
    International Precious Metals Institute
    4905 Tilghman Street, Suite 160
    Allentown, PA 18104

Lundy, David "The Mining and Refining of South African Platinum"
    American Jewelry Manufacturer October 1978 pp. 26-34
    November 1978 pp. 52-54

Lundy, D. E. and Zysk, E. D. 1983 IPMI Seminar
    International Precious Metals Institute
    4905 Tilghman Street, Suite 160
    Allentown, PA 18104

Mazia, Joseph "In Search of the Golden Fleece" Metal Finishing
    August 1981 p. 81

McClelland, G. E., Wrobleski, M. D. & Eisele, J. A.
    Production of Hi-Purity Gold from Zinc Precipitates and Steel Wool Cathodes by Hydrometallurgical Refining
    Bureau of Mines 1C9002

McMillon, Walter G. Electric Smelting and Refining 1904
    2nd English Ed.
    Chas. Griffin & Son
    Translation of Dr. W. Borchers - German Book

McQuiston, Jr., Frank W. and Shoemaker, R. A.
    Gold and Silver Cyanidation Plant Practice II 1981
    Society of Mining Engineers
    American Institute of Mining, Metallurgical and Petroleum Engineers, Inc.

Mellor, J. W. Inorganic and Theoretical Chemistry 1967
    Vol. VIII Suppl. 11 Nitrogen (part II)
    NOCl p. 421 $2NO + Cl_2 = 2NOCl$ much information NOCl
    pp. 420-433

Milazzo, Gulio <u>Electrochemistry</u> 1963
    Elsevier Publishing Co.

Mishra, R.K. (Ed) <u>Precious metals 1993</u> p 181
    Silver Chloride by Loewen
    International Precious Metals Institute
    4905 Tilghman Street, Suite 60
    Allentown, PA 18104

Morris, Norman <u>Cyanide Reduction of Metal Finishing Wastes</u>
    Precious Metals 1986
    U.V. Rao Ed.
    International Precious Metals Institute
    4905 Tilghman Street, Suite 160
    Allentown, PA. 18104

Nebergall, Wm. H., Schmidt, Frederich C. & Holtzclaw, Henry F.
    <u>College Chemistry</u> 5th Ed. 1976
    D. C. Heath & Co.
    Lexington, Mass.

Nicol, M. J. Report #1844 National Int. for Metallurgy 1976 and 1981
    Johannesburg, South Africa

NIOSH <u>Criteria for Recommended Standards</u>
    <u>Occupational Exposure to Hydrogen Cyanide and Cyanide Salts</u>
    by U. S. Dept. of Health Education and Welfare
    Public Health Service Center for Disease Control
    National Institute for Occupational Safety and Health October 1976

Oddy, Andrew "Assaying in Antiquity"
    <u>Gold Bulletin</u> Vol. 16 No. 2 pp. 52-59 April 1983

Parker, Peter D. <u>Chloride Electrometallurgy</u> 1982
    The Metallurgical Society of AIME
    420 Portland Place
    Warrendale, PA 15086
    Copper Electrowining pp. 167-203

Pitocco, Janine Verbal communication,
    B. A. Ballou & Co.
    E. Providence, RI

Potter, Geo. M.
    <u>Some Developments in Gold and Silver Metallurgy</u>
    pp. 128-136
    Review of recovery from ore - references

Puddephatt, R. J. <u>The Chemistry of Gold</u>
    Elsevier North-Holland, Inc.
    52 Vanderbilt Avenue
    New York, NY 10017

Rao, U. V. <u>Precious Metals</u> 1986
    International Precious Metals Institute
    4905 Tilghman Street, Suite 160
    Allentown, PA 18104

Reddy, Rawana G. and Mishra Rajesh K. "Recovery of Precious Metals by Pyrometallurgical Processing of Electronic Scrap"
    pp. 135-146 <u>Precious Metals 1987</u>
    International Precious Metals Institute
    4905 Tilghman Street, Suite 160
    Allentown, PA 18104

Rice, J. E. "Explosion Accidents in the Coating of Mirrors"
    <u>Journal of Chem. Ed.</u> ii 231 1939

Rimmer, B. F. "Refining Gold from Precious Metal Concentrates by Liquid-Liquid Extraction" <u>Chemistry and Industry</u>
    January 1974

Roberts, Michael, Private communication
    Warwick, England

Salter, R. S., Wyslouzll, D. M. & McDonald, G. W. (Eds.)
  <u>Proceedings of the International Symposium on Gold Metallurgy</u>
  Winnipeg Canada 1987
  Pergamon Press
  Maxwell House, Fairview Park
  Elmsford, NY 10523

Schalch, Eugen and Nicol, Michael J. "A Study of Certain Problems Associated with the Electrolytic Refining of Gold"
  <u>Gold Bulletin</u> Vol. 11 No. 4 October 1978 pp. 118

Schaler, Alfred, Verbal communication
  B. A. Ballou & Co.
  E. Providence, RI

Schnabel, Dr. Carl <u>Handbook of Metallurgy</u> 3rd Ed. Vol. 1 1921
  Macmillan & Co.

Schneller, David "The Recovery of Precious Metals from Used Casting Investment" <u>Santa Fe Symposium</u> 1987
  Met Chem Research
  P. O. Box 3014, High Mar Station
  Boulder, Colo. 80307

Schneller, David "Silver Chloride" Recovery, <u>Reclamation and Refining of Precious Metals - San Diego 1981</u>
  International Precious Metals Institute
  4905 Tilghman Street, Suite 160
  Allentown, PA 18104

Schumb, Walter C., Satterfield, Charles N. & Wentworth, Ralph L. <u>Hydrogen Peroxide</u> American Chemical Society Monograph
  Reinhold Publishing Co.
  New York, NY

Seidell <u>Solubilities of Organic & Inorganic Compounds</u> 2nd Ed. 1919
  D. Van Nostrand & Co.

Simpson, Douglas K. "Hydrazine: A Powerful Metal Reductant"
  <u>Metal Finishing</u> April 1985 pp. 57-60

Sketchfield, John H. "Electronic Scrap Treatment at Engelhard" pp. 147-154
   Precious Metals 1987
   International Precious Metals Institute
   4905 Tilghman Street, Suite 160
   Allentown, PA 18104

Smith, Ernest A. The Sampling and Assay of the Precious Metals 2nd Ed. 1946
   Charles Griffin & Co. Ltd.
   Republished by Met-Chem Research, Inc.
   P. O. Box 3014 High Mar Station
   Boulder, Colo. 80307

Stanley, G. G. The Extractive Metallurgy of Gold in South Africa 2 Vols. 1987
   South African Institute of Mining and Metallurgy
   Kelvin House, 2 Hollard St.
   Johannesburg 2001

Statham, E. F., Coyle, T. J. and Howat, D. D. "Some Aspects of Electrolytic Gold Refining as Applied to South African Mine Bullion" Journal of the South African Institute of Mining and Metallurgy June 1978
   Johannesburg, South Africa

Suslick, Kenneth S. "The Chemical Effects of Ultrasound"
   pp. 80-86 Scientific American February 1989

Thompson, Maurice deKay Theoretical and Applied Electro-chemistry
   3rd E. 1939
   The MacMillian Company
   New York, N.Y.

Tolley, W. K. and Tester, L. S. Super Critical CO_2 Solubility of $TiCl_4$
   Report of Investigations 9216 (1989)
   United States Bureau of Mines

Turkevitch, John "Colloidal Gold" Parts I & II
   Gold Bulletin 18 No. 3 pp. 86-91 18 No. 4 pp. 125-131

Wälchli, Walo & Vuilleumier, Pierre "Touchstone Testing of Precious Metals"
   Aurum #24 pp. 36-45

Wälchli, Walo "Touching Precious Metals"
   Gold Bulletin Vol. 14 #4 October 1981

Wälchli, Walo & Vuilleumier, Pierre "Assaying Gold by Cupellation" Aurum No. 29
   pp. 56-64

Wise, E. M. (Ed) Gold - Recovery, Properties and Applications 1964
   D. Van Nostrand Co., Inc.
   120 Alexander St.
   Princeton, NJ

Young, Roland S. Chemical Analysis in Extractive Metallurgy 1971
   Barnes & Noble, Inc.

Young, Roland S. "Analysis for Gold"
   Gold Bulletin Vol. 13 No. 1 January 1980

Zysk, E. D. Platinum Group Metals Seminar 1985
   International Precious Metals Institute
   4905 Tilghman Street, Suite 160
   Allentown, PA 18104

Zysk, E. D. and Bonucci, J. A. Precious Metals 1985
   International Precious Metals Institute
   4905 Tilghman Street, Suite 160
   Allentown, PA 18104

FURTHER READING

Ammen, C. W. Recovery and Refining of Precious Metals 1984
    Van Nostrand & Co. Ltd.
    135 West 50th Street
    New York, NY 10020

"Analogies between Liquid Ammonia and Water" Inorganic and Theoretical
    Chemistry p. 276

Davis, C. W. W. Methods for Recovery of Platinum, Iridium, Palladium, Gold and
    Silver from Jewelers Waste (1924)
    Bureau of Mines Pamphlet - out of print

Fink & Carrol Standard Handbook for Electrical Engineers 10th Ed. 1968 Section 23
    "Electrochemistry"
    McGraw - Hill

Gadja, George Gold Refining (1976)
    Privately published
    P. O. Box 1846
    Santa Monica, CA 90406

Gee, George E. Recovering Precious Metals from Liquid Residues 1920
    E and F Spon Ltd.
    57 Haymarket SW 1
    London, England

"Gold and Ammonia" American Jewelry Manufacturer March 1981 p. 16

Hayward, Carle R. An Outline of Metallurgical Practice
    3rd Ed. 1961
    D. Van Nostrand Co., Inc.

International Precious Metals Institute
    4905 Tilghman Street, Suite 160
    Allentown, PA 18104

> A series of conference proceedings from 1972 (now about 16 volumes) on nearly all aspects of precious metals.

Jolly, Wm. L. The Inorganic Chemistry of Nitrogen Theromodynamics of Nitrogen Compounds pp. 115-120

> Gives heats of formation, etc., including redox potentials.

Kirk-Othmer Encyclopedia of Chemical Technology Volume 11
pp. 972-995 Review of gold and gold compounds.

Kubaschewski, O. & Alcock, C. B. Metallurgical Thermo-chemistry
5th Ed. 1979
Pergamon Press

Loewen, Roland Small Scale Silver Refining and Recovering Gold from Jewelry Sweeps published by the Goldsmiths Company, London
Available from:
International Precious Metals Institute
4905 Tilghman Street, Suite 160
Allentown, PA 18104

Mazia, Joseph "Coatings Corner" VII thru XII - Metal Finishing
March 1981 through August 1981
also "Precious Metal Potpourri"
Metal Finishing January Through April 1982 also July and October 1982
A series of columns by a man who grew up with a refinery.

McHugh, Mark A. and Krukonis, Val J. Supercritical Fluid Extraction 1986
Butterworth

Mellor, J. W. Comprehensive Treatise on Theoretical & Inorganic Chemistry
Properties of anhydrous ammonia pp. 115-120

> An old and still useful reference of many volumes. Available in the reference section of many libraries. Vol. 3 devoted largely to precious metals.
> Fulminating Silver Vol. 3 p. 381
> Fulminating Gold Vol. 3 p. 582
> Fulminating Platinum Vol. 16 p. 336

Moore, J. I. Chemical Metallurgy 1981
    Butterworth & Co. Ltd.
    London - Boston

"Non Aqueous Chemistry - Ammonia" Comprehensive Inorganic Chemistry
    pp. 158-175

Parker, R. H. An Introduction to Chemical Metallurgy 1978
    Pergamon Press, Ltd.

Roberts, E. R. The Extraction of Non-Ferrous Metals 1950
    Temple Press, Ltd.
    London

Rose, T. Kirk The Precious Metals Comprising Gold, Silver and Platinum 1909
    D. Van Nostrand & Co.

Salter, R. S., Wyslouzll, D. M. and McDonald, G. W. Gold Metallurgy
    Proceedings of the International Symposium, Winnipeg, Canada, 1987
    Pergamon Press
    Maxwell House, Fairview Park
    Elmsford, NY 10523

Seabrook, John "A Reporter at Large Gold Mining" New Yorker
    April 24, 1989 pp. 45-81

    A narrative of modern gold mining (Carlin) in Nevada how it is done
    and the discovery of "invisible" gold

Sisler, Harry H., Vanderwerf, Calvin A. and Davidson, Arthur A.
    General Chemistry 1959
    The Macmillan Co.
    New York, NY

Smout, Arthur (Chairman) The Refining of Non-Ferrous Metals 1950
    The Institution of Mining and Metallurgy

Thorpe's Dictionary of Applied Chemistry see Gold: covers history mining, refining,
    chemistry, etc.

Williams, P. Recovery of Precious Metals from Jewelry Scrap
International Precious Metals Institute
Seminar - Skytop Lodge, PA 1980
also Symposium - San Diego, CA 1981

Good outline description of refining processes for Gold-Silver, Gold-Platinum - Palladium, Palladium-Ruthenium and Platinum - Ruthenium and Platinum Iridium types of scrap.

International Precious Metals Institute
4905 Tilghman Street, Suite 160
Allentown, PA 18104

OTHER READING - HISTORY

Birmingham, England Assay Office
    Has a private library covering many subjects including a considerable number of the older books (ca 15th to 19th century) on gold and silver and platinum metallurgy.

    May possibly be visited by addressing the Assay Master above.

Del Mar, Alex <u>History of the Precious Metals</u> 1902 reprinted 1968
    Burt Franklin
    235 E. 44th Street
    New York, NY

Dennis, W. H. <u>A Hundred Years of Metallurgy</u> 1963
    Gerald Duckworth & Co. Ltd.
    3 Henrietta Street
    London WC 2

Dibner, Bern <u>Agricola on Metals</u> 1958
    Burndy Library
    Norwalk, Conn.

Healy, J. F. <u>Mining and Metallurgy in the Greek and Roman World</u> (1978)
    Thomes and Hudson
    500 Fifth Avenue
    New York, N.Y. 10036

Jabir <u>The Works of Geber</u> "Englished by Richard Russell 1678"
    E M Deut & Sons Ltd., London
    E P Dutton & Co., Inc., New York

Theophilus <u>On Divers Arts</u> translated from the Latin by John G. Hawthorne and
    Cyrus Stanley Smith (1979)
    Dover Publications, Inc.
    180 Varick Street
    New York, N.Y. 10014

Thompson, Charles J. <u>Alchemy</u> 1897 reprinted 1974
   Sentry Press, New York

Tylecote, R. F. <u>The Prehistory of Metallurgy in the British Isles</u> 1986
   Institute of Metals, London

U. S. Geological Survey <u>Bibliography of the Metals of the Platinum Group 1748 - 1917 - 1919</u>

INDEX

Acidity Control - See pH	206
Activated Carbon	85, 87
Activated Charcoal	210
Air Lift	206
Air Pollution	193
Air Pollution Chemistry	210
Alcohol	96
Alluvial Gold	216
Alumina	62
Aluminum	84, 93
Aluminum Oxide	32, 51
Amalgamation	182
Ammonia	119, 131, 136, 158, 182, 226
Ammonium Chloride	4, 157, 158, 160, 162
Ammonium Chloro Palatinate	160
Ammonium Chloro Pallidate	160
Ammonium Chloro Pallidite	160
Ammonium Hydroxide	135, 137, 140, 143, 152
Amyl Nitrite	84
Aqua Regia	2, 78, 93, 97, 99, 115, 123, 127, 158, 159
Aqua Regia Recovery Chlorine System	201
Aqua Regia Refining	201
Aqua Regia Self Destruction	123
Aristra	217
Aspirator	104
Assay Ton	18, 28
Assaying	11, 18
Assaying Other Methods	
Absorption Spectrography	20
Density	20
Emission Spectrography	20
Neutron Activation	20
Plasma Arc	20
X-Rays	20
Automobile Catalysts	165
Automobile Mufflers	90

Bacteria	86
Ball Mill	17, 28, 71
Barren Solution	119
Base Metals	19, 125
Bioleaching of Gold	224
Bisulfite	130
Bleach	95
Blowers	41
Bombing	1, 81
Bombing Solutions	77, 79
Borax	37, 40, 51, 61, 63, 69, 71, 88, 120, 152, 154, 155
Borax Glass	61
Boric Acid	61, 71, 120
Boron Oxide	61
Brass	12
Brine	117
Brine - See Sodium Chloride	117
Bromine	169, 185, 225
Bronze	12
Brown Fumes	99
Buchner Filter	138
Buchner Funnels	102
Bullion	19
Burner	23
Burning	193
Butane	46
By-Product Recovery	224
Cadmium	19
Calcium Sulfate	36, 64, 89
Carbamide - See Urea	110
Carbon	64, 85
Carbon Dioxide	40, 61, 153
Carcinogen	131, 134
Carpets	36
Caustic	142
Caustic Soda	134-137, 140
Caustic Soda - See Sodium Hydroxide	3
Cementation	120, 127, 133, 157, 177, 205
Charcoal	136, 147

Chemistry Platinum and Palladium	166
Chlorination	86
Chlorine	2, 81, 86, 97, 123, 175, 180, 190, 201, 211, 226
Clorox	95
Colloids	126
Concentrating Table	75
Copper	3, 12, 93, 100, 120, 135, 138, 203, 206, 213
Copper Compounds	203
Copper Poisoning	3
Copper Retrieval	209
Copperas	111, 114, 127, 160
Corn Syrup - See Dextrose	134
Cornet	19
Crucible	40, 95, 120
Crucibles	36, 38, 136
Cupel	19
Cupel Furnace	19, 186
Cupellation	170, 182, 185
Cupric Chloride	111, 117, 130
Cuprous Chloride	111, 115, 117, 119, 130
Cyanate	88
Cyanidation	182, 218
Cyanide	1, 18, 75, 79, 89, 169, 219, 222
Cyanide Antidotes	84
Cyanide Destruction	86
Cyanide First Aid	80
Cyanide Testing	86
Cyanogen Chloride	86, 87
Destruction of Cyanide	85
Dextrose	3, 133, 136, 137, 140, 142
Diamonds	99
Diatomaceous Earth	36
Dietzel Cells	184
Electrode Potentials	124
Electrolysis	179
Electrolytic Refining	133, 182
Electromotive Series	125
Electronic Scrap	77, 89

Electroplating	79
Electrostrip	79, 81
Emery	32
Eutectic	65
Explosive Gold	119
Explosive Silver Compounds	135
Eye Protection	2, 96
Eyeglass Frames	77
Ferrous Sulfate - See Copperas	111, 114
Filter Paper	104, 110
Filtering	102, 117, 146
First Aid Kit	83
Fizzer Cell	172, 178
Flame Temperatures	46
Flotation	182, 222
Fluorspar	37, 40, 51, 62, 63, 69, 88, 154
Flux	18, 36, 37, 40, 59, 60, 67, 70, 88, 120, 152
Formaldehyde	111, 129, 133
Fulminating - See Explosive	119
Fulminating Compounds	136
Fume Hood	2, 94, 134
Furnace	37, 41, 153, 154
Furnace Home Built	40
Furnace Starting	45
Gas	45
Glass	51, 65, 69
Gold	1, 14, 19, 21, 59, 63, 69, 70, 75, 93, 111, 133, 138, 161, 188, 215, 224
Gold Chemistry	122
Gold Chloride	95, 110, 111, 114, 189
Gold Cyanidation	226
Gold Filled	77, 85
Gold Mills	219
Gold Mono Chloride	189
Gold Oxide	191
Gold Precipitation	126
Gold Refining	2, 185
Golden Fleece	215
Graphite	14, 121, 122, 147

Green Gold	97, 100
Hammermills	17
Heap Leaching	222
Hydrated Cuprous Oxide	131
Hydraulic Cone Classifiers	219
Hydrazine	3, 111, 129, 131, 144, 145, 150
Hydrochloric Acid	2, 94, 97, 114, 119, 123, 131, 136, 159, 190, 211
Hydrofluoric Acid	59
Hydrogen Cyanide	79, 82, 85
Hydrogen Peroxide	175, 176
Hydroquinone	3, 111, 129, 131, 148, 151
Hypochlorite	81, 145
Incinerator	23
Ingot	14, 136, 147
Investment	36, 69, 77, 89
Ion Exchange Resins	210, 213
Iron	3, 28, 64, 126, 208, 213
Iron Chloride	208
Jaw Crusher	71
Jewelers Bench Scrap	16
Jewelers Sweeps - See Sweeps	16
Karat Gold	121
Kieselguhr	32
Lead	18, 36, 62, 93, 104, 126, 186, 224
Lead Nitrate	126
Lead Sulfate	102, 104, 110, 126
Lemel	16
Lemel - See Jewelers Bench Scrap	16
Lime	62
Liquid-Liquid Extraction	182, 183
Liquidity	65
Liquids Sampling	17
Litharge	18, 70, 185, 186
Lye - See Sodium Hydroxide	3
Magnesium Hydroxide	209, 213
Magnet	28, 32, 96
Magnetic Material	17
Manganese Dioxide	36, 62, 63, 150
Manganese Oxide	60

Matte	64
Melting	40, 46, 120, 147, 148, 194
Mercury	169, 184, 217
Mercury Poisoning	218
Metabisulfite	114
Metal Hydroxides	205, 212
Miller Chlorine Process	186
Mining	215
Molten Metal	14
Natural Gas	46
Nickel	93, 224
Nitric Acid	2, 19, 94, 97, 100, 110, 123, 133, 134, 136, 138, 158, 159, 183, 200, 201
Nitrogen	211
Ore	91
Ores	19
Oxalic Acid	111, 129
Oxidizer	36
Oxygen	147, 200, 227
Packed Tower	194, 200
Palladium	4, 19, 93, 157, 160
Parkes Process	182, 224
Parting	133, 176, 181
PGM's	165, 226
pH	206, 212
Phase Diagrams	65
Picric Acid	82
Placer Gold	215
Plastic	28, 36, 69, 94
Plastic Saddle	194
Plating	81
Plating Solutions	77
Platinum	4, 19, 93, 111, 157, 160
Platinum and Palladium	162, 226
Platinum Group Metals - See also PGM's	164, 182, 224
Poisoning	79
Polishing Dust	22
Pollution	179, 193
Pollution Melting Refining	194
Pollution Scrubber	196

Pollution Sweeps Burning	193
Polypropylene	94
Potassium Chloride	158
Pulsed Current Electrolysis	190
Pumice	32
Rag Plant	215
Reduction-Oxidation Reactions	129
Refineries Copper	165
Refineries Miller Chlorine	170
Refineries Other Methods	169
Refining	96, 194
Refining Platinum and Palladium	159
Refractory	41
Remelting	52
Rhodium	89, 157
Rod Mill	17, 28
Rolled Gold	77
Rouge	28, 32, 36, 51
Black	36
Green	36
Red	36
White	36
Yellow	36
Safety	1, 81, 93, 134, 135
Safety Data Sheets	4
Salt	137
Salt Brine	133, 134
Salt Cell	175, 180
Salt Solution	134
Sampling	11, 14
Sand	37
Scrap Gold	99
Screen	31, 32, 71
Scrubbed Liquid	198
Scrubber	2, 196
Selenium	215
Shot	59, 121
Silica	36, 60, 63, 64, 89
Silicon Carbide	32

Term	Pages
Silver	14, 19, 69, 75, 93, 100, 124, 133, 138, 142, 182, 189, 224
Silver Carbonate	153
Silver Chemistry	149
Silver Chloride	12, 61, 64, 93, 100, 110, 124, 133, 134, 136, 139, 142, 145, 148, 152, 154, 177, 183, 189
Silver Compounds	203
Silver Electrolysis	183
Silver Nitrate	139
Silver Oxide	63, 136, 142, 150, 151, 153
Silver Refining	3, 138, 176
Silver Sulfite	124
Sink Trap Sludge	28, 69, 77, 88
Slag	40, 47, 59, 63, 96, 154, 155
Slag Liquidity	47
Slag Metal Molds	51
Slags	59
Sluice Boxes	216
Soda Ash	37, 40, 51, 61, 64, 69, 89, 100, 133, 144, 148, 152, 154, 155, 206
Sodium Bisulfite	111, 117, 129, 158
Sodium Borohydride	133
Sodium Chlorate	4, 158-160
Sodium Chloride	139, 155
Sodium Dithionite	133
Sodium Hydroxide	3
Sodium Metabisulfite	130
Sodium Nitrate	37, 62-64, 120, 148, 151, 211
Sodium Nitrite	211
Sodium Sulfite	117, 129
Sodium Thiosufite	152
Sodium Thiosulfate	143
Solder	36
Solvent Extraction	226
Spot Plate	114
Spot Test	78
Stamp Mills	217
Stannous Chloride	78, 114, 115, 126, 163
Stripping	1
Sulfur	114, 225

Sulfur Dioxide	111, 117, 129
Sulfuric Acid	2, 70, 102, 104, 126, 135, 137, 144, 159, 183, 211
Sweeps	21, 59
Sweeps Ashes	28, 59
Sweeps Burners	23
Sweeps Melting	22, 31
Sweeps Quality	32
Teflon	94
Telephone Scrap	77, 90
Tellurides	222
Tellurium	215
Temperature	152, 154
Test for Silver Chloride	143
Test Kits	81
Thiourea	169, 184, 225
Thum Cell	133
Tin	93, 104
Torch Melting	52, 162
Touchstone	11
Tripoli	32, 51
Tripolite	32
Tumbling Mud	77, 88
Ultrasonic Agitation	190
Ultrasonic Vibration	100
Urea	110, 127, 159, 163
Vacuum	104
Vee Mold	52
Vein Gold	217
Washing	119, 146
Watch Bands	77
Watch Batteries	77, 91
Water Pollution	203
Water Pollution Chemistry	211
Wohlwill	188
Wohlwill Cell	171
Zadra Cells	69, 227
Zinc	3, 84, 87, 93, 122, 157, 219, 224, 227